Western
HOME
LANDSCAPING
by Ken Smith, Landscape Architect

Publisher: Bill Fisher; Editor-In-Chief: Carl Shipman; Editor: Jon Latimer; Art Director: Don Burton; Book Design & Assembly: Chris Crosson; Typography: Cindy Coatsworth, Connie Brown; Drawings: Bruce Smith; Lettering: Karen Bellamy; Photography: William Aplin, Denny Everett, Ken Smith.

Published by H.P. Books, P.O. Box 5367, Tucson, AZ 85703 602/888-2150
Paperback: ISBN: 0-89586-003-1; Hardcover: ISBN: 0-89586-012-0
Library of Congress Card Number: 71-51897 © 1978, Fisher Publishing, Inc. Printed in U.S.A.

Cover photo: William Aplin
Landscape design: Eric Johnson

Contents

Landscape And You

Bargains are hard to find nowadays but here's a big one: Imaginative development of outdoor space can make a small house *live* like a large one. Patios, fences, lawns and trees still cost much less than floors, walls, carpeting and roofs. And you don't have to be an expert to install them.

All it takes is common sense, lots of hard work, and a little guidance along the way. That's what this book is all about. Garden construction and planting can be fun—when they're done right. Do-it-yourself projects are not only satisfying, but they really do save money.

You can benefit from good landscape ideas even if your estate is limited to a small condominium patio, a tiny mobile-home lot or a miniscule balcony. In fact, the smaller the area, the more important it is to make the most of the limited space.

PURCHASING OR BUILDING A HOME

It takes a great deal of time and effort to select a new home. It's usually the most important purchase made by a family in a lifetime and it can have a profound effect on health and happiness.

Let's assume the house is of sound construction and pleasing design. It should also have ample space and be located in a desirable neighborhood, convenient to shopping, fire and police services, schools, recreation areas and transportation. Hopefully, it's also within the financial reach of the family, with a little left over for basic outdoor work. After all these, there are still many landscape considerations that can make the purchase a wise or an unsound one.

When you start, you may doubt that you can achieve even this much, but consider what this looked like a few months before, as shown in the picture below.

This low concrete planter box looked like this before it was planted with an olive tree, gazanias and daylilies, and lawn was planted around it. Planning and a little patience can pay off handsomely.

Make a budget allowance for at least some immediate landscape costs such as fencing, trees and paving.

Choose an orientation suited to the specific climate. A southern or western exposure of major glass areas may be desirable for a cool, coastal site, but unbearable in a hot, inland valley or desert situation.

Determine what use areas will be needed. Is there room for a swimming pool or spa, an ample patio, game court, vegetable garden or whatever else is required? Look for good indoor-outdoor relationships so that outdoor living areas will be convenient and the garden will be part of the house.

Check utilities to see if there are sewers, gas, reliable water supply, or unsightly power lines. Find out if there are easements, deed restrictions or other requirements that might limit development of the property.

An inviting patio can help transform an average house and lot into a pleasing and comfortable living environment.

Verify property lines—there should be surveyor's stakes marking the corners.

Visit the site and talk to local residents to see if there are seasonal or prevailing winds that could be a problem or an asset. Study site plans and zoning maps to determine what will be built on adjacent property. Will there be a two-story house looking down on your back yard? Will there be apartments or a gas station across the street?

Inspect soil conditions, slopes and grading to avoid crippling extra costs. If the builder is required to plant the slopes, will it be a permanent solution? Will adequate sprinklers be included? Evaluate existing trees, boulders, views and other outstanding features that may turn out to be a bonus or a liability.

Anticipate room additions and future developments and make sure there is sufficient area and access.

If the house is to be built or is not yet completed, ask the builder to provide an oversize water service line to accommodate sprinklers. Install electrical stub-outs with indoor switches for garden lighting and a pool or spa. Protect all paving from damage during construction or pour after all work has been completed. Plaster, wood, concrete and other trash should be thoroughly cleaned-up and removed from the site—not buried.

If landscaping is included in the cost of the home, ask the builder for an itemized breakdown of what is included. After all, you're paying for it. Frankly, it's usually not very well done. It's better to get a credit for the work than to end up doing it over anyway.

Investigate the workmanship of tract subcontractors before having them do any paving, walls, sprinkler installation or other work. The price may be right, but they may not be set up for custom work.

Try to picture the completed living environment of house and garden. Can it be "just what you want" or will it always be an unsatisfactory compromise?

This back yard is truly an outdoor room. A carpet of dark blue water contrasts with a floor of brick. The walls are covered with lush foliage. There's room for lounging under the handsome shade structure or for sun-bathing on the brick decking.

A tile floor extends the feeling of the house and a wood screen creates a cozy corner for outdoor dining and relaxing. Table can be positioned in the shade of the tree or moved out into the sun on chilly days.

Here the pool and planting were planned to complement each other. The garden has been modified through the years, but the major elements remain intact. The trunks are a 15-year-old soft-tip yucca that was part of my original design for Dr. and Mrs. Jerry Sievers.

So maybe you'll have to settle for a little bit less than your ideal. Obviously no property is perfect. Some small items you can easily live with or handle yourself. But try not to overlook any *major* problems. Years ago, the United States Government had a complex rating system for land suitable for housing. One site was rated far above any others, somewhere around 96 percent. Years later it was discovered what the missing 4 percent represented. The land was subject to periodic flooding.

It's easy to panic when you find yourself surrounded by a barren yard with only dust or mud and weeds to look at. The temptation is to call a "concrete man" to pour a patio or an irrigation company to install a sprinkler system. Stay away from the phone and try to resist the urge to rush outside and start planting trees.

There is a logical order that a landscape professional normally follows when a complete garden is to be installed at one time. This is shown in the accompanying box. Actually, there is considerable overlapping and coordination, but the general order prevails.

A strained budget, site conditions and special priorities may modify this sequence. Fencing is often needed immediately upon moving in. A spa or shade trellis can be a future addition. Erosion control is usually the first order of business on a hillside lot.

When you have to modify this sequence, it's important to allow for work that you plan to do later. Install pipes or sleeves that must go under paving. Include footings where posts will occur in a patio. Keep plants and piping clear of future construction. Leave room for equipment access. A little foresight now can save a great deal of time, effort and money later.

TOLERANCES

You're *likely* to notice that I use *most, many, probably, often, generally, could, sometime, such as, if, but, however, approximately, usually* and similar qualifying words throughout this book. It's not that I don't know what I'm talking about. It's that there are many variables, especially

Landscape contractor Dave Geller enjoys his handiwork with a friend. An old flagstone patio was expanded and a wood seat built in the shade of a large Southern magnolia tree. Note the lattice built on top of the concrete block wall for added privacy.

Logical Order of Installation
1. Design
2. Rough Grading and Retaining Walls
3. Spas and Swimming Pools
4. Paving
5. Finish Grading and Drainage
6. Fencing
7. Sprinkler Systems
8. Lighting and Electrical Work
9. Shade Trellises and Patio Roofs
10. Miscellaneous Construction
11. Soil Preparation and Weed Killers
12. Planting
13. Lawns
14. Furniture and Finishing Touches

Do you have a problem with a narrow side yard? Landscape contractor Jim Keener of Landscape Associates turned this previously unusable space into a pleasant sitting area.

Here the logical order of installation means installing walls and fences first to keep pets and children in or out. Wide side yards give easy access for patio and other future construction.

Installing your own landscaping is easier and more fun when the entire family participates. Jason isn't old enough to sweep or mix mortar, but he's good with a hose.

in regard to personal preferences and living plants.

We may live in the age of the computer, but rigid formulas are as difficult to apply to the landscape as they are to people. It would be nice to have a chart that would say, "Apply 2.3 liters of water every 36-1/2 hours and 8 kilograms of 6-10-4 commercial fertilizer every 44 days." Or, "Install 378 square feet of concrete paving and 12-2/3 cubic yards of topsoil." It just doesn't work that way. You must consider the alternatives, assess the possibilities and make a decision best suited to the specific situation which is *probably* constantly changing. If there is any rule at all, it's: *Generalizations are no good—including this one.*

Tolerance is a closely related subject. Don't try to apply the fine standards of the furniture or aircraft industries to the landscape. You'll only be frustrated. It's impossible to impose a hundredth-of-an-inch tolerance to a brick or a plank when they themselves may vary a quarter of an inch. Overall straightness, level, plumb (verticality) and pattern are *usually* more important than precision of the individual parts. When installing any landscape work, stand back occasionally to see if it looks "right." This is *often* a better test than the tape measure or level.

A FIRST STEP

A garden is a highly complex organism with many interrelated parts. Make a list of your specific requirements and what you want your garden to be. Take a drive to see what appeals to you and what leaves you cold. Get a pile of garden magazines and clip out photos of what you like. Study the descriptions of the various garden styles and decide what overall feeling you want to achieve.

Restrain yourself for a little longer. It's time to start designing, but no digging yet.

STYLES

Style should not just be a copy from some other time or culture. A design is most successful when it is adapted to the specific site, climate and way of life. However, we don't have to reject centuries of garden art—we can borrow some of the elements that fit our conditions. In this way we can achieve a *flavor* of what we admire from the past while creating new and vital solutions of our own.

By definition, a successful garden of today would be *contemporary* or *of the times*. But the following styles or motifs may be appropriate to a specific house and site and family. Oriental—Serene, natural, but neat

A gentle slope with carefully placed boulders and Japanese black pines reflect the *Oriental* style of this house. The Japanese stone lantern is the definitive touch.

A *Natural* style was chosen here to take advantage of the sloping site. Boulders, rough textured wood and flowing lines are complemented by low maintenance planting.

Tile, wrought iron and rough plaster walls set the style here. Red clay pots accent the *Spanish-Mediterranean* appearance. Landscape architecture by Lang and Wood.

This lush garden in Costa Rica is as *Tropical* as they come. You can achieve similar results by using big-leaved plants and colorful foliage and flowers adapted to your climate.

and orderly. Ponds, pebbles and boulders. Stone lanterns, bridges and bamboo tubs. Korean grass, mondo grass, baby's tears, black and other pines, blue atlas cedar, junipers, cycad, camellia, nandina, golden and other bamboos, and *podocarpus.*

Spanish-Mediterranean—Informal, antique, simple. Slumpstone, adobe, wrought iron and tile. Pergolas, fountains, clay pots and decomposed granite. Yuccas, bird of paradise, aloes, geranium, olive, dracena, prickly pear, century plant, barrel cactus, fan palms, California pepper and Aleppo pine.

Tropical—Lush, overgrown, cool, dramatic. Logs, mounds, volcanic rocks. Waterfalls, lagoons and aviaries. *Philodendron selloum,* hibiscus, golden and giant bamboo, aralia, tree ferns, bougainvillea, jacaranda, Algerian ivy, coral tree, palms, Nile lily and *Agave attenuata.*

Natural—Relaxed, flowing lines, rough textures, contours, rambling. Railroad ties, boulders, split rail and grapestake fences, stone walls. Flagstone, pebble concrete, redwood tubs and barrels. Xylosma, junipers, sycamore, oak, eucalyptus, iris and other bulbs, daylily, periwinkle and wildflowers.

This *Natural* stream bed is actually in a small front yard. Dichondra ground cover provides lushness and dwarf Nile lilies grow between the boulders. Design and installation by the owner, Kirk Aiken.

The *Formal* style of the louvre is appropriate for its setting, but I doubt that you'd want to keep your yard this way.

Personally, I prefer natural plant shapes, but the rectangular forms of these carefully trimmed wax-leaf privets are in good proportion with the house and the plants are full and healthy.

Sophisticated—Balanced, geometrical, polished, refined. Terrazzo, slate and brick. Fountains, topiary, sculpture and large pots. Boxwood, Italian cypress, Indian laurel fig, magnolia, natal plum, English and Hahn's ivy, tree roses, holly, wax-leaf privet, stone pine, star jasmine, and beds of color.

Other categories—*Desert* is similar to Spanish-Mediterranean with more emphasis on native plants, crushed rock, sand and boulders. *Alpine* combines some of the feeling of Oriental and Natural with groves of trees, conifers, meadow-like lawns and rock-garden plants. *Ranch* is characterized by a casual layout with used brick, rail fences, climbing roses and orchard trees. *Modern* is sophisticated in a striking manner, with angles, structure and unconventional use of plants.

Sophisticated materials and forms are used in this pool garden. If it has to have a name, I'd call it *Modern* or *Sophisticated.*

This is a "real" Japanese garden designed by famed professor Nakane of Osaka. Except it's in Singapore and the plants, like the striking yellow flame tree, are tropical. It shows that you can adapt almost any style to almost any locality and still have a successful design.

The strong, horizontal lines of this entry patio and wall feel at home in a flat Tucson site. A motor court of crushed rock, compatible plant materials and an old saguaro cactus complete this *Desert* scene created by landscape architect Warren Jones.

First Comes the Design | 2

Every garden is designed by someone. Complex projects call for the services of a professional, but the average yard can often be designed successfully by an amateur—with proper guidance. If you decide to design your own garden, the first rule is to learn to sift through the free advice offered by friends, relatives, neighbors and everyone who has ever laid a brick, built a fence or planted a plant. Some of their suggestions can be helpful, others disastrous.

This book should answer most of your questions. See page 182 for other books and places to get assistance. If you still get stuck, you might consult with a professional on a limited basis.

PLANNING

Regardless of who is doing the designing, there is a general procedure that is advisable for both amateurs and professionals.

First, prepare an accurate plan of your land at a scale of either 1/8 or 1/4 inch equal to one foot. Graph paper makes it easier to convert the measurements to the plan. Show existing conditions such as the house, property lines, easements, underground and overhead utilities, paving, walls, fences, trees, slopes and so forth. Include doors, windows and overhangs. Also mark down the direction of the prevailing wind, views (good and bad), north arrow, drainage flow and similar items.

Lay a piece of tracing paper over the plan. Now is the time to explore, experiment, dream, reject, erase— all the while trying to picture the completed garden. Think in terms of the

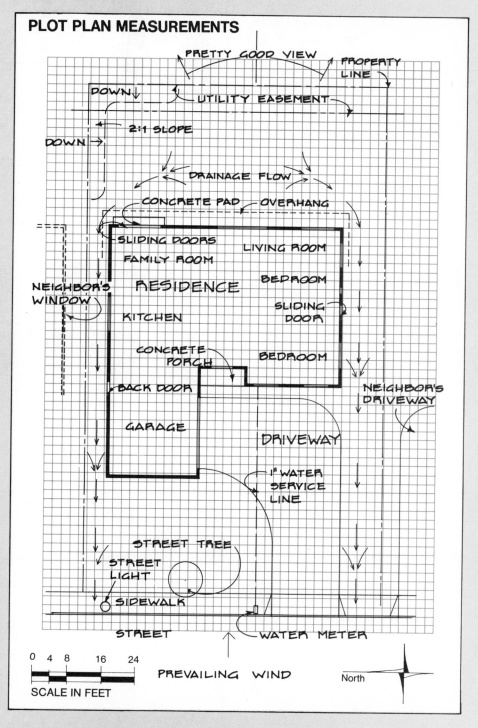

PLOT PLAN MEASUREMENTS

PRETTY GOOD VIEW — PROPERTY LINE
DOWN — UTILITY EASEMENT
2:1 SLOPE
DOWN
DRAINAGE FLOW
CONCRETE PAD — OVERHANG
SLIDING DOORS — LIVING ROOM
FAMILY ROOM
RESIDENCE — BEDROOM
NEIGHBOR'S WINDOW
KITCHEN — SLIDING DOOR
CONCRETE PORCH — BEDROOM
BACK DOOR — NEIGHBOR'S DRIVEWAY
GARAGE — DRIVEWAY
1" WATER SERVICE LINE
STREET TREE
STREET LIGHT
SIDEWALK
STREET — WATER METER
0 4 8 16 24
SCALE IN FEET
PREVAILING WIND
North

Beautiful design compositions require a skillful blending of form, color and texture, and knowledge of construction and plants. Landscape Architect: Lee Sharfman.

style you've selected as described in Chapter 1.

A diagrammatic layout of use areas, as shown here, is a good way to begin. Carefully integrate circulation, privacy, wind, noise, views, drainage and sun/shade patterns with the overall organization.

As your ideas begin to crystallize, you can draw in the paving and other structures such as walls, fences and shade trellises. Next, decide what uses the plants are to serve, where they should go and how big they should get. Shade, privacy, noise reduction, windbreak and erosion control are a few of the important uses for plants. Then make tentative selections based on the plant lists in Chapters 6 and 13.

BEAUTY

Sadly enough, a garden can function quite well and still not be pleasant to look at or to be in. Try to apply basic art principles to your design. Proportion, color, texture, unity and rhythm are just as important to a garden as they are to a painting. Think of your garden as three-dimensional—even four-dimensional when movement through time and the ever-changing nature of living plants is considered. Coupled with all the practical factors, this makes a garden infinitely more difficult to create than other art forms. But don't be overwhelmed. Here are a few suggestions:

● Limit the number of construction materials and repeat those that are used in the house wherever possible. Likewise, stick with the house colors.

● Don't try to use every plant in the nursery. Think in terms of areas, groups and masses. One-of-this and one-of-that usually looks terrible.

● Start out with simple and restrained plans. Many plants will eventually provide a bonus of seasonal displays that may not be evident when they're first planted. You can add accents later if you still feel something is lacking.

● Concentrate on the overall concept and avoid fussy details and gaudy gimmicks. Be bold. If in doubt, make it larger, not smaller.

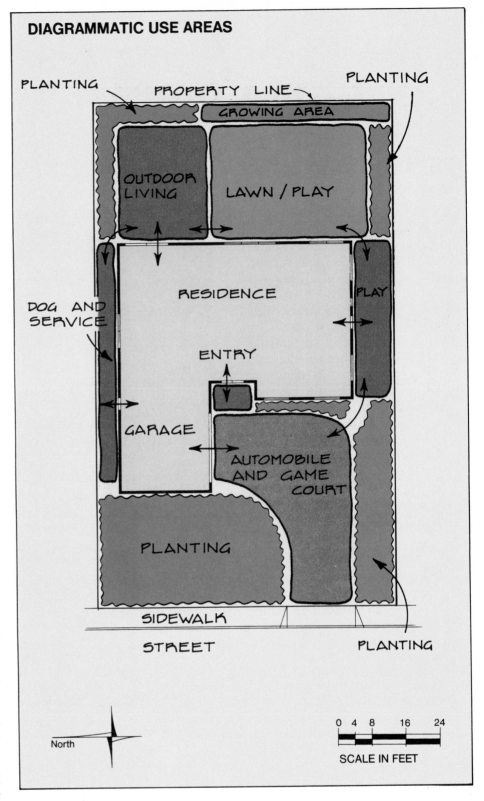

DIAGRAMMATIC USE AREAS

Famous "Sand Garden" in Kyoto is for meditating, not family entertaining or touch football. Decide what functions your garden must accommodate before you design.

Front entrance was laid out first with stakes and string to get a feeling of size. Footing was then dug for railroad tie wall.

CHECKING YOUR PLAN

This is a good time to give a critical eye to what you've come up with so far. If you have trouble picturing it, it might be helpful to go outside and make a "mock-up" with stakes and strings. Pretend you're having friends over for a barbeque, or you're one of the children, or even the dog. Does the proposed plan serve everyone well? Does it accomplish all your desired uses? Involve the entire family—if the plan passes the test at this stage, you're on the right track.

Make sure the plan meets local building codes and deed restrictions, and doesn't violate any setbacks or easements. Technical plans for structures, sprinklers, lighting and drains don't have to be completed until you are ready to install them, but they should be roughed-out at this time. This will allow you to include sleeves, stub-outs and footings where they will be needed. Don't forget to consider possible future additions such as a swimming pool, spa, playhouse or extra bedroom.

Before making final decisions on materials, size of plants and the extent of paved areas, you'd better make an overall cost estimate. If you intend to have all or part of the work done by others, call in a reputable contractor and ask for a bid. If the price comes in much higher than you can or want to invest, this is a good time to consider substitutions. Maybe the patio will have to be made of concrete instead of brick. Or all the plants will have to be smaller to start with, or the lawn will have to be planted from seed instead of being sodded. Rather than cut on the basic quality, some items can be set aside as a future phase and installed when finances allow. One of the advantages of a good plan is that everything will fit together, even if it's not all installed at one time.

HOW MUCH WILL IT COST?

There's not much you can do about house payments and property taxes. Furniture, carpeting and drapes are usually essential. With the outdoors you have more choice. It would be nice to have a completed landscape the day you move in. More often it's a matter of setting priorities, doing the most important items first and

Landscape Costs			
Type of Work	Typical Cost Range in $		
Design	200	to	600
Rough Grading	100	to	200
Paving	1000	to	2000
Finish Grading & Drainage	200	to	400
Fencing (Assumes cost split with neighbors)	500	to	1500
Sprinkler System	500	to	1000
Lighting	100	to	200
Miscellaneous Construction	200	to	400
Soil Preparation	200	to	400
Planting	600	to	2000
Lawns	200	to	800
Furniture & Finishing Touches	200	to	500
Total	$4000	to	$10000

It takes considerable skill to construct a 6-foot masonry wall. There are many other landscape projects better suited to doing-it-yourself.

waiting for the remaining until the budget recovers from the shock of moving.

Once you have a plan worked out, you can come up with a reasonable estimate of cost. It will undoubtedly differ from the chart on page 15 to some extent, but the basic items and general costs will most likely be similar. The chart is based on the *average* builder-constructed house in the $40,000 to $80,000 price range on a level 7,500 square foot lot. All material and labor are provided by a landscape contractor. Do-it-yourself items normally save approximately 50 percent of the contracted figure.

Few homeowners have the time, capability or desire to do everything. Unless you've had previous experience or can get experienced help, it's best to leave certain items to the experts. Concrete paving, masonry walls, chain-link fences, 110-volt electrical work, gas lines, spas and swimming pools, and planting large specimen trees should be attempted only after careful consideration. Brick-on-sand paving, wood fences, sprinkler systems, minor construction, simple trellises, low-voltage lighting and most planting can be successfully handled by an amateur. Getting the family involved is not only fun, but can really speed up a project and be a rewarding experience for children.

Ten to fifteen percent of the cost of the house and property is considered a reasonable investment by most realtors. The cost of a spa, swimming pool, patio roof and other major construction would be additional.

Financing is readily available for construction work, but is sometimes more difficult to arrange for planting. The best way is to have landscape costs included in the first mortgage—when possible. Going to a personal loan means interest of 12 percent or more on the total amount for each year of the loan—a very expensive way to go if the payments are stretched out over several years. Also, in most cases, the interest is pre-charged so you don't save anything by paying it off ahead of time.

When you need $3,000 or more, and if you have a reasonable amount of equity in your home, it's better to use the property as collateral and benefit from simple interest on the declining balance, the same as on a first mortgage. A second mortgage or home equity loan that permits you to use the money for any purpose has an interest rate of around 12 percent. And you can get 80 percent of your equity. A similar loan that requires proof of improvement of the property carries a lower percentage rate and you can get 100 percent of your equity. Usually you can pay off either one of these loans early without a penalty charge.

CAPITALIZE ON YOUR CLIMATE

Indigenous architecture usually takes advantage of the best characteristics of a site and helps overcome some of the disadvantages. The prairie sod house, the arctic igloo and the thatched hut of tropical climes are well suited to their location. They are also oriented to benefit from desirable sun and breeze, and to exclude unwanted elements.

Unfortunately, we have no such luck. The typical mass-produced house is plopped indiscriminately down on the lots of a tract with no regard for exposure. The sliding glass doors are

This Palm Springs garden capitalizes on the unique low desert climate. The swimming pool and small lawn are complemented by heat-loving oleanders, Mexican Fan Palms and colorful petunias. Design: Eric Johnson.

likely to face the hot sun and the wide overhang often occurs on the north side where it's least beneficial. Insulation is needed to help correct mistakes and forced-air heating or air-conditioning must be run most of the year to make the place tolerable.

Few people have the opportunity to start from scratch and design a house to truly fit the site and climate. But most of us *can* do something with the landscape. Locate the major patio area in the most desirable exposure. For hot climates this usually means the east or north side of the house. Along the ocean where cool breezes are an almost daily occurrence, the south or west side may be more comfortable. Sometimes a small, secondary sitting area can be a sun-trap for winter warmth, or it can be a very shaded area to escape from summer heat. Shade trellises can break the sun on patios and house walls. A removable covering such as the shade cloth used by nurseries can be changed with the season. If winds are a problem, even narrow windbreaks can filter strong winds and reduce their intensity.

In our desire for year-round effect, we often overlook the advantage of deciduous trees. They can shade the house during the hot months and then conveniently drop their leaves to allow the welcome sun to enter during

This house in Borneo works *with* the climate. The high-peaked, thatched roof permits hot air to excape and provides protection from torrential rains. Stilt construction allows cool air and high water to flow under the house, and discourages cobras from entering.

the winter. Indoor temperatures can be lowered as much as 10 to 20 degrees when the roof is heavily shaded. High-branching trees on the east and south sides, and low-branching ones on the west are most effective.

Shrubs can also be helpful in shading walls and windows. Lawn and ground covers can reduce glare and radiation, significantly affecting the temperature of the surrounding area. Not only is the general comfort increased by using garden structures and plants as climate modifiers, but there are significant savings in heating and cooling costs.

LEGAL CONSIDERATIONS

In a society as complex as ours, even landscaping is subject to restrictions, codes and laws. As in all business transactions, it's advisable to deal only with properly licensed and insured companies, to have signed contracts that clearly define the work, and to receive labor and material releases before making final payment.

Be sure to verify property lines before starting any work. Check for easements or rights-of-way that might limit use of the property. Locate septic tanks and cesspools if there is no sewer service. Find out if there are any deed restrictions and if there is

Fran Harris enjoys her new front yard. The old back yard patio is larger and more convenient to the kitchen, but too chilly except on rare hot summer days in her cool coastal climate.

Built before air conditioning was common, this old ranch house is cool in summer because it's surrounded by large shade trees. It's also warm in winter because the trees are deciduous and allow the sun to reach the entire roof area.

an architectural committee that has to approve the plans. Cooperation with neighbors on fencing, planting and views may not be legally required, but it is almost always mutually beneficial.

BUILDING CODES

Most cities and counties have building codes and may require permits for landscape work. Check with the agency having jurisdiction in your area. Here is a list of common restrictions.

Grading—Cuts exceeding five feet, fills exceeding three feet, or more than 50 cubic yards of material require permits. Most lots must drain into the street or storm drain, not over banks or onto neighboring property.

Banks—Approved erosion control, ground cover, shrubs and trees are required. Hazardous brush must be removed and replaced with fire-resistant plants in fire danger areas.

Spas and Swimming Pools—Engineering and installation require permits. Power lines may not cross over. Pumps or other equipment cannot be located in a *required* side yard.

Fences—There is usually a 42-inch height limitation within a front yard setback, 6 feet for side and rear yards. Pool fences must be 54 inches or 5 feet high with self-closing gates and lockable latches.

Retaining Walls—Normally, no permit is required for walls less than 4 feet high, including footing, without a slope behind, called a *surcharge*. Still, it must be an approved wall.

Sprinklers—Supply lines must be of approved size and material. Heavy plastic is accepted by most agencies if buried 18 inches deep. Anti-siphon devices to prevent backflow of possibly contaminated water into potable supply is often required for sprinkler heads at ground level.

Lighting and Electrical—Permits are required for all work except low-voltage types. Conduit must be buried 12 inches deep or protected under paving. Direct burial cable is now accepted by some departments.

Parkways—Property lines normally begin 6 inches back from the sidewalk, leaving from 3 to 10 feet of

Why can't you cut down a street tree or plant one you like better? Because it's really not on your property. But, in most cities, *you* have to take care of it. Actually, this ginkgo tree is an excellent choice for this narrow parkway.

parkway owned by the city or county, but maintained by the property owner. Paving and planting are usually restricted within this area. For example, street trees cannot be removed or changed without permission. Where the sidewalk is adjacent to the street, the property line or an easement is located in the yard to allow for street trees.

Patio Roofs—Design and installation need approval. Aluminum and canvas awnings, and detached pergolas of 400 square feet or less are usually exempted. No power lines can pass over, however. Shade trellises in fire zones must have wide enough spaces to allow air-borne embers to fall through.

Gas—All piping, valves and equipment must be approved. Some uses are prohibited entirely.

Cantilevered Decks—These are usually strict requirements when constructed over a bank. A variance is sometimes called for, in addition to a building permit, for slopes steeper than 2 to 1.

Building departments are usually quite strict about hillside decks because they have a way of slipping and collapsing if not built properly. Landscape architects Lang and Wood designed this one to last.

CONTRACTOR'S RESPONSIBILITY

Poor drainage, concrete cracks and plant guarantees sometimes become legal problems. Some small amounts of standing water are virtually unavoidable, especially after a heavy rainstorm. However, large areas that don't drain and paving or planting areas that obviously slope towards the house usually indicate the need for correction by the contractor, and possible payment for water damage if the area drained properly before the work was performed.

Hairline cracks in concrete are inevitable and do not indicate defective work. Also, some shifting and cracking may occur in expansive soils even if proper precautions are taken. Large cracks from too thin a pour, laying over dry adobe soil with no precautions, and lack of expansion joints in obvious locations are usually considered the responsibility of the contractor.

Because maintenance is almost always assumed by the homeowner as soon as planting is completed, the question often arises as to who killed the plant, the contractor in planting it or the owner in not caring for it properly. Normally, the contractor gives a 30 or 60 day guarantee and allows for the replacement of a few plants, regardless of the cause. If the garden is bone dry—or extremely wet—and many plants succumb, the responsibility may lie with the owner, especially if watering needs were properly explained. Failure of seed to germinate is almost always due to improper watering. Extensive weed growth is hardly ever brought in with the seed or fertilizer.

THE LANDSCAPE INDUSTRY

Few people know what the differences are between the several divisions of the landscape industry. The various roles used to be played by one person—now it takes an entire cast. To further complicate matters, there is still considerable overlapping of the parts. The following clarification should help you to know whom to call for what.

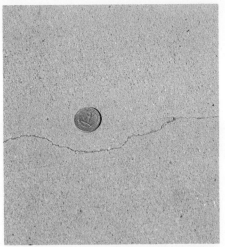

No need for concern if a few hairline cracks appear in your concrete. They really don't hurt anything. We used to use a dime to indicate scale, but it's up to a quarter now.

Landscape Architect—The landscape architect is required to be licensed in most states and is the planning expert best qualified to design outdoor areas. Training is comparable to that of an architect or engineer. He or she usually holds a degree from an accredited university and often has additional experience in the other phases of the industry. The initials *AILA* (American Institute of Landscape Architects) or *ASLA* (American Society of Landscape Architects) signify membership in a professional group similar to the the *AMA* (American Medical Association) in the medical profession.

The landscape architect does not sell a specific plant or product, but wants only to create the best living environment possible for the client. He receives remuneration through professional fees rather than through discounts or profits. He considers total site development, including structural elements along with planting and sprinklers. When possible, he should be called in while the tract house is still under construction and, on custom houses, to collaborate with the architect when the house is being designed.

Landscape Contractor—Also licensed by most states, the landscape contractor is the person who is able to install the garden from the plans of the landscape architect. Not only does he handle planting, he will usually include the paving, sprinklers and structure as well. Sometimes his own crew will do all the work, at other times he will function as sort of a general contractor, seeing that various sub-contractors perform their work properly. Most landscape contractors belong to an association such as the *CLCA* (California Landscape Contractors Association) or the *ALCA* (Arizona Landscape Contractors Association), through which they keep abreast of latest developments and methods.

Nurseryman—The nurseryman is charged with the important job of supplying plant material for a garden. Most of the time he grows at least some of the plants himself, ordering the rest from wholesale growers. He does his utmost to keep a stock of healthy, well-grown plants of a size suitable for the container indicated on the plant list. He will not substitute plants that may be difficult to find, but will advise the owner to ask the landscape architect if a substitute is in order. He is usually qualified to offer general planting and maintenance advice, and quite often is an expert on local climatic conditions. If a nurseryman has state *certification,* that means he has passed an examination in regards to competency. Most nurserymen are devoted to their work and belong to the *AAN* (American Association of Nurserymen) and horticultural societies.

Gardener—Gardening is a highly complex art requiring many years of training and experience. Unfortunately, there is no state registration act that assures the homeowner that a gardener is qualified. City licenses are for tax purposes only. Frankly, most of the really good gardeners are in such fields as golf course, park, cemetery, estate and commercial maintenance.

The homeowner must carefully assess the ability of the individual gardener, supervise the work with him—most watering is done by the owner—and be prepared to pay a fair price for his time. Partial services for cutting and edging lawns, and general clean-up and weeding are more common than complete care.

When a gardener is to be completely in charge of a garden, he receives the finished product from the landscape contractor and guides it to its ultimate form. He must be receptive to the intent of the landscape architect and owner, yet he will have to make many interpretations of his own as the years go by. If you're thinking of a casual, natural effect and your gardener is of the old school and shears everything into a sphere or cube, there's bound to be trouble. It's wise to explain what your personal preferences are before hiring someone. One day with the hedge clippers can destroy years of growth.

Landscape Designer—This title is often used by those engaged in landscape design but unlicensed as landscape architects. Some are well-qualified, some are not. The public has no way of knowing from the name alone. A landscape designer may be in business for himself or work through a contractor or nursery. Some are deeply involved and give considerable personal attention to their work. Those with commercial ties are more apt to function as a salesperson and tend to concentrate on profit and money derived from plant discounts rather than professional service.

Multiple Roles—Much confusion is caused by the fact that some nurserymen and gardeners design and install gardens, some landscape contractors offer planning services, and some landscape architects are also landscape contractors. With proper licensing, this is not illegal and there is much to be said in favor of the efficiency possible under such multiple businesses. Natural gardens are difficult to capture on paper and are often better created during installation. On the other hand, commercial interests can limit design, and the spreading of talent and energy over several fields can result in lower quality services.

LANDSCAPE DESIGN SERVICES AND FEES

There seem to be three main reasons why more homeowners don't hire a landscape architect to design their property. First, they think it will be too expensive. Second, they're afraid their own ideas will be disregarded. Third, many landscape architects are totally involved in large projects and are not available for residential design.

Expense—Fees vary considerably with the job and the individual landscape architect. Most have a consultation fee of $50 to $100 to visit the site and to offer ideas and advice. This is a relatively inexpensive way to get a professional's input without being obligated any further. If additional consultation or a plan is desired, many landscape architects charge for all services on an hourly basis, usually with an estimated range of time for specific work. Others charge a percentage of construction cost or a lump-sum fee.

Typical basic plan cost for an average residence is between $600 and $1,000 depending on the complexity of the site, amount of structure, overall budget and client/designer relationship. This basic plan service normally includes an initial meeting on the site; one preliminary plan, cost estimate and site review; and construction drawings based on the approved preliminary plan. Preparation of the basic plot, major revisions or changes in the scope of the work, securing of bids, and supervision would be additional.

For a small property, a portion of a garden or a very simple development, some landscape architects will provide a one-trip service by drawing a plan on the site. Drafting and details are completed at the office and final prints are delivered by mail. This method eliminates a considerable amount of drafting and travel time, while still providing the essential design concept. This very efficient way of working ranges in cost from $200 to $500.

A landscape architect can also provide valuable services other than drawing plans for a new garden. Among them are: property selection, siting of house and collaboration with the building architect on the basic house design, selection of a house

There seems to be no purpose in butchering these wax-leaf privets. It not only looks bad, but it wastes gardening time that could be put to better use.

already built, general consultation, addition of a patio roof, shade trellis, swimming pool or spa, design of part of a garden, remodeling an existing garden, and maintenance advice.

Your Wishes—Most landscape architects encourage as much client participation as possible. Having a list and portfolio of clippings beforehand is very helpful.

Availability—This is quite often a problem. Springtime and fall are usually the busiest seasons, so it's sometimes easier to find one during summer or winter. When a registered landscape architect isn't available, it's possible to get the help you need from a landscape designer. Fees are usually lower than a landscape architect's but in many cases, charges and method of operation are quite similar.

INTRODUCTION TO MASTER LANDSCAPE PLANS

My mathematically minded son tells me that if I took the four basic lot types, with four basic styles, four basic climates and four different orientations to the sun, this would mean a total of 256 example master plans. And that if I added the factors of family composition, budget and maintenance preference, it would be an astronomical figure.

What I'm trying to illustrate is how the overall feeling of a certain style and the needs of a family determine the garden uses, and how climate and orientation also influence design—especially plant selection.

The example plans in this chapter and elsewhere in the book are intended to enable you to choose the ideas and solutions that apply best to your specific situation. They may appear complicated and confusing at first, but after looking them over several times they should start to become clearer. If you're lucky, you might even find that you're one of those people that can project the plan into 3 dimensions in your mind.

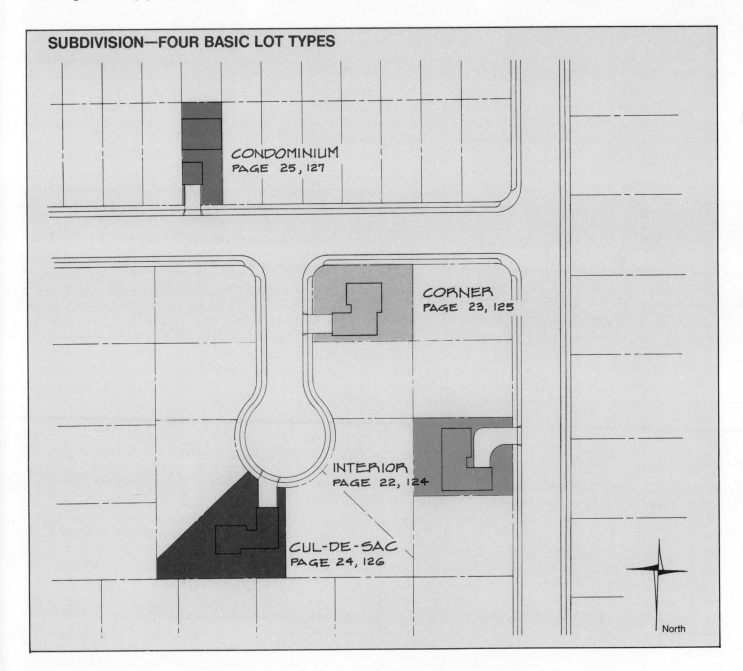

SUBDIVISION—FOUR BASIC LOT TYPES

CONDOMINIUM
PAGE 25, 127

CORNER
PAGE 23, 125

INTERIOR
PAGE 22, 124

CUL-DE-SAC
PAGE 24, 126

North

MASTER PLAN—Interior Lot

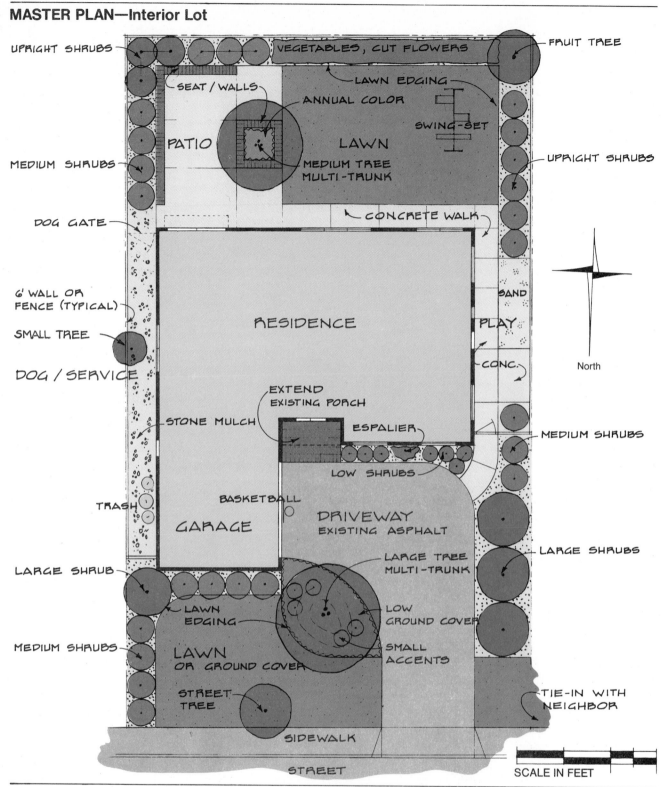

Labels on plan:
- UPRIGHT SHRUBS
- SEAT / WALLS
- VEGETABLES, CUT FLOWERS
- FRUIT TREE
- ANNUAL COLOR
- LAWN EDGING
- PATIO
- LAWN
- SWING-SET
- MEDIUM SHRUBS
- UPRIGHT SHRUBS
- MEDIUM TREE MULTI-TRUNK
- DOG GATE
- CONCRETE WALK
- 6' WALL OR FENCE (TYPICAL)
- SAND
- PLAY
- SMALL TREE
- RESIDENCE
- DOG / SERVICE
- CONC.
- North
- EXTEND EXISTING PORCH
- STONE MULCH
- ESPALIER
- MEDIUM SHRUBS
- LOW SHRUBS
- TRASH
- BASKETBALL
- GARAGE
- DRIVEWAY EXISTING ASPHALT
- LARGE SHRUBS
- LARGE SHRUB
- LARGE TREE MULTI-TRUNK
- LAWN EDGING
- LOW GROUND COVER
- MEDIUM SHRUBS
- LAWN OR GROUND COVER
- SMALL ACCENTS
- STREET TREE
- TIE-IN WITH NEIGHBOR
- SIDEWALK
- STREET
- SCALE IN FEET

Assumed Conditions
- Interior lot.
- Cool, coastal climate.
- Young family with small children.
- *Contemporary* style.
- Modest budget.
- Medium maintenance.

Design Considerations
- Driveway basketball area and separate side entrance for use by children when they get older.
- Side yard adjacent to bedrooms has sand box, storage space for toys and future bicycles.
- Back yard has open lawn for swing set and general play.
- Patio is extended beyond afternoon shadow of house to take advantage of sun. No shade trellis is needed for east exposure in cool climate.
- *Contemporary* style has an organized feeling with straight lines, controlled curves and simple shapes.

MASTER PLAN—Corner Lot

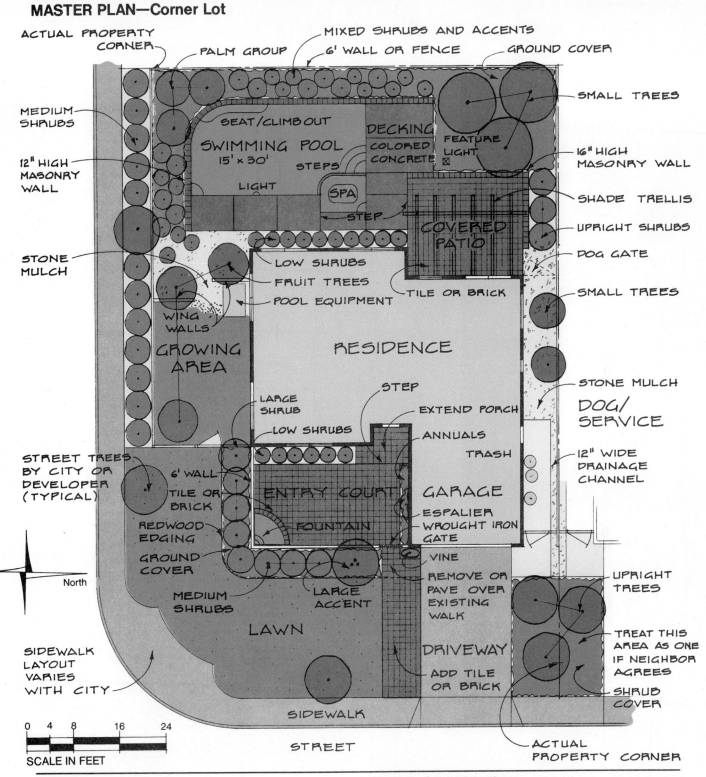

ACTUAL PROPERTY CORNER

PALM GROUP

MIXED SHRUBS AND ACCENTS

6' WALL OR FENCE

GROUND COVER

SMALL TREES

MEDIUM SHRUBS

SEAT/CLIMBOUT

SWIMMING POOL 15' x 30'

STEPS

DECKING COLORED CONCRETE

FEATURE LIGHT

12" HIGH MASONRY WALL

LIGHT

16" HIGH MASONRY WALL

SHADE TRELLIS

SPA

STONE MULCH

STEP

COVERED PATIO

UPRIGHT SHRUBS

DOG GATE

LOW SHRUBS

FRUIT TREES

POOL EQUIPMENT

TILE OR BRICK

SMALL TREES

WING WALLS

GROWING AREA

RESIDENCE

STEP

STONE MULCH

DOG/ SERVICE

LARGE SHRUB

EXTEND PORCH

LOW SHRUBS

ANNUALS

TRASH

12" WIDE DRAINAGE CHANNEL

STREET TREES BY CITY OR DEVELOPER (TYPICAL)

6' WALL

TILE OR BRICK

REDWOOD EDGING

GROUND COVER

ENTRY COURT

FOUNTAIN

GARAGE

ESPALIER

WROUGHT IRON GATE

VINE

North

MEDIUM SHRUBS

LARGE ACCENT

REMOVE OR PAVE OVER EXISTING WALK

UPRIGHT TREES

LAWN

DRIVEWAY

TREAT THIS AREA AS ONE IF NEIGHBOR AGREES

SIDEWALK LAYOUT VARIES WITH CITY

ADD TILE OR BRICK

SHRUB COVER

SIDEWALK

0   4   8   16   24

SCALE IN FEET

STREET

ACTUAL PROPERTY CORNER

Assumed Conditions
- Corner lot.
- Warm, sub-tropical climate.
- Active couple with no children. Frequent parties and entertaining.
- *Spanish-Mediterranean* style.
- Ample budget.
- Medium to high maintenance.

Design Considerations
- Paving added to driveway allows room for both cars and people. Enclosed entry court is comfortable for evening sitting.
- Covered patio and small swimming pool with a built-in spa are ideal for entertaining.
- Growing area or greenhouse makes use of large, sunny side yard.
- *Spanish-Mediterranean* style utilizes plaster or slump type block walls, wrought iron, tile or brick, and a classic Spanish fountain.

MASTER PLAN—Cul-de-sac Lot

Assumed Conditions
- Cul-de-sac lot.
- Moderate climate.
- Family with teen-age children, lots of relatives.
- *Natural* style.
- Average budget.
- Medium to low maintenance.

Design Considerations
- Extra parking is included for RV and teen-ager's cars.
- Multi-use game court and open lawn are for family games with a separate entrance to the game area.
- Patio has choice of sun or shade. Fire pit is for evening use.
- *Natural* style includes contours, boulders, stone mulch, wood path lights, stone walls and paving, and free-flowing lines.

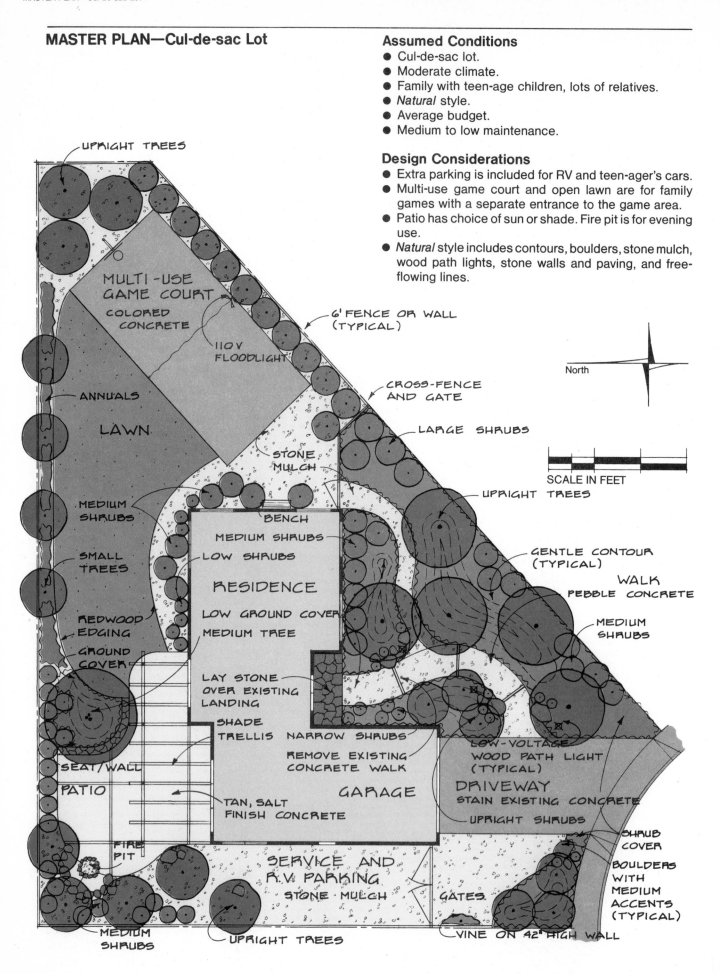

UPRIGHT TREES

MULTI-USE GAME COURT
COLORED CONCRETE

110 V FLOODLIGHT

6' FENCE OR WALL (TYPICAL)

CROSS-FENCE AND GATE

North

SCALE IN FEET

ANNUALS

LAWN

STONE MULCH

LARGE SHRUBS

UPRIGHT TREES

MEDIUM SHRUBS

BENCH
MEDIUM SHRUBS
LOW SHRUBS

RESIDENCE

LOW GROUND COVER

MEDIUM TREE

GENTLE CONTOUR (TYPICAL)

WALK
PEBBLE CONCRETE

MEDIUM SHRUBS

SMALL TREES

REDWOOD EDGING

GROUND COVER

LAY STONE OVER EXISTING LANDING

SHADE TRELLIS   NARROW SHRUBS

REMOVE EXISTING CONCRETE WALK

LOW-VOLTAGE WOOD PATH LIGHT (TYPICAL)

SEAT/WALL

PATIO

TAN, SALT FINISH CONCRETE

GARAGE

DRIVEWAY
STAIN EXISTING CONCRETE
UPRIGHT SHRUBS

FIRE PIT

SERVICE AND R.V. PARKING
STONE MULCH

GATES

SHRUB COVER

BOULDERS WITH MEDIUM ACCENTS (TYPICAL)

MEDIUM SHRUBS

UPRIGHT TREES

VINE ON 42" HIGH WALL

MASTER PLAN—Condo Lot

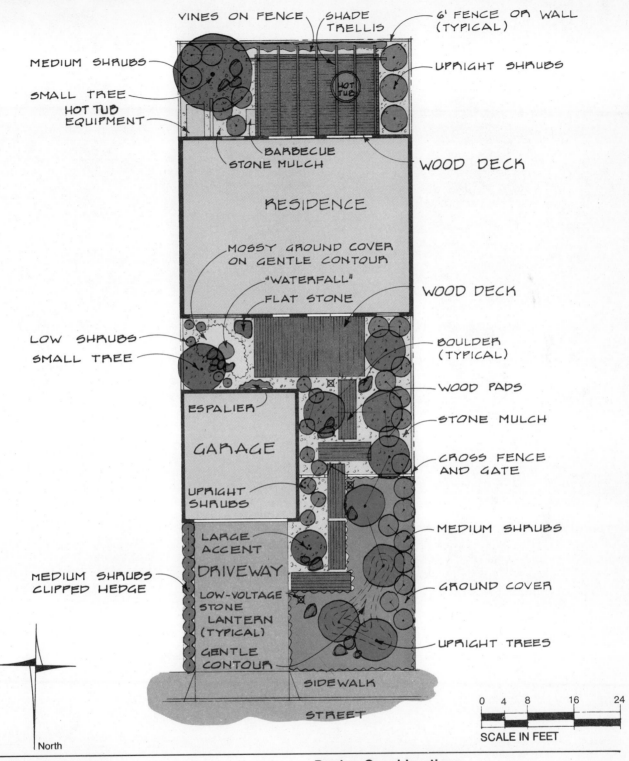

VINES ON FENCE

SHADE TRELLIS

6' FENCE OR WALL (TYPICAL)

MEDIUM SHRUBS

UPRIGHT SHRUBS

SMALL TREE

HOT TUB EQUIPMENT

HOT TUB

BARBECUE STONE MULCH

WOOD DECK

RESIDENCE

MOSSY GROUND COVER ON GENTLE CONTOUR

"WATERFALL"

FLAT STONE

WOOD DECK

LOW SHRUBS

SMALL TREE

BOULDER (TYPICAL)

WOOD PADS

STONE MULCH

ESPALIER

GARAGE

CROSS FENCE AND GATE

UPRIGHT SHRUBS

MEDIUM SHRUBS

LARGE ACCENT

MEDIUM SHRUBS CLIPPED HEDGE

DRIVEWAY

GROUND COVER

LOW-VOLTAGE STONE LANTERN (TYPICAL)

GENTLE CONTOUR

UPRIGHT TREES

SIDEWALK

STREET

North

0 4 8 16 24

SCALE IN FEET

Assumed Conditions

- Condominium lot.
- Severe climate.
- Retired or working couple, no children.
- *Oriental* style.
- Ample budget.
- Low maintenance.

Design Considerations

- Front wood walk and deck provide a gracious entry and sitting area.
- Water feature can be viewed from both the front deck and living room.
- Back deck with hot tub is protected by a shade trellis. Fences, shrubs and vines are used for privacy.
- *Oriental* style features wood decks, boulders and stone mulch, natural water feature, bamboo tubs and stone lanterns.

Relaxing & Entertaining | 3

Travel is expensive. Beaches, campgrounds, parks and other vacation spots are crowded. Home recreation is convenient, inexpensive and often more restful than harried trips.

Think of your yard as an outdoor room that needs a floor, walls and a roof. Incorporate some of your family's favorite activities. Allow for cooking and gracious entertaining. Now you have a garden that not only looks good, but truly serves your living and recreational needs.

Begin with the entrance. Because most arrivals will be by automobile, make sure there is adequate parking and unloading space. Standard driveways can be widened to allow for easier walking and extra parking. If you have a boat, trailer or camper, perhaps it can be accommodated unobtrusively alongside the garage.

Guests will appreciate a landing strip next to the curbing. A wide, gracious walk is an inviting approach to the front door. When you inherit a typical 3-foot wide walk, consider adding to it so it's more in scale with the house and property. Even a brick strip along each side will help considerably. If the only way from the street to the front door is via the driveway, it may be wise to build a separate walkway.

A generous landing or porch with a convenient bench is good for saying hello as well as goodbye to departing friends. Here again, you'll probably have to expand what's already there to improve the scale and usability.

Driveways don't have to be ugly. Brick with grass strips serves people as well as cars in this San Francisco front yard.

Concrete driveway is widened with generous tile walk and landing.

Brick strips make an attractive and inviting curbside landing.

Stone mulch landing also gives a place for trash cans on collection day. Trees are young Italian stone pines.

Space next to garage is put to good use for trailer parking.

Your landscape can be both intimate *and* a gathering place for family and friends.

Rather than have guests walk up the driveway, landscape architect Roy Seifert designed this separate entrance for the Katleman family in San Diego. Then he reinforced it with plantings to make it look like it had always been there.

Is your driveway too steep to walk on? These concrete steps are safer and keep cars away from the retaining wall.

PATIOS

Patios are for people. As discussed in the last chapter, they should be located to make the most of your specific climate and orientation. Or you may need more than one to give a choice between warm-and-protected or cool-and-breezy.

A successful patio must be large enough for entertaining guests, but should also have an intimate feeling for family use. An 8 by 10-foot space may hold a table and chairs, but would obviously feel cramped. Approximately 15 by 25 feet could be considered a minimum size. This allows for furniture, a barbecue and some storage, with room to move and without stubbing a toe.

Privacy, wind protection and the relationship to the kitchen or family room should also be considered. If a patio is too far from the house, placed in the prevailing wind or within view of the neighbors, it probably won't get much use.

Properly located, a patio may be comfortable without any additional shade. However, in most Western climates, a shade tree or shade trellis is usually essential. Solid roofs are less popular than an open grillework that filters the sun because a solid roof tends to keep light out of adjacent rooms. A solid roof also costs considerably more and is more diffi-

The Don Thompsons asked me to design an outdoor room that would be comfortable for everyday use, but still accommodate an occasional large group. The secret is the built-in seating and spaciousness carefully broken up by the fire pit and Brazilian pepper tree.

cult to build. In areas of typically low rainfall, the lack of rain protection is not a major problem. A partially solid, partially open roof provides a place to keep furniture dry without

the drawbacks of a totally solid one. For rainier northern climates, a solid patio roof can rescue many an outdoor barbecue or party from disaster.

These shade trellis posts are set on top of retaining wall. The built-in wood bench eliminates the need for space-consuming furniture.

A trellis can shade your patio without cutting out light into adjacent rooms.

Vinyl-treated canvas is good for about 5 years and requires only a simple pipe frame.

TRELLISES AND PATIO ROOFS

Shade trellises and patio roofs are kind of an orphan in the construction industry. Most general building contractors find the job too small—they'd rather build houses. Many landscape contractors consider them a nuisance, and try to avoid getting involved. Most homeowners are overwhelmed with the thought of building one themselves. Try to find a company specializing in patio construction. If you can't, one solution is to work along with a carpenter, contributing as much as you have time and experience for.

The basic framing is the same whether the roof is solid or open. Lumber costs are approximately $200 for an overhead area of 200 square feet. Add $75 for 2x2s, or $150 for 1x6 sheathing and mineral-coated roll roofing. A good price from a contractor doing all the work would be $4 per square foot for a shade trellis and $5 per square foot for a solid roof, including footings. The patio and staining or painting would be additional. Shingle and tile roofs require a steeper pitch and cost considerably more than roll-type roofing.

Even if you hire experienced helpers, most of them are strong on construction and weak on design. If you know of an example that you like, have them take a look at it before giving a bid.

By using one wall of the house for support, it's a simple task to attach a patio roof or trellis. The trick is to make it look like part of the original construction and not an unrelated afterthought. Repeating existing house materials and colors will make it more harmonious.

Oversize rafters, beams and posts are more in scale with the outdoors than minimum dimensions. Use 3x6 or 4x6 rafters rather than 2x6s. Standard 4x4 posts and 4x8 beams can be enhanced with "plant-ons" of 1x2 or larger strips for a built-up effect. Most building departments have span charts indicating minimum lumber sizes and can offer over-the-counter advice. A building permit is required for a shade trellis and footings must be inspected before pouring any concrete. Set-back requirements must also be complied with.

SHADE TRELLIS CONSTRUCTION

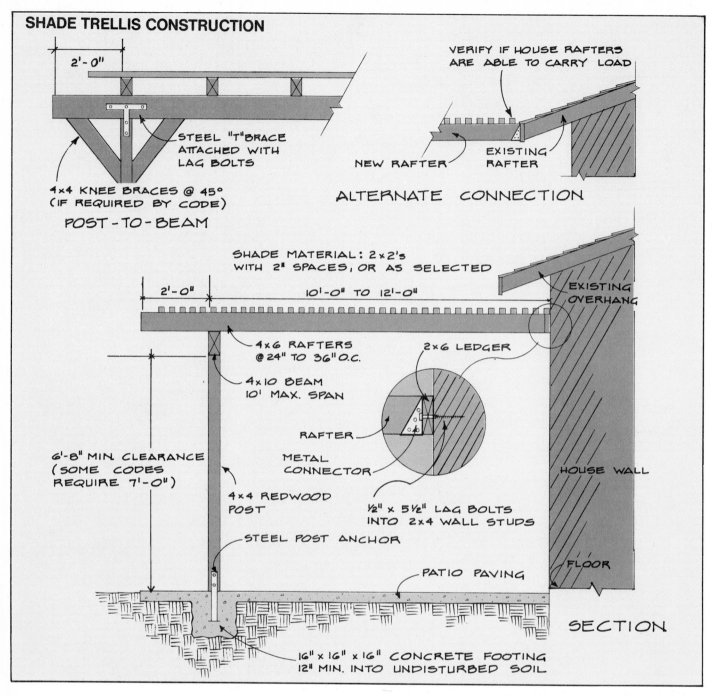

2'-0"

STEEL "T" BRACE
ATTACHED WITH
LAG BOLTS

4x4 KNEE BRACES @ 45°
(IF REQUIRED BY CODE)

POST-TO-BEAM

VERIFY IF HOUSE RAFTERS
ARE ABLE TO CARRY LOAD

NEW RAFTER   EXISTING
              RAFTER

ALTERNATE CONNECTION

SHADE MATERIAL: 2x2's
WITH 2" SPACES, OR AS SELECTED

2'-0"   10'-0" TO 12'-0"

EXISTING
OVERHANG

4x6 RAFTERS
@ 24" TO 36" O.C.

2x6 LEDGER

4x10 BEAM
10' MAX. SPAN

RAFTER

6'-8" MIN CLEARANCE
(SOME CODES
REQUIRE 7'-0")

METAL
CONNECTOR

HOUSE WALL

4x4 REDWOOD
POST

½" x 5½" LAG BOLTS
INTO 2x4 WALL STUDS

STEEL POST ANCHOR

PATIO PAVING

FLOOR

16" x 16" x 16" CONCRETE FOOTING
12" MIN. INTO UNDISTURBED SOIL

SECTION

This built-up post is made with two 2x8s with a 4x4 inside.

Another way to build up a post is to nail 1x2s on all four sides of the 4x4.

CONSTRUCTING A SHADE TRELLIS

Post-anchor was set in concrete patio with footing below. Bolts will be put through the post to prevent shifting. If you must leave a post-anchor unused for any period, cover it with an overturned plastic container to avoid accidents.

Connecting the rafters with steel fasteners directly to a ledger lag bolted to the house wall is stronger and usually preferable to attaching to an existing roof overhang. Existing fascia is notched to receive the rafters.

Steel fasteners are also used for post-to-beam and rafter-to-beam connections. They are stronger than toenailing and bolts are stronger than nails.

The 2x3s are shifted to test desired shade density before nailing permanently.

This is a *knee brace* required by most building departments to eliminate side sway or *shear*. The "T" brace is too small to do the job alone.

Effectiveness of 2x3s is shown by the shade pattern on the previously sun-drenched wall.

Woven reed is an inexpensive covering ideal for plant areas. It usually lasts 3 or 4 years before replacement is necessary. It is also sharp edged and can give nasty cuts. Wear gloves and long pants when working with it.

Sometimes an open framework is all that's needed. This magnificently pruned tree is a fern pine.

Rafters alone are seldom enough to provide sufficient shade. Usually a stripping made of 2x2s or lath is added on top at right angles to the rafters. The spacing determines the amount of shade—the closer together, the less sunlight gets through. Grapestakes, 2x3s, 1x2s, bamboo poles, netting and various types of shade cloth can also be used. Removable panels allow for more sun during the cool months, but are a nuisance to take off and store.

The best way to determine how much shade you want is to finish the framework first. Then lay whatever material you've selected on top, without nailing, for a trial run.

An obvious disadvantage of using a shade tree to cool a patio is growing time. Even fast-growers such as fruitless mulberry, evergreen elm and white alder take four or five years to do the job when starting with a 5- or 15-gallon size. Where there is access, a large specimen tree can be planted for about the same cost as a shade trellis as shown in Chapter 9. This way you can sit under its spreading branches the very day it is planted. Shade trees don't have to be evergreen. Deciduous trees permit the sun to enter during the winter just when you need it most.

Other structural considerations are footings, sizing of posts, connec-

Ferns thrive under this shade cloth stretched over 4x6 rafters. Design: Bill Peterson.

The west wall of this house is cooled by a long shade trellis. The Japanese *engawa* or floor-like deck is handy for sitting.

tion to house, shear bracing and sheathing. A 16-inch-cube concrete footing with a steel post-strap to receive the post is adequate for most situations. If there is a possibility that the patio may be enclosed as a room some day, a continuous footing should be included at the future wall line.

Sizing of posts is seldom an engineering problem because a redwood 4x4 or a 2-1/2-inch steel pipe column is more than adequate to support any

patio roof. You may want to use 6x6 posts if you're looking for a heavy timber effect. Pipe columns look better if encased in brick or concrete block.

It's poor practice to attach anything other than a light shade structure to an existing overhang. The best procedure is to bolt a 2x6 ledger to the house wall directly underneath the existing overhang. Attach the rafters to the ledger with metal connectors.

Shear bracing is needed to keep the roof from moving sideways, parallel to the house wall. This can be accomplished by *knee braces* at the posts. They do the job but look lousy. Steel *"T" braces* lag-bolted to the post and beam is a better way if your local building department will accept it. Steel pipe columns set 36 inches deep in concrete provide shear support and eliminate the need for braces.

Sheathing is especially important for patio roofs because it's seen from below. One by six tongue-and-groove is standard and easy to install.

PERGOLAS AND GAZEBOS

Pergolas and gazebos are another way to provide immediate shade. A *pergola* is a freestanding structure, usually consisting of simple posts, beams and rafters of heavy timber. Bougainvillea, grape, wisteria, blood red trumpet and similar large-scale vines are frequently planted at each post for additional shade.

Gazebos are also freestanding, but they are lighter weight and semi-enclosed. Hexagon shapes are most popular, although squares are easier to build. Lath is a common gazebo covering, either in a right angle or diamond pattern, for a somewhat Victorian look. Pre-cut kits, ready to assemble, can simplify the job considerably. You can still have fun and save part of the cost by putting it together yourself.

Change the materials and design to fit in with your chosen garden style. You can create an Oriental teahouse, or a rustic ramada reminiscent of the early West, or an ultra-modern geodesic dome. They all serve the same general purpose of providing an inviting, shady sitting area.

This lath gazebo nestles nicely in the corner of this back yard. Design and construction by Bill Bidle.

Another gazebo created by Bill Bidle. This one is elegant and airy.

BARBECUES AND FIRE PITS

Cooking outdoors is a natural for mild climates. Prefabricated gas barbecues consume no more fuel than indoor cooking, or you can use charcoal instead. Portable barbecues have the advantage of being movable out of the wind and stored out of sight when not in use. Built-in counters and storage spaces save repeated trips indoors.

Fire pits extend comfort into the chill evening hours. It's great to gather 'round a friendly fire after a session in a pool or spa. Now that natural gas has become a precious resource, the old wood campfire is a logical substitute. Be sure to check to see if there are restrictions concerning open wood fires in your area.

This fire pit uses radiant heat from volcanic rock to make the most of natural gas fire.

Built-in gas barbecue is efficient and unobtrusive.

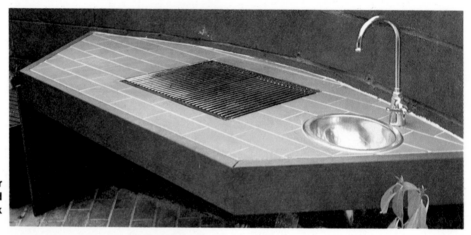

This combination cooking grill, tile counter and sink was designed for George and Myrna Weiss by landscape architect Jack Smith.

Swing sets have almost universal appeal. This one is actually in far-off Malacca.

PLAY AREAS

Play and game areas can serve all members of the family along with providing fun activities to share with guests. The main problem is to avoid creating an expensive and unattractive white elephant that takes up space and is seldom used. Family interests vary throughout the years. Children will outgrow sandboxes and swing sets. Teenagers may play a certain game for months on end and then turn to some other pastime away from home. Grown-ups are just as fickle in their preferences. It all adds up to the fact that temporary, expendable, convertible and multi-use areas are often better than unchangeable, permanent installations.

A 30 x 60 foot multi-use game court turned this back yard into a popular recreation area for family and friends. Construction by Sport Court of Encino, California.

Pre-schoolers may accept being fenced-in for a while, under the watchful eye of mother from the kitchen window. In a year or so they outgrow the enclosure and are happier if allowed to roam the entire yard rather than one small area. They also, along with older children, seem to go out of their way to snub elaborately contrived apparatus and often end up digging a hole in the dirt or building a house out of boxes and scrap lumber. Imagination and creativity are more important than a sophisticated structure that pleases the parents. However, don't overlook swing sets. They are universally popular and, when placed on a lawn, require no garden remodeling after removal. A sandbox or, better yet, a pile of sand is always a favorite with young children and easily disposable when obsolete.

Standard-size playing courts for badminton or volleyball take much more space than is generally realized, especially when proper clearance is allowed for safety and to avoid damage to nearby plants. The chart on this page shows the space required for a specific activity. Make a cut-out the same scale as your plan and see where it fits best.

You'll probably find that you just don't have the total space required. Don't despair. Fortunately, most playing courts can be scaled-down considerably and still be fun. Even as small an area as 20 by 40 feet can work reasonably well as a multi-use badminton, volleyball, tetherball and half-court basketball court.

If it's a choice between having a lawn or paving the entire back yard, remember that badminton, volleyball and croquet are perfectly at home on a tough grass such as hybrid Bermuda or alta fescue. Grass is also usable for mini-games of baseball and football. If you have a wide enough driveway or a motor court, perhaps it can serve double-duty for games such as basketball and tetherball. Of course, it has to be fairly level and safe from street traffic. If you live in a classy neighborhood, you may want to use removable poles and a fold-down basketball backboard so as not to offend the neighbors.

Ping-pong is enjoyed by all ages. The table is easy to move around or store if interest wanes temporarily. It can be played on a lawn, but paving is better. The garage is fine for the average game. Outside, it should be located out of the wind and with some shade for daytime games.

Dancing, archery, catch and similar activities that require no special or elaborate installation are no problem. You just do them. A horseshoe court can be installed at relatively small cost, to be used or abandoned with no great loss. Shuffleboard can be marked off on any long and relatively smooth concrete area. A full-size specially constructed court is seldom worth the cost unless it's going to be played quite often.

Tennis courts are major investments and space-takers. They should be built only after very careful investigation. A possible alternative is paddle tennis. It requires about one-half the space and is a challenging game in its own right. Give swimming pools just as much thought before rushing into having one built. Pools, spas and hot tubs are discussed in Chapter 4.

A shaded place where spectators can sit, be it a low wall, steps or bench, is a welcome addition to a recreation area. To save wear and tear on the kitchen and mother's nerves, a drinking fountain is also a good idea. Adequate lighting should be provided for evening use, but avoid glare on neighboring property.

Space Requirements for Outdoor Activities

Name	Actual Size in Feet	Total Space Required in Feet
Badminton	20 x 44	30 x 60
Basketball	50 x 94	60 x 100
Croquet	30 x 60	40 x 75
Horseshoes	8 x 50	12 x 60
Paddle Tennis	20 x 44	35 x 70
Ping Pong	5 x 9	12 x 20
Shuffleboard	6 x 52	10 x 60
Spa or Hot Tub	6 (diameter)	14 (diameter)
Swimming Pool	16 x 36	28 x 52
Swing-Set	6 x 12	16 x 20
Tennis	36 x 78	60 x 120
Tetherball	6 (diameter)	20 x 20
Volleyball	30 x 60	45 x 80

PAVING

By now it's apparent that a large part of a garden is often covered with a solid surface. Function should dictate the form and size the paved area will take. Don't skimp on size. Generous areas of well-designed paving not only increase the usability of a garden and reduce maintenance, but they can also be attractive.

Use also determines which materials are most suitable. Appropriateness to site and personal preference narrow the choice down a little further. Finally, cost rears its ugly head once again and influences the final decision.

Once you've recorded the shape and extent of the various paved areas on the plan, then you can concentrate on the selection of which kind. The following descriptions and the paving materials chart on page 51 will help you wade through the bewildering number of options.

PAVING CONSTRUCTION

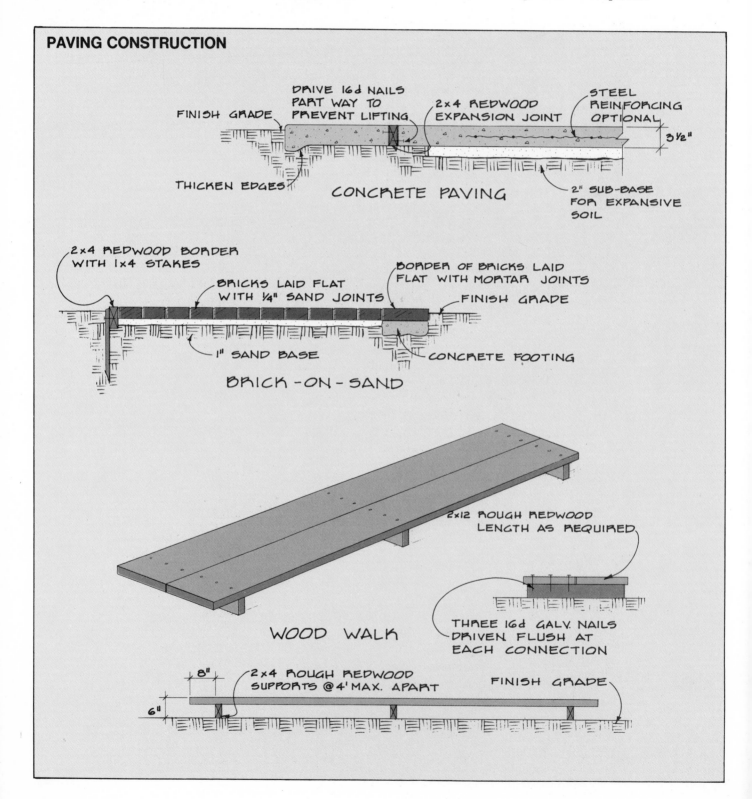

LAYING CONCRETE

Forms made with 2x4s are easy to work with and strong enough to hold the fluid concrete in place. A 2-inch base of rock dust, decomposed granite or similar material helps prevent cracking with any soil, but is essential with clay soils.

Concrete is struck off or *screeded* with a straight 2x4. Low spots are filled in along the way.

Using a *bull-float* takes a delicate touch. A float with no handle, called a *darby*, is used for walks and small areas.

An edger is used after initial troweling, while the concrete is still workable. Edges that aren't rounded look bad and break off easily. Final troweling or brooming will determine the surface texture.

CONCRETE

Concrete is the most widely used garden paving material because it is practical, durable, relatively inexpensive and available in a variety of types and treatments. The surface should be non-skid, colored or textured to break glare, and divided for design interest and to prevent cracking. Expansion joints should be placed at corners and stress points, and through areas larger than 200 square feet. Redwood 2x4s, vinyl dividers and deep-driven joints are better looking than commonly used fiber strips. Shallow scribe lines are of little or no value in preventing cracks.

Adobe soils that expand when wet can cause raising and cracking. Subsoil should be soaked before laying concrete and a 2-inch rock-dust or decomposed granite base used in this type of soil. Wire mesh or steel bar reinforcing is an added safeguard against major cracks. Hairline cracks are almost unavoidable and are not a signal for concern.

Concrete needs 1/8- to 3/16-inch pitch per foot for good drainage. Allow a little bit more, 3/16 to 1/4 inch, for pebble and patterned finishes. Pouring concrete, especially large areas, is not a job for an amateur. A good procedure for the homeowner who wants to do part of the job himself is to do the grading, lay the forms and then assist an experienced finisher. One cubic yard of ready-mix will cover about 80 square feet, 3-1/2 inches thick, but order a little extra so as not to run short. Another approach is to use redwood or other dividers to cut the job into small units that don't have to be done all at one time. Ready-mix comes in minimum loads of 3 to 6 cubic yards. Mix it yourself in a wheel-barrow or rent a mixer when doing only a few square feet at one time.

TIP—A good Concrete Mix:
- 1 part cement.
- 2-1/2 parts washed sand.
- 2-1/2 parts 3/4-inch crushed rock aggregate.
- 5 gallons of water per sack of cement.

VARIATIONS WITH CONCRETE

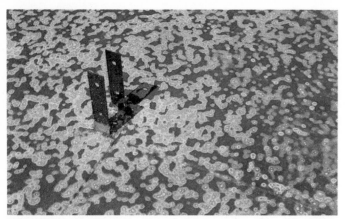

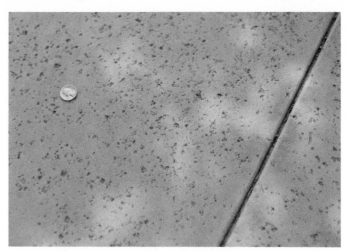

Rock-salt is sprinkled on wet concrete at a rate of 5 to 10 pounds per 100 square feet and tamped-in with a wood float. It's dissolved with water after the concrete hardens. Post anchor is for 4x4 post.

Tan, salt-finish concrete with a deep-driven joint.

Concrete is a fluid material, its shape is determined by the forms. This entrance walk has a stone-like quality. Landscape architect: Roy Seifert for Dr. and Mrs. George Zucconi of San Diego.

Plain concrete, exposed pebble concrete and railroad ties are combined in these handsome steps by landscape contractor Bill Peterson in Camarillo. Note the louvered step lights recessed into the railroad ties.

Rounded beach stones sprinkled on the wet surface contrast with smooth concrete in a grid pattern. *Cold-joints* between the two different pours prevent cracking.

Owner John Mrak did a neat staining job to give this concrete walk a flagstone appearance.

Colored concrete is impressed with a patented steel form to impart an antique paving block effect.

LAYING COBBLESTONE

Cobblestone paving is a good do-it-yourself item. First, large round stones are tapped into a 2-inch bed of sand until level.

Mortar is used to fill in between the stones and tooled until firm.

Surface is cleaned with a brush and water so that stones are visible.

Finished paving fits perfectly with railroad ties and looks a hundred years old. Landscape architect: Jack Smith.

PEBBLE CONCRETE with a redwood 2x4 divider. This crushed rock was part of the concrete mix. It was rough troweled and then exposed with a fine spray of water.

I took this photo in Singapore. Hand-set stone paving is great where labor costs are low or if you do it yourself. The contracted cost is quite high in the United States.

BRICK-ON-SAND is set on a 2-inch sand base. A 2x4, notched the thickness of a brick, levels the sand to the proper depth.

Fine sand is swept into the joints to make a firm surface.

BRICK

Because of its various sizes, colors and patterns, brick is an outstanding garden paving. Common red bricks are of medium hardness and texture, approximately 4x8 inches and a little more than 2 inches thick. Allow five bricks per square foot to cover some breakage. You can also get bricks that are smoother or harder or thinner or thicker or wider or longer. They come in other colors such as light red, dark, red, yellow, buff, brown and splotchy "used." You can lay them flat, on-edge, side-by-side, diagonally, overlapping and a hundred other ways. They can be laid on sand or concrete, the joints swept with sand, filled with mortar or planting. Beside all that, brick paving is cool, glare-free and not slippery.

Perhaps the only drawback is that installed cost is significantly more than concrete. However, about half of that cost is for materials. Do it yourself and save the difference. Unlike concrete, you don't have to finish it immediately once you've started. Lay as many bricks as you want at one time and come back to it whenever it's convenient. Another way to cut cost is to lay bricks over existing concrete. This way you don't even have to tear out and haul away the old paving.

Make sure you stop and square your pattern every 3 or 4 feet. Otherwise you may get an unpleasant surprise when you step back to admire your completed project.

BRICK PAVING PATTERNS

Running Bond

Basketweave

Stacked

Herring Bone

TIP—A good Mortar Mix:
● 1 part cement.
● 3-1/2 parts washed sand.
● 1/2 part lime or fire-clay.
● Plus enough water to bring to a plastic workable consistency.

TIP—Brick paving absorbs water which helps it dry out, but a pitch of 3/16 to 1/4 inch per foot helps, especially in shaded areas.

If you're mixing a lot of mortar, better use a full-size *contractor's wheelbarrow.* It's also handy for mixing concrete and for hauling soil and materials.

A professional brick mason brought this brick water-saw to the job. Some supply yards will saw bricks, tile, stone and pre-cast concrete for 10 to 25 cents per cut.

These bricks are laid over an old concrete patio. Bricks are tapped into level position on a 1/2-inch mortar setting bed. Mortar joints will be filled later, all at one time.

SETTING BRICKS ON MORTAR

Used bricks are set on a mortar base several inches thick.

A homemade grout bag is filled with mortar made from sack of pre-mixed mortar.

Grout bag is used to squeeze mortar into joints like cake frosting.

Rustic joints are finished by hand wearing a heavy work glove. Precision is unnecessary and virtually impossible with railroad ties and used bricks.

ASPHALT

Asphalt should not be ruled out as a valid paving for certain garden uses. If you've ever tried to keep grease spots off a concrete driveway, you'll agree that asphalt is more practical where cars are involved. It's also quite satisfactory for game courts and service yards. Softness and heat accumulation during summer and an uninspiring appearance make it unsuitable for uses such as patios and entrances.

The main advantage of using asphalt is to save money. Even with the tremendous increase in the cost of petroleum and related products, it still costs much less than its nearest rival, concrete, *if* there is a clear access for the large trucks and rolling equipment, and *if* the area is large and open.

Asphaltic concrete, as it is correctly called, is laid 2 inches thick over a 2-inch rolled base of rock dust, decomposed granite or a similar material for most residential uses. Weed killer keeps Bermudagrass and other intruders from breaking through. Edges should be sturdy redwood 2x4s securely staked and laminated for curves. Concrete, brick or steel borders can also be used—at added cost. Pitch should be at least 1/4 inch per foot. Any depressions or *dishes* in the surface should be corrected before the final bill is paid.

This is not a do-it-yourself item unless you happen to own a big, dirty dump truck and a ten-ton roller.

FLAGSTONE

Flagstone is a beautiful paving—if it just didn't cost so much. If you live near a quarry, it *might* come out about the same as brick. With transportation costs, it's often prohibitive.

Colors range from almost white through tan, pinks and browns in sandstone to grays and blues for granite and slate. Thickness is from 1/2 to 4 inches and sizes of individual pieces go up to several feet across. The wide variety and natural appearance make it easy to fit into any garden.

A concrete base with mortar joints is usually best for patio-type uses. For informal areas, flagstone can be

This asphalt driveway was widened with brick which curves around a Japanese black pine, making a gracious entry.

A 3-inch thick flagstone makes a sturdy and good looking step.

Bouquet canyon stone has an interesting grayish-blue color.

Pinkish *Arizona* flagstone cantilevers over pool edge for natural effect.

laid in sand or just dug into the ground with grass or creeping plants growing in the cracks. Flagstone is not the easiest paving to lay. It's hard to get the feel of it. Amateurish jobs look just awful. If you want to tackle it yourself, look at some good examples to see how the joints were fitted and how the mortar was installed. Plan to lay out the stones ahead of time allowing 1/4 inch per foot for drainage unless water can soak into the sand or soil base.

TILE

Tile comes in as many colors and even more shapes and sizes than its close relative, brick. Textured and casual finishes are more at home in most gardens than slick and precise types. The effect has a Spanish or Mediterranean feel and fits in well with rough plaster, slumpstone and tile roofs. Cost and installation methods are similar to brick. Tolerances are a little tighter, but if you can lay brick, you can lay tile.

PRE-CAST CONCRETE

This is a good way to let the manufacturer take the worry out of your trying to finish concrete. Of course, you pay for the advantage. There is an amazing range of shapes, sizes, colors and finishes on the market. Look them over and you might find some you prefer to brick or tile, which some of them resemble. Installation is similar to brick and tile. Design so you can use full-size pieces or you'll have to cut them with a masonry saw.

ADOBE BLOCKS

Adobe blocks won't melt in the rain—they're now made with an asphaltic stablizer or fired like a brick—but they tend to wear out a little and are kind of dusty. They're perfect for a Spanish courtyard, especially if the house or garden walls are also made of adobe or slumpstone. The 8x6x4 inch size is heavy and tiring to handle, but they're a good owner-builder item if you take it slowly. Lay the blocks on a sand base like bricks, except don't tap them too sharply or they'll crack. Space them one inch apart to allow for irregularitites and fill the joints with mortar or topsoil.

Mexican paving tiles tend to wear with time—but that's part of their charm.

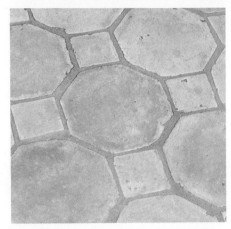

This is one of the many tile pavings available.

Interlocking pre-cast concrete paving units fit together like a jigsaw puzzle. They can be installed on a 1-inch sand base with sand joints.

Redwood 2x4s hold the edges in place and define the planting areas. Designed and installed by Jim Keener, Landscape Associates.

WOODEN GARDEN FLOORS

Wood is a great garden paving material and can give many years of service when used properly. Some of the requirements are:

● Use pressure-treated or a decay-resistant species such as heart redwood, when in contact with the ground or footings. Preservatives applied without pressure are usually of little value.

● Thin boards tend to warp when subjected to outdoor conditions. Two inches thick is minimum and they should be securely nailed to hold in place.

● Rough surfaces are less apt to be slippery when wet and don't show marks and defects as readily as smooth finishes. The texture usually looks better anyhow. Slivers are not as big a problem as generally anticipated. Go over the edges with a wood rasp and hit the surface lightly with coarse sandpaper to make it a little more comfortable for bare feet.

● Paints and shiny finishes deteriorate rapidly. It's better to apply a stain or just let the wood weather naturally.

● Nails should be galvanized, aluminum or stainless steel. Drive them flush in a pleasing pattern rather than try to hide them by setting.

You can lay railroad ties, log cuts, six-inch-long end pieces cut from 4x4s or larger, 2x4s and similar boards directly in the ground. It is simple and effective, and fun to do. A sand base or sandy soil helps in the leveling.

Lumber is expensive—material alone will be a dollar a square foot or more. If you can find a cheap source of scrap lumber, it will help keep the cost down, but remember that the wood must be pressure-treated or decay-resistant.

DUCK BOARDS AND DECKS

Duck boards and low-level decks are another way to use wood as garden paving. They're just as easy to build as laying the wood in the ground. In fact, there's usually less digging to do. Rough redwood 2x4 or 4x4 stringers are laid directly on the ground or

Here is an easy way to build a curbside or any wood walkway. Two redwood 2x4s laid on edge support 2x4 planks.

Here a 16d galvanized nail is used as a spacer as another is driven into the edge of the 2x4 to hold it in place. Then two nails are driven straight down, flush with the surface. You may want to skip driving the nail into the edge, but it does give extra holding power.

Finished result is neat and simple. Note the low-voltage redwood path light by Sylvan Lights designed to tie-in with angles of the 2x4s. Landscape architect: Ken Smith.

on concrete or brick supports. The planking is nailed to the stringers and the weight holds it in place. Space the stringers to suit the planking. Flat 2x4s will span two feet with a little flexing. Placed on edge and nailed together, they'll reach 6 feet. Boards 2 by 6 and wider are okay for 3-foot spans. Planking clear of the ground can be Douglas fir or other untreated type, which cuts cost considerably.

As the deck gets higher, construction becomes trickier and most build-ing departments will require a permit You'll also probably need a railing and steps for any height beyond 18 inches. It's best to work with a carpenter unless you have experience and confidence. Standard pier and girder undersupport is satisfactory for most situations. For normal deck loading, 4x6 girders spaced 3 feet apart will span 6 feet between piers.

Hillside decks are another story. Most agencies require a structural engineer to calculate the spans and footings. Contractor's costs are high and it's an overwhelming project for most homeowners. If you have enough level space on solid land that will serve the need, it's almost always better to avoid the complication and expense of a deck precariously cantilevered out over a hillside. If your usable space is limited and you have a sensational view, by all means consider a dramatic deck to gain full use of your property.

Landscape contractor Dave Geller designed and installed this walk of redwood 4x6s. Note the piece tapered to fit the subtle bend in the walk. The ground cover at top is star jasmine.

Railroad ties laid in dichondra lawn cost less than a solid walk and add a feeling of spaciousness.

A walk made of redwood log cuts with sand in between gives a pleasant rustic effect.

What could be simpler? Two rough redwood 2x12s were nailed to redwood 2x4 supports to create a fun walkway that took only a few minutes to build.

DECK CONSTRUCTION

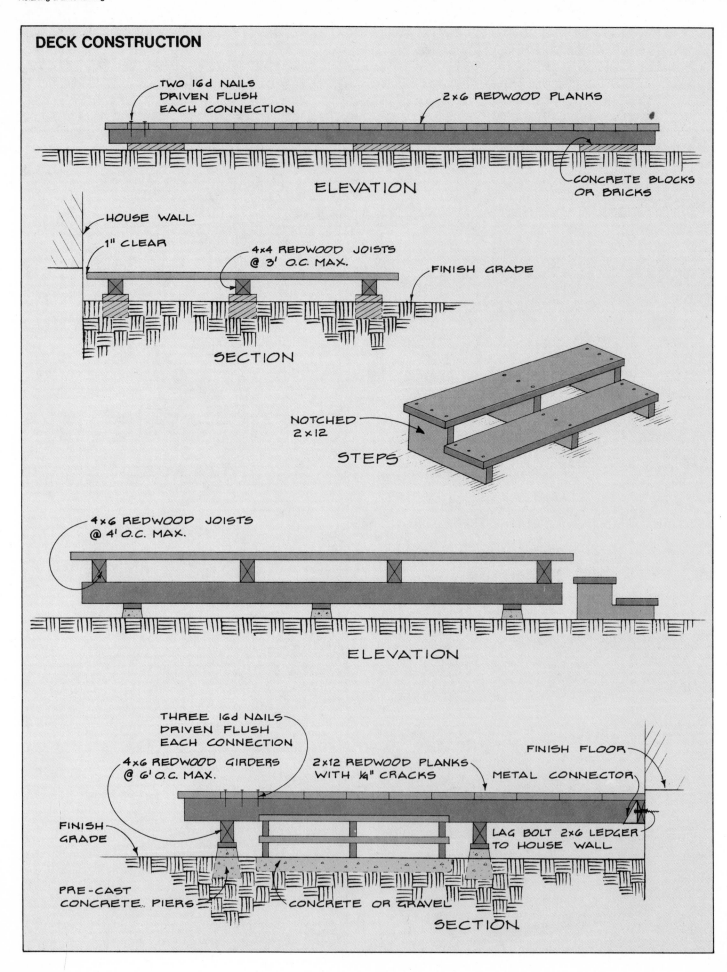

TWO 16d NAILS DRIVEN FLUSH EACH CONNECTION

2×6 REDWOOD PLANKS

ELEVATION

CONCRETE BLOCKS OR BRICKS

HOUSE WALL

1" CLEAR

4×4 REDWOOD JOISTS @ 3' O.C. MAX.

FINISH GRADE

SECTION

NOTCHED 2×12

STEPS

4×6 REDWOOD JOISTS @ 4' O.C. MAX.

ELEVATION

THREE 16d NAILS DRIVEN FLUSH EACH CONNECTION

4×6 REDWOOD GIRDERS @ 6' O.C. MAX.

2×12 REDWOOD PLANKS WITH ¼" CRACKS

FINISH FLOOR

METAL CONNECTOR

FINISH GRADE

LAG BOLT 2×6 LEDGER TO HOUSE WALL

PRE-CAST CONCRETE PIERS

CONCRETE OR GRAVEL

SECTION

BUILDING A DECK

Jane and Billy join in as Bill Becher digs holes for pre-cast concrete piers. The piers must be carefully leveled or the whole deck will be crooked.

Rough redwood 2x4 stringers are nailed to the piers and finished redwood 2x6 planks are laid across them. Planks are extended over the old concrete step, instead of tearing it out. Leave a 1 inch space between the wood and the house as a protection against termites.

String tells nailer where 2x4 is underneath.

Chalk-line is snapped to mark a straight edge.

A portable rotary saw is used to trim off excess wood. Edges are smoothed with a rasp or a former.

Not bad for a day's work. They deserve a rest before doing the planting.

SEMIPAVINGS

What to do with an area that doesn't require a solid paving, yet is unsatisfactory for lawn, ground cover or bare dirt? For example, take the side yard where you want to keep some firewood and walk on occasionally. Or a path to the back corner that isn't worth going into concrete or brick. What is needed is a material that drains rapidly, is easy to install, low in cost, can be walked on, is reasonably free of mud and dust, fairly stable, low maintenance and pleasant appearing. Believe it or not, there are quite a few common granular, stone and bark materials that fill the bill rather well. You can grow shrubs and trees directly in them and when conserving water is crucial, some of these materials can also be used as lawn and ground cover substitutes.

The do need borders such as curbings or redwood 2x4s to help keep them in place and they should be limited to reasonably level ground to prevent erosion. Weeds can be pulled by hand or controlled by sprays as shown in Chapter 13. All it takes to install semipavings is a little common sense and a strong back—no previous experience necessary.

Sacked products are convenient, but expensive for all but small areas. Most of these materials are sold in bulk, by the cubic yard, ton or skip load at a much lower cost. You can haul them yourself in a pick-up or trailer, or arrange for large deliveries with a dump truck. Cost varies considerably with quantity, availability and distance of haul. It takes a mathemetician to calculate how much of which to cover what. The safest way is to measure how many square feet you have to cover. Convert that number to cubic feet by dividing by 6 for a 2-inch thickness. Then, divide by 27 to get cubic yards. Ask the supply yard to give you the equivalent amount—plus a 10 percent safety margin—no matter how it's sold.

Granular Materials—These include decomposed (disintegrated) granite, rock dust, select natural base and brick dust. Laid 2 or 3 inches deep, they pack solidly and take to raking

rather well. They're good for walks, parking areas and even game courts. Color range is gray, tan, brown and red. They'll scratch floors, so it's best to keep them away from the house.

Stones and Gravels—These start at pea size, about 1/4-inch diameter, and go up to 2 inches and larger. Heavy, 3/4-inch mixed stays in place the best and is easiest to walk on. Earth colors are most pleasing and don't show leaves and debris as much as light colors and white. Lay at least 2 inches deep and keep slightly below the border or adjacent paving to prevent scattering. Loose stones can be a nuisance in parkways or along public sidewalks. Avoid lightweight volcanic types unless well-confined.

An occasional raking keeps decomposed granite looking neat.

Water-filled roller is used for packing select natural base or other granular materials.

A layer of 3/4-inch mixed stone is walkable with shoes on. These rich colors are found in *Lomita* or *Rusty* types.

Grayish tones are easier to find. Here they blend well with concrete pads in Polly Martin's garden in Ojai.

Volcanic rock is neat looking, but tends to displace more easily than heavier types. I ran out of quarters.

Bark Products—Not only can these be walked on, they make excellent mulches for plants when placed at least 2 inches deep. Large chunks look good, but can float or wash away and should be kept away from moving water. Smaller sizes can be mixed in with the soil so they stay in place a little better. Shredded bark placed 6 inches deep is safe for under swing sets and slides. All types of bark decompose and need replenishing at least once a year. Pecan and walnut shells serve a similar purpose and are longer lasting, but have sharp edges that are hard on bare feet.

In some areas bark products may be a problem, particularly if you have pets. Ticks and other undesirable insects will sometimes take up residence and become pests.

COSTS

The chart on page 51 gives estimated costs of various paving materials. In general, you can assume that flagstone will cost 3 or 4 times as much as gray concrete and that asphalt is usually the cheapest of the solid types. Actual cost often depends on how busy contractors happen to be and how much competition there is. Small areas less than 500 square feet are almost always more expensive than large areas. If you have hard soil, difficult access and need extra grading, footings and complex forming, you're obviously going to have to pay for it. If a contractor's bid seems too high, get a comparison figure. If you plan to do it yourself, you can figure that materials alone will be approximately one-half the installed cost.

GRADING

After you've made a choice as to what kind of pavings you'll be using, you're almost ready to start with the installation. But first you have to prepare the ground.

Shredded bark is walkable and useful under play equipment.

Newly planted shrub areas look good right away when mulched with bark chunks.

Walnut shells make fairly good paths. They're also good for mulches in planting areas and can even be rototilled into the soil as an amendment.

Mexican beach stones combine beautifully with gray granite boulders and dwarf Japanese garden juniper. Landscape architect: Ken Smith.

Rough grading of most lots is performed by the builder. The typical lot is graded to drain away from the house to the street. A building department inspector is usually needed to approve the work. This existing drainage pattern should be carefully preserved during subsequent grading and construction to protect the house, prevent erosion and avoid damage to neighboring property. Earth berms, or low dikes at the top of banks can usually be made less obvious by flattening them out a little, but their function of keeping water from flowing over the bank must not be impaired.

If paving patterns, terracing, contouring or other features that might affect grading can be anticipated, a few passes with the tractor can save much hand work later on. Be sure to reroute drainage flow if the old route is blocked by added paving. Side yards are frequently a problem. A good way is to leave an open channel at least a foot wide along the property line. Lawn and planting areas should be approximately 2 inches below adjacent paving rather than flush, to allow for soil from planting holes and the addition of soil amendments.

Don't do any planting until you're sure that your entire property drains properly. Approximately 1/4 inch per foot slope is advisable for lawn and planting areas. This means 2-1/2-inches fall for every ten feet, or at least 2 feet in 100 feet. Testing the drainage first by observing the flow of rain or applied water and correcting low areas is much easier before planting.

Stockpiling of topsoil to be replaced in planting areas is highly desirable, but usually only possible if the house is constructed singly rather than in a tract. Burying concrete, plaster, lumber and other debris should be avoided. Boulders and rock outcroppings should be looked upon as potential features. They can often be incorporated into the design rather than hauled away at considerable expense.

Grading permits are usually required for any cut exceeding 5 feet or any fill exceeding 3 feet, or if more than 50 cubic yards of material are involved. When large portions of a garden are paved, soaking-in of rainwater is eliminated. Water coming from a paved area often reaches such volume and velocity that erosion and flooding result, unless drainage to the street or storm drain is provided. If roof water must drained to the street, unsightly surface gutters of asphalt or concrete should be avoided. Walks and driveways can often serve as drainage channels, but underground lines are often advisable. When there are existing drain lines, it's easy to tie into them at relatively little expense.

Sloping and hillside lots require careful grading design. Strict ordinances must be complied with, and in most instances, some retaining walls are necessary to fully utilize the site. Ideally, the basic layout by the architect should consider grading as an integral part of his design. Collaboration with the landscape architect at this stage is quite rewarding.

LAYING PAVING

Here are some basic steps which are quite similar for laying any paving:

● Stake out the proposed area on the ground and make last minute modifications if necessary.
● Decide what finish elevation the top of the paving will be. Sometimes you can raise or lower it a little and save lots of digging or filling.
● Grade for the slope and thickness required by the specific paving. Allow extra depth for sub-base, if used. Include footings and post anchors and arrange for any required inspections.
● Build forms and mark where dividers and expansion joints will be.
● Install reinforcing and piping, conduit and sleeves that need to go under paving.
● Soak the ground thoroughly to minimize expansion of clay soils.
● Lay the paving of your choice, referring to the description, detail sketches and photos. Watching a professional for a few minutes on a job similar to your own is the next best thing to hiring him.

Painters, plasterers, and other workmen raise havoc with paving that is installed too soon during construction of a house. If possible, obtain an allowance from the builder and have it installed after other work is completed. This will also give you time to consider the design more carefully. If loan requirements necessitate earlier installation, insist that it be protected against damage.

To return to the outdoor room concept, we've talked about the floor and the roof in this chapter. Without the walls, most people will feel exposed and uncomfortable. This brings us to "Make Your Garden a Private Retreat"—coming up next.

The use of exposed pebble concrete and a low stone wall combines well with planting that is allowed to assume its natural form. As you choose each element for your yard or patio, consider how it fits in with your total plan.

SUMMARY OF PAVINGS

Type of Paving	Installed cost per Square Foot	Type of Paving	Installed cost per Square Foot
Concrete		**Pre-Cast Concrete**	
Basic Gray—Can be monotonous and will glare in sunlight. Broom, sweat and swirl finishes are safer and more interesting than smooth, steel-troweled surfaces which tend to be slippery.	$1.00 to $1.50	**Sand or Earth Base**—Avoid thin types that will crack.	$1.50 to $3.00
		Concrete Base—Same advantages as tile.	$2.00 to $4.00
Colored—It's easier to order color mixed in with the concrete direct from the ready-mix company, rather than dusting it on the poured surface. Select colors from samples, not just names. Remember that they fade unless sealed or waxed.	$1.25 to $1.75	**Adobe Blocks**	
		Often hard to find both blocks and someone to lay them.	$2.00 to $4.00
Salt-Finish—Very popular because it's fairly easy to do. Just press rock salt into the troweled surface while it's still soft. The pitted effect adds interest and fits into most garden scenes. Often used with colored concrete.	$1.25 to $1.75	**Wood Paving**	
		Railroad Ties—Laid directly in the ground with 8-inch side up. Not a smooth surface. Can be spaced to include lawn or walkable ground cover between.	$2.00 to $4.00
Pebble or Exposed Aggregate—Workmanship and types vary considerably. Be sure to look at samples before giving the go ahead. The unevenness can be a problem for furniture and is difficult to keep clean.	$2.00 to $3.00	**Log Cuts**—Odd shape between cuts are a problem. Concrete looks bad, stone or bark move around. Lawn or a low ground cover works best and also keeps logs moist which helps prevent cracking.	$1.50 to $3.00
		End Pieces—Lots of labor involved, but very effective.	$4.00 to $6.00
Patterned—A steel form is used to impress soft concrete to give a brick, cobblestone or tile-like effect. Installation is by franchised contractors only.	$2.50 to $4.00	**Laminated 2x4s**—Parallel lines give it a sophisticated quality.	$2.50 to $5.00
Brick		**Duck Boards and Decks**	
Sand Base—Quite stable when the sand is 1 to 2 inches deep and well-compacted. Best when held in place with a redwood 2x4 or other type of permanent border. One of the few materials you can practice with or start over if you don't like the results.	$2.00 to $4.00	**Duck Boards**—Pallet-like modules fit together for walks and patios. Easily moved about.	$2.00 to $4.00
		Low-Level Decks—Perfect way to eliminate the common 6-inch step down from a sliding door.	$2.50 to $5.00
Concrete Base—Usually laid with mortar joints. This makes it easier to sweep clean than a sand base. Install on new concrete or over existing, which saves the cost of a new base. Used bricks are best laid this way to allow for irregularities. Cost of old bricks is even higher than new bricks in most areas due to limited supply.	$4.00 to $5.00	**Medium-Height Decks**—Cost doesn't include steps or railings.	$3.00 to $6.00
		Hillside Decks—Can easily cost twice as much when you include engineering, permits, footings and railings.	$10.00 and up
		Semi-Pavings	
		Decomposed Granite—The best-looking is tan or brown with a uniform texture about the same as coarse sand.	$.40 to $.60
Asphalt		**Rock Dust**—Mixed gravel with *fines* often used as a base under concrete or asphalt. Usually a neutral gray and not especially decorative.	$.25 to $.50
The larger the area, the better the price. Redwood edging, weed killer and 2-inch base are included.	$.50 to $.75		
Flagstone		**Select Natural Base**—Fine mineral deposits dug directly out of the ground. Looks like tannish-gray dirt but packs like concrete and isn't too muddy. More utilitarian than pretty.	$.20 to $.30
Sand or Earth Base—Grow lawn or a walkable ground cover in the joints for a natural effect. Easy to change.	$3.00 to $4.50		
Concrete Base—Mortar joints make it more practical for furniture and general use.	$4.00 to $6.00	**Brick Dust**—Red color goes well with tile roofs and brick work.	$.25 to $.50
Tile		**Bark**—Brownish-red chunks available in 1/2-inch to 2-inch sizes. Use shredded bark where softness is important.	$.40 to $.60
Sand Base—Weak tile will crack unless firmly bedded. Sand joints are not as satisfactory as with brick.	$1.50 to $2.50	**Walnut and Pecan Shells**—Usually not shipped, so you have to live near the orchards.	$.20 to $.30
Concrete Base—Excellent for laying over existing concrete because of the thinness of tile. This saves the cost of a new base.	$3.00 to $5.00	**Common Stones and Gravels**—Whatever you can find at the local building materials yard. Look for brownish tones and non-garish colors.	$.25 to $.50
		Special Stones—Water-worn, beach stone and similar types bring premium prices. Excellent for dramatic effects.	$.50 and up

Make A Private Retreat | 4

Privacy seems to be of more importance to people in the Western United States than it does in many other places. Build a solid fence or wall around your back yard in the Midwest or East and you're considered anti-social. Out here it's the first order of business, perhaps it's because of our year-round outdoor season. At any rate, you don't have to be a sunbather or skinny-dipper to enjoy freedom from the prying eyes of your neighbors. It's nice to be able to relax in your own little world and do your own thing.

In most cases, privacy is desirable for everyone involved. This means a solid structure, or heavy planting if you're willing to wait at least a year for it to fill in. A masonry wall or a well constructed wood fence is usually the best solution. Hardly anyone wants to wait for plants.

Even with a 6-foot solid enclosure, plants are still almost always necessary to achieve total privacy. Shrubs that grow above a wall or fence not only add to privacy but help block wind and noise as well. They also soften the harsh lines of the structure. Where width is limited, choose upright plants that can be kept narrow without constant trimming. Well placed trees can screen a neighbor's second-floor window that looks down on your patio. Where the situation is uncomfortable, consider putting in good-size trees rather than having to wait years for results.

Hillside lots are more of a problem, especially if you happen to be on the down-hill side. It's best to talk it over with your neighbor before planting a forest that will block their panoramic view. With cooperation and careful plant selection you can both be satisfied. Sometimes a shade trellis can be

Sometimes an extra-high fence is needed to achieve total privacy. The height of this fence is doubled by colorful oleanders.

This fence is almost 8 feet high, but it looks lower because of the stone wall base.

used as a horizontal screen to cut off a disturbing line of sight into your windows.

Walls and fences normally look better if their tops are level. It's preferable to jog or definately slope the top of the fence to adjust to a change in grade rather than make it slightly crooked. However, informal rail fences, rustic stakes and see-through fences can usually follow the land.

Before you decide what kind to build, there are several other benefits to consider in addition to privacy.

First, a wall or fence is usually needed to provide protection for children and pets, and to deter intruders. Walls can also help break the wind. Surprisingly, a fence that filters the breeze works better than a solid wall that the wind may go up and over. Finally, sound from neighbors, highways, playgrounds and other sources can be reduced by solid fences and walls.

Many gardens have a nice view in one direction, but need privacy in another. By dropping-in a section of see-through fencing, it's possible to have both a view and privacy. In a small yard, see-through panels give a feeling of openness.

Allen Fong designed this elegant restyling of a plain backyard to accommodate large groups, yet provide an intimate retreat for the family. Photo: Leyland Y. Lee.

A horizontal screen and lots of container plants are used here to cut off the view into the bedroom from a higher lot. Landscape contractor: Howard Olsen for Mr. and Mrs. Jack Howard.

Change in grade is turned into a design feature by jogging fence sections rather than precisely following the slope of the land.

Ornamental wrought iron panel relieves closed-in feeling of solid wall. Planting provides privacy.

Planting is helpful in relieving bare expanse of a block wall. This is tan, slump-type block which is attractive and popular.

This 4-foot-high block wall afforded no privacy at all. A 2x4 sill was bolted to the wall to support the added wood section.

BEFORE YOU BUILD

Be sure to verify property lines before building *any* wall or fence. The maximum allowable front-yard height is normally 42 inches. Backyard height is usually limited to 6 feet. There are places where a 6-foot fence isn't quite high enough. If you and your neighbor both agree, there should not be any problem to build one a little higher, or to add on to an existing one.

Masonry walls over 6 feet high should have extra reinforcing, so it's easier to use wood. Some cities require permits for all walls and fences, and may frown upon *any* type over 6-feet high. It's a good idea to check before you build. Incidentally, if there's any chance you might add a swimming pool, hot tub or spa, you might as well plan all fences to meet applic-

able ordinances.

You'll get a lower bid for several hundred lineal feet—or better yet, for several neighboring yards done at one time. Good access can also lower cost, especially for concrete block. Material-to-labor ratio is close to 50-50 for most types. Cost doesn't include painting or staining. Add $50 to $75 for each 3-foot wide gate.

54

Concrete block walls enclosing condominium patios are plastered to match buildings.

The 1x6 tongue and groove cedar used on the balcony is repeated in a diagonal pattern on the fence.

CHOOSING A STYLE

Unless you've been through it before, it's hard to believe the hassles that can develop over fencing. Try picturing three adjacent neighbors who want three different types of fencing—all different from the kind you prefer. Assuming you want to split the cost, it's worth considerable effort to come to a mutually agreeable choice.

Often the style is set by what's already existing in the neighborhood. Hopefully, it will be compatible with the houses. For example, grapestakes look fine with shake roofs and wood sliding; plastered block or slump type wall is a natural for Mediterranean style; and picket fences should be reserved for Cape Cod architecture. Look over the following descriptions of various types of walls and fences and the cost chart on page 64. They should help you make a choice.

MASONRY WALLS

They're sturdy, permanent, practically maintenance-free and have the additional advantage of cutting out quite a bit of sound. Although brick, stone, adobe and poured concrete are sometimes used, concrete blocks, especially lightweight cinder and slump types, are by far the most common type of garden masonry walls.

These blocks come in a wide range of sizes, colors and textures, or they

These blocks have recessed ends and the top course has vertical grooves.

can be plastered to match the house. Blocks 6- or 8-inches wide, 8-inches high and 16-inches long are standard. Blocks 4-inches wide are economical, but require pilasters every 16 feet and additional steel for extra support.

The main drawbacks of block walls are their relatively high cost and their tendency to give a closed-in feeling, especially in a small yard. Using panels of grille blocks or wrought iron will relieve the prison effect and allow welcome breezes to enter. Generally, it's better to have block walls installed by a contractor unless you have lots of time, muscle and experience. If you're undaunted by this warning, then follow this construction procedure.

BUILDING MASONRY WALLS

Always locate property corners and set string lines *before* digging the foundation. For normal soils, a 12-inch by 12-inch concrete footing with one 1/2-inch horizontal steel reinforcing bar is sufficient. Soft edges of fill slopes offer poor support for heavy walls. Extend the footing at least 12 inches into undisturbed soil to avoid settling and cracking.

The base row, called a *course,* is either set into the wet footing or added with a layer of mortar later. I recommend using vertical reinforcing bars centered 24 inches apart, and another horizontal bar in the top course. The vertical bars are embedded in the footing and connected to

The base course is embedded in concrete footing. The pilaster contains steel bars and will be filled solidly with grout. Note step-up pyramid for holding string line.

It's important to get the base course level. This one is especially tricky because of the jog.

the horizontal bars with tie-wire. Fill all cells containing steel solidly with concrete grouting. When mixing grout by hand, use one part cement, two parts sand and two parts pea gravel, and pour in the cells. Some building departments require permits for all masonry walls and can usually give advice and free plans to follow. Retaining walls should always be constructed

according to an engineered plan.

Build the corners first like step-up pyramids. This gives a handy ledge to stretch a guide line for filling-in the blocks in between. Move it up as you complete each horizontal course.

Joints are approximately 1/2 inch wide. By adjusting each one just a little bit, the blocks can be fitted-in with a minimum of cutting. Usually the joints are left open in the bottom course to allow water to flow through. Mix just enough mortar to last you half an hour or so using the mix on page 40. *Butter* the lower block and the edge of the block to be set with mortar. Tap the block gently with the trowel handle until it's in line and level in both directions. It takes a while to get the hang of it. Low planter walls are good practice before attempting the 6-foot variety.

Finish the joints with a joint tool or piece of 3/4-inch pipe as soon as the mortar is firm but still workable. Or you can cut the joints deep, called *raking,* for a shadow effect.

Fill the top cells for a flush or rounded concrete cap. Or use a solid block for the top course. Or a matching concrete brick. Or a clay brick. Or attach a 2-inch-thick wood plank with bolts set into the top cells. Concrete glue brushed on or mixed in the mortar helps prevent dislodging of the cap course.

BRICK WALLS

Structural bricks with hollow cells are just as easy to lay as concrete blocks. They cost approximately 50 cents each for an 4 x 8 x 12-inch brick or about twice as much as a concrete block of comparable size. This is still much more economical than building a solid brick wall or applying solid bricks as a veneer. However, bricks are an excellent covering for an existing wall that needs improving.

The reason that walls of solid brick are more difficult to build is bricks are smaller than blocks and there are no convenient cells for the steel reinforcing and concrete grout. The most common method is to lay two separate walls about 4 inches apart and use the space between for

A curving brick wall is stronger than a straight one. Thomas Jefferson designed one like this for the University of Virginia.

Low planter walls are a good use of brick.

reinforcing. The top can be finished flush with solid grouting, or a 12-inch long brick can be laid cross-wise as a cap course.

Mortar is handled similarly to hollow block work, except it's laid out on top of each brick and *furrowed* with the trowel point to form a setting bed. Because of the high cost, few brick walls are built over 3 feet high. An 18-inch height is convenient for sitting.

Hollow structural brick is made like a concrete block.

Modern, asphalt-stabilized adobe blocks hold up fairly well even under constant sprinkling.

When it's important for the ends and the backs to look good, use structural bricks that are textured on all four sides. Steel and solid grout add strength.

Low-fired adobe blocks are similar to soft bricks and make excellent low walls. Orange-flowering lantana thrives in desert heat.

Laying a veneer of flagstone over concrete block doesn't take nearly as much stone as building a solid wall.

ADOBE WALLS

Adobe walls are built like brick except they're normally only one block wide. This leaves no space for vertical steel, so strengthening pilasters are needed for heights greater than 30 inches.

STONE WALLS

Stone is another story altogether. The most common method is to treat it as a facing veneer over a concrete wall. This is something you might want to tackle, especially if the wall is low. Adding concrete glue to the mortar won't help during construction but once it's dry, the wall will be practically indestructable. Solid stone walls require a great quantity of material and skill. In fact, it's almost a lost art. If you have a lot of free stone that you don't want to haul away, then it might be worth your while. Otherwise, forget it.

CONCRETE WALLS

Properly laid, broken concrete can give a stone-like appearance at much less cost. It's heavy enough to be used for low terracing walls without mortar, which gives a pleasing casual effect. Laid in mortar with regular courses, it can be surprisingly attractive.

Poured concrete is fine for curbings, seat walls and low retaining walls. Except, by the time you build sturdy enough forms, you could have built it from block. The main justification is if you want to create some far-out free-form shape or you want a pebble-finish surface.

WOOD FENCES

Wood is softer appearing and generally less expensive than masonry. Wood fences are available in an almost infinite variety and can fit any situation. You don't have to be a cabinet-maker to build a simple wood fence, which makes them great for the owner-builder. When allowed to weather naturally, they require little maintenance. Redwood, cedar and rough textures are best. If color is desired, staining is preferable to painting.

Posts must be *pressure-treated* or *decay-resistant* wood. Even then, they are subject to deterioration, but no one seems to worry too much about it. They'll usually last for quite a few years without falling over. Steel pipes can be used if permanency is extremely important, but at additional cost.

Once you decide on the basic frame, you can select from the many choices of materials and patterns. Or you can modify the framing for non-wood materials described under miscellaneous fences.

BUILDING WOOD FENCES

Start by lining up the fence with a string-line. Be sure not to encroach

Low walls of hand-set, rounded stones are fun to build and fun to look at. I don't know how the creator of this one plans to finish off the top.

This dry-laid, broken concrete wall is softened by creeping thyme. Design by Jack Smith, Landscape Architect.

on property lines. Locate the 4x4 posts *inside* the line at a maximum of 8 feet apart. The boards laid across the space between posts are *stringers*. They'll sag if they're any farther apart. Unless your lot line happens to be an exact multiple of 8, divide the length into equal spaces not to exceed 8 feet, rather than ending up with an odd panel at the end. If you are working with pre-cut stringers, the posts have to be set carefully or the pieces won't fit properly.

A hand auger or clam-shell digger is fine for a few holes or for soft soils. Use a power auger if many holes are involved and if digging is tough. The idea is to end up with a hole not much larger than 6 inches in diameter—so don't use a shovel. A hole 24 inches

deep will leave 6 feet above ground if you start with an 8-foot post. Or you can use 7-foot posts and let the boards extend 12 inches above the top stringer for a 6-foot height. You can pack crushed rock around the posts, but concrete will hold them more securely. A little extra depth and additional concrete is advisable for gate posts and at the top of slopes. Some building codes require banking the cement against the posts to form a mound above ground level.

Set the corner posts first. Brace them securely and run a *taut* string to line up and determine the top of the posts in between. Be sure the string doesn't sag. For long runs, it's better to set the posts extra high and cut off the excess later.

A 2-man power auger is considerably faster than the clam-shell post-hole digger in background.

WOOD FENCE CONSTRUCTION

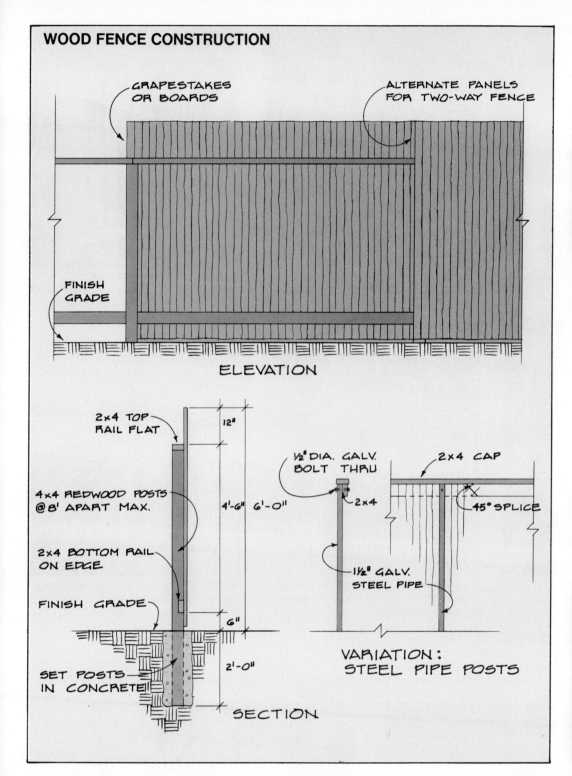

GRAPESTAKES OR BOARDS

ALTERNATE PANELS FOR TWO-WAY FENCE

FINISH GRADE

ELEVATION

2×4 TOP RAIL FLAT

12"

½" DIA. GALV. BOLT THRU

2×4 CAP

2×4

45° SPLICE

4×4 REDWOOD POSTS @ 8' APART MAX.

4'-6" 6'-0"

2×4 BOTTOM RAIL ON EDGE

1½" GALV. STEEL PIPE

FINISH GRADE

6"

SET POSTS IN CONCRETE

2'-0"

VARIATION: STEEL PIPE POSTS

SECTION

The ends of the bottom stringer are cut-in and toenailed to the posts. The top stringer is nailed flat.

Boards are nailed vertically. Note how these extend above the top stringer for full 6-foot height.

Let the concrete cure for a day or longer before nailing on the stringers. Running the bottom 2x4 stringer on-edge adds vertical strength. Using the top 2x4 flat helps keep the fence in line. Nailing the top stringer to the posts with two 16d nails is easy. The bottom one is harder because it's cut to fit between the posts and toenailed in place with two or three 8d nails. If you don't have a helper to hold the stringer while you nail, a temporary block to rest it on saves frustration.

Applying the boards, grapestakes, panels or whatever is a snap. Decide what size nails are needed and how far apart they'll be. Two 6d nails are normally used at the top and the bottom for 1x6 boards. One 8d nail, at each connection point is common for grapestakes. Where rust streaks will be detracting, use stainless steel or aluminum nails.

Most materials are applied vertically. Check frequently with a level to avoid tilting. Add a middle rail for thin boards and fences more than 6 feet high. A 2x4 or 2x6 cap gives a clean top line, but then the posts have to extend full length for nailing.

WOOD FENCE VARIATIONS

BOARD-AND-BOARD allows air circulation and looks the same from both sides. Gray stain soaks in and will not require restaining.

BOARD-ON-BOARD makes a solid fence. Panels must be alternated to avoid one-sided effect. Redwood can be stained or allowed to weather.

A rustic rail fence defines yard boundary without looking heavy or unfriendly.

One-sided pecky cypress board fence shows frame on the other side. It will weather to a tannish-gray.

The posts extend 6 inches above the top of the boards to support a 2x6 cap for added interest.

This grapestake fence has alternating panels. Watermarks are sometimes a problem on unstained wood fences where sprinklers continually hit the same area.

This handsome fence of overlapping, horizontal boards is stained a weathered gray.

WROUGHT IRON

This is preferable to chain link for an open fence when close-up viewing is important. Hollow bars are commonly used—at a much lower cost than the old solid type. Even with that, cost is still approximately *double* that of chain link. Metal primer and high-quality paint should be used to minimize the need for repainting. Wrought iron isn't well-adapted to the do-it-yourselfer. Some welding is usually necessary at the site. However, there are prefabricated panels available that can be used without any welding if you measure very carefully.

CHAIN LINK

This is a perfectly good solution where immediate solid enclosure is unnecessary or undesirable. Chain link also costs considerably less than masonry or wood. To make it less obtrusive, leave off the top rail and use black vinyl-coated mesh. Where semi-privacy is desired, wood strips can be inserted. It's also an ideal support for vines and shrubs. Eventually the framework will be totally hidden by foliage. Chain link isn't really difficult to install with the proper tools, but it's not much fun, and the prices are fairly low anyway, so there's little to save by doing it yourself. Call on a good professional and get the job done right.

Chain link fences make an excellent support for vines and supple shrubs that can be woven into the wire. An existing chain link fence can be made higher by slipping pipes into the existing posts and running horizontal wires 6 inches apart along the top of the fence. Hall's honeysuckle, Algerian ivy and other rapid growers will quickly cover the added portion and create a solid green wall. The chart on the following page lists some of the best plants to use with chain link. Plant lists in Chapter 6 give additional information on each variety.

Climbing roses add color without closing the view through wrought iron fence. Concrete block columns appear very substantial.

Owner Curt Reedy built this brick wall and added ornamental wrought iron according to my plan.

Black vinyl-coated chain link is less obtrusive than standard galvanized type.

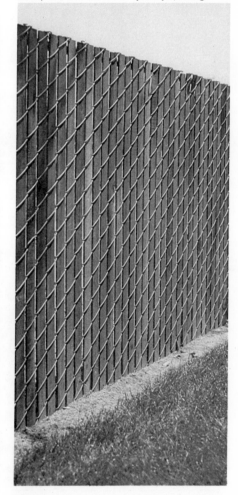

Redwood lath strips are slipped into chain link mesh for added privacy. Privacy isn't total, but the effect is quite pleasing.

Plants for Chain Link Fences

Common Name *Scientific Name*	Degree of Privacy	Remarks
English Ivy *Hedera helix*	Solid	Slow growth. Easy to control. Space plants 2' to 4' apart.
Carolina Jessamine *Gelsemium sempervirens*	Open	Moderate growth rate. Gets top heavy. Space plants 3' to 5' apart.
Hall's Honeysuckle *Lonicera japonica halliana*	Solid	Rapid grower. Needs cutting back. Space plants 3' to 5' apart.
Pyracantha *Pyracantha coccinea*	Open	Moderate growth rate. Thorns add security. Space plants 4' to 6' apart.
Climbing Rose *Rosa species*	Open	Moderate growth rate. Bare in winter. Thorns add security. Space plants 4' to 6' apart.
Parney Cotoneaster *Cotoneaster parneyi*	Partial	Moderate growth rate. Easy to control. Space plants 4' to 6' apart.
Fraser Photinia *Photinia fraseri*	Partial	Moderate growth rate. Easy to control. Space plants 4' to 6' apart.
Shiny Xylosma *Xylosma congestum*	Partial	Slow starter. Easy to control. Space 4' to 6' apart.
Algerian Ivy *Hedera canariensis*	Solid	Rapid growth needs cutting back. Space plants 3' to 5' apart.
Cape Honeysuckle *Tecomaria capensis*	Solid	Rapid growth, tends to sprawl. Space plants 6' to 8' apart.
Blood-Red Trumpet Vine *Phaedranthus buccinatorious*	Solid	Rapid growth. Gets very large. Space plants 6' to 8' apart.
Bougainvillea *Bougainvillea species*	Partial	Rapid growth; rampaging. Thorns add security. Space plants 6' to 8' apart.

CHAIN LINK COVERS

Carolina jessamine, see page 105.

Hall's honeysuckle, see page 105.

Cape honeysuckle, see page 181.

Bougainvillea, see page 105.

OTHER MATERIALS

In special situations, materials such as glass, plastic, shingles, bamboo, plywood, canvas, expanded metal and precast panels may be a good answer to a fencing problem. The limiting factor is usually cost. These custom type fences are best used to enclose or divide a small area adjacent to the house rather than an entire lot. Usually you can use a wood frame similar to that described under wood fences. Just make sure the spans fit the size of the material that you've selected and the frame is strong enough to support the weight.

Cozy alcove is shielded by colorful canvas wind screen. Landscape architect Roy Seifert designed the panels for easy replacement every five years or so.

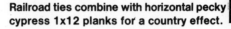

Railroad ties combine with horizontal pecky cypress 1x12 planks for a country effect.

Handsome and simple, this fence is made of exterior siding plywood which comes in 4x8 foot panels. Various grooved patterns and textures are available.

Custom fence of 1x12 and 1x2 boards allow air circulation without loss of privacy.

Rather than introduce a new fencing material, I suggested that the house shingles be extended. Shingles are a good homeowner's fencing material if you're not in a big hurry and are willing to pay the price for materials.

The back side is surprisingly attractive. To cover both sides would be very expensive.

SUMMARY OF FENCES

Type of Fence or Wall	Installed cost per linear foot for six foot height	Type of Fence or Wall	Installed cost per linear foot for six foot height
Wood Fences		**Stone**—First you build a concrete block wall—then you apply stone veneer.	$5.00 to $10.00 (3 feet high)
Boards—1 x 8-inch roughsawn redwood or cedar are quite common but boards come in various widths and many patterns.	$6.00 to $8.00	**Poured Cement**—For retaining walls and low seats.	$5.00 to $10.00 (3 feet high)
Woven Boards—Interlaced, flexible boards. Pre-cut packages are easy to install.	$5.00 to $7.00	**Chain Link Fences**	
Grapestakes—One of the most popular wood fences. Casual appearance. Rough texture requires no stain, ages well. Add 50¢ per lineal foot for 2x4 cap.	$6.00 to $8.00	**Standard**—Looks commercial and offers no privacy. Secure and maintenance-free. Vines and shrubs can be added.	$5.00 to $7.00
1x1s, 1x2s, Combed Stakes—More sophisticated than grapestakes, but not as strong. 2x2s are sturdier, but cost more.	$6.00 to $8.00	**Standard with Wood Inserts**—Look surprisingly well. Privacy isn't total. Filters wind.	$7.00 to $9.00
Woven Palings—Sturdy poles woven with wire. Not common in the west.	$8.00 to $10.00	**Colored Link**—Black vinyl is almost invisible when the posts are painted black.	$6.00 to $8.00
Plywood—Use *textural exterior* types only. Neat, strong and easy to nail. Back is blank; not for situations where both sides will be seen.	$8.00 to $10.00	**Wrought Iron Fences**	
Louvers—Greatly overrated. Difficult to build; warp easily. For special uses only.	$10.00 and up	**Standard**—The best answer for pool fencing. Especially appropriate with Mediterranean style house. Embellishments are okay for gates, but simple uprights are usually preferable.	$8.00 to $12.00
Lath—Prefab panels and wired rolls save labor and are stronger than individual pieces. Good way to add height to an existing wall or fence.	$5.00 to $8.00	**Prefabricated**—Good drop-in panels, if you make sure the spacing is correct.	$6.00 to $8.00
Shingles—Great choice when the house has shingle walls. Can be applied over an existing wood fence.	$10.00 and up	**Miscellaneous Fences**	
Rail—Obviously not for privacy or security. You can set the posts in gravel or directly in the ground. Looks well with ranch houses and shake roofs.	$3.00 to $5.00 (3 feet high)	**Glass**—For view and wind protection. Safety requires 1/4-inch tempered plate glass. Plexiglass is somewhat cheaper, but scratches.	$15.00 and up
Picket—Better for keeping out animals and people than a rail fence. Looks best painted to coordinate with house.	$4.00 to $8.00 (3 feet high)	**Plastic**—Corrugated fiberglass isn't very classy. Some flat panels are quite handsome, but hard to obtain in exterior grades. Lets light through for small garden enclosures.	$10.00 and up
Custom—Tends to be gimmicky unless done tastefully. Have fun, but don't get carried away.	$10.00 and up	**Bamboo**—Quite a chore to install individual canes. Sometimes available in wire-woven rolls. Woven reed is cheap but temporary and has sharp edges.	$10.00 and up
Masonry Walls		**Wire Mesh**—Inexpensive see-through fence, easy to install. Needs frame on all sides or will wobble around.	$5.00 to $7.00
Concrete Block—Plain, colored, slump, grille and textured. Avoid fancy patterns.	$9.00 to $14.00	**Expanded Metal**—Can look commercial. Needs rust-proofing.	$10.00 and up
Plaster over Concrete Block—Good way to tie in with a plastered house or to upgrade an old wall. The problem is to find a plasterer.	$10.00 to $15.00	**Canvas**—New vinyl coatings last for about five years. Nice colors available.	$10.00 and up
Structural Brick—Available in several colors. Makes a handsome wall. Strong and costs less than solid bricks.	$12.00 to $15.00	**Various Panels**—Asbestos cement, pebble surfaces, pressed fibers and others. Good possibilities when well-designed.	$10.00 and up
Standard Brick—Best for low retaining walls and low seats.	$8.00 to $10.00 (3 feet high)	**Railroad Ties and Poles**—Striking when set vertically in the ground. Can be used as low retaining walls. Repeat clusters as accents.	$10.00 and up
Adobe—Slump-type concrete blocks look similar, but are stronger and less expensive.	$5.00 to $7.00 (3 feet high)		

This gate is simple, with no latch exposed.

A Z-brace resists downward pressure and keeps the gate from sagging.

Double gate has cane bolt set in the paving so that one side can be opened. Spring at lower left pulls gate closed if left open.

Wrought iron gate provides security without destroying the effect of the graceful archway.

This elegant and practical wrought iron gate enhances the entrance of the Myron Mendelson's Encino home.

GATES

These are a necessary evil that go along with walls and fences. No matter how solidly a wooden gate is built, it always seems to sag or bind. Try to use lightweight, dry wood if possible, along with the extra-heavy-duty hinges and adequate bracing. Allow an extra 1/4 inch for swelling when the wood gets wet. Avoid wooden gates more than 4 feet wide. If you must have a solid driveway gate, build it on a steel frame and install a running wheel to relieve the strain. Chain link gates work fine, but look bad and afford no privacy. Wrought-iron gates are the most desirable for both workability and appearance, when seeing through doesn't matter.

PLANT SCREENS AND HEDGES

Plants can be used both for privacy and for protection. A tall hedge will not only keep people and animals out of a yard, it will also absorb noise and soften wind. Hedges and screens are also usually better looking than many types of fencing.

There are two major drawbacks. First, you must wait the year or more it will take for a hedge or screen to grow and fill in. This is a long time to wait for privacy. Second, plants require maintenance both to keep them alive and to maintain their appearance. Maintenance can be reduced if you select a plant that will naturally stay the height and width you want with minimal clipping. This will not only save a lot of unnecessary labor, but will also look more natural and usually more pleasing. For example, if you want a screen or hedge at least 8 feet tall, but you only have an allowable space 4 feet wide, common eugenia, golden bamboo or yew pine would be good choices. The plant list on the facing page suggests some of the best screens or hedges and their approximate sizes. The lists in Chapter 6 gives additional information such as best exposure, climate and a description of each plant.

About as reliable as they come, wax-leaf privet can be trimmed several feet high or allowed to reach 6 feet or more. Charlie Hoyt has kept this one in shape for twelve years.

Naturally a little sprawly, Frazer photinia takes a bit of pruning to encourage upright form. New red growth is a distinctive feature.

Versatile Commom eugenia can be sheared as narrow as 2 feet and kept any height from 2 to 20 feet or more.

Victorian box, *Pittosporum undulatum,* is a large shrub, small tree or a clipped hedge. It grows best near the coast and tolerates only a few degrees of frost.

Plant Screens and Hedges

Common Name *Scientific Name*	Approximate Size	Remarks
Wax-Leaf Privet *Ligustrum texanum*	6' by 4' wide	Good hedge plant. Moderate growth rate. Space 3' to 4' apart.
Laurestinus *Viburnum tinus*	6' by 5' wide	Moderate growth rate. Space 4' to 5' apart.
Yew Pine *Podocarpus macrophyllus*	8' by 4' wide	Slow growth rate. Space 3' to 4' apart.
Wilson Holly *Ilex altaclarensis 'Wilsonii'*	8' by 5' wide	Moderate growth rate. Space 5' to 6' apart.
Purple Hop Bush *Dodonaea viscosa 'Purpurea'*	8' by 5' wide	Rapid growth rate. Space 5' to 6' apart.
Blue Pfitzer Juniper *Juniperus chinensis pfitzeriana glauca*	8' by 6' wide	Moderate growth rate. Space 5' to 6' apart.
Golden Bamboo *Phyllostachys aurea*	10' by 4' wide	Rapid growth rate. Space 5' to 6' apart.
Oleander *Nerium oleander*	10' by 8' wide	Moderate growth rate. Space 5' to 6' apart.
Carolina Laurel Cherry *Prunus caroliniana*	10' by 5' wide	Good hedge plant. Moderate growth rate. Space 4' to 6' apart.
Italian Buckthorn *Rhamnus alaternus*	12' by 5' wide	Rapid growth rate. Space 4' to 5' apart.
Glossy Privet *Ligustrum lucidum*	12' by 6' wide	Good hedge plant. Rapid growth rate. Space 3' to 5' apart.
Peruvian Pepper *Schinus polygamus*	12' by 6' wide	Rapid growth rate. Space 4' to 5' apart.
Myoporum *Myoporum laetum*	14' by 10' wide	Rapid growth rate. Space 5' to 10' apart.
Common Eugenia *Syzygium paniculatum*	20' by 4' wide	Good hedge plant. Rapid growth rate. Space 3' to 5' apart.
Leyland Cypress *Cupressocyparis leylandii*	20' by 10' wide.	Rapid growth rate. Space 5' to 8' apart.
Indian Laurel Fig *Ficus retusa nitida*	25' by 12' wide	Moderate growth rate. Space 6' to 10' apart.
Athel Tree *Tamarix aphylla*	25' by 12' wide	Good hedge plant. Moderate growth rate. Space 6' to 10' apart.

Yew Pine, see page 93.

Purple Hop Bush, see page 92.

TUBS AND SPAS

It's strange how most of us are comfortable at a crowded pool or at the beach with thousands of people, but dislike swimming or sun-bathing in our own yard without total privacy. Full-size swimming pools are difficult to screen from every angle. Small pools, tubs and spas are easy to tuck into a secluded corner beyond the view of nosy neighbors. They also take less space, are comparatively inexpensive, don't require as much energy to heat or water to fill, are less of a chore to keep clean and don't add as much to your tax bill.

For sociable soaking and tension relief, nothing can beat a hot tub or spa. They're actually miniature swimming pools with aerated bubbles and water jets for massaging action. The water is heated to approximately 106 degrees F, but because there is less than 1,000 gallons, combined gas and electric cost is only $10 to $20 per month with average use.

Redwood hot tub blends beautifully with wood deck, railroad tie wall and barrel planters. Removable lid keeps water clean and conserves heat.

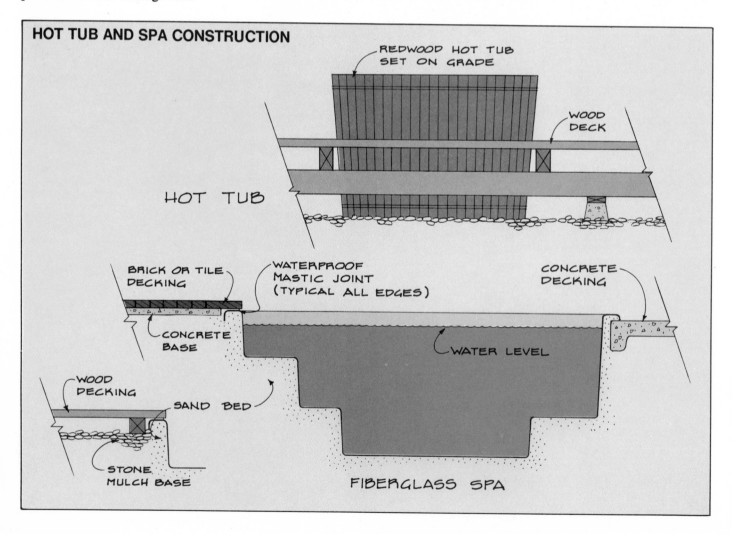

HOT TUB AND SPA CONSTRUCTION

REDWOOD HOT TUB SET ON GRADE

WOOD DECK

HOT TUB

BRICK OR TILE DECKING

WATERPROOF MASTIC JOINT (TYPICAL ALL EDGES)

CONCRETE DECKING

CONCRETE BASE

WATER LEVEL

WOOD DECKING

SAND BED

STONE MULCH BASE

FIBERGLASS SPA

Complete kit prices including wood tub or fiberglass spa, heater, pump, filter and hardware range between $1,000 and $2,000 for most models. You can just about double the kit price to get a pretty good estimate of how much the basic hook-up and installation will be. Access, distance to gas and electricity, and other site conditions will of course affect the cost.

If you've been doing some mental calculations and figure you can start soaking for as little as $2,000, you're only partially correct. Even if you already have an existing garden in which to place a tub or spa, better allow at least another $1,000 for decking and additional planting. The big back-breaker could be whether or not your existing fencing complies with the pool fencing ordinance. Better check it out before signing up.

Gunite® spas made of sprayed-on reinforced concrete are only economical when constructed as part of, or along with a swimming pool. Otherwise, the cost of a Gunite® spa is approximately twice as much as a comparable size fiberglass type.

Both hot tubs and fiberglass spas can be installed by a homeowner. Building departments require permits and inspections—it may be a good idea to hire licensed contractors for the electrical and plumbing work if your experience is lacking in these areas.

A good way of achieving privacy for tubs and spas is to place them under a shade trellis or in a gazebo. The shade is welcome on hot days and the protection appreciated during evening use. Add some lush plants that will thrive in the warmth and humidity and you've created a cozy, intimate spot all your own.

SWIMMING POOLS

Don't rush into installing a full-size swimming pool without carefully weighing all the advantages and disadvantages. Probably no other garden element presents as many problems. Practical considerations such as noise, glare, drainage and safety impose rigid limitations. Added to these is the problem of budget. The cost of the pool itself is only the beginning. If enough money isn't allowed for decking, fencing, planting,

Hot tubs are small enough to set on any convenient deck, but make sure it is properly supported. Photo courtesy of California Cooperage.

Interior designer Fran Elson wanted a spa that would take advantage of the view, so I terraced it into the slope. The shade trellis affords seclusion without casting too much shade for the cool Ventura climate.

Plan ahead and you can make your hot tub really work. This one is completely private, yet has a beautiful view to enjoy while the owner soaks. Photo courtesy of California Cooperage.

Blue-gray plaster and tile lends enchantment to this small pool. The angular shape was carefully contrived to make it look larger. Co-designers: Michael and Nina Foch Dewell; Ken Smith.

Stone wall built at the pool edge allows planting adjacent to water. Note underwater seat in corner for resting and safety. Grayish pindo palms arch gracefully over the edge.

lighting, furniture, interest on the loan, taxes, operating costs and maintenance, the project is apt to be a financial burden. The average pool costs closer to $10,000 than the tempting $4,995 "girl-in-the-bikini" ad of the Sunday supplement.

The simplest solution is a plastic pool sitting on the back lawn. It's not very glamorous, but for a mere $500 or $600 including the filter system, you can have a spot of water for you and the kids to paddle around and cool off on hot days. Sink it into the ground and add some decking and it becomes fairly presentable.

If you have ample space, *if* the budget will stand the strain and *if* you're convinced that a full-size permanent pool will really be enjoyed, then go ahead. But do it right. You can trade-in a lemon car—a pool you're stuck with forever.

In terms of water conservation, it takes a lot of gallons to fill a pool—approximately 24,000 gallons for a 16 by 36 foot size. With good maintenance, a pool will rarely need draining and refilling. It will require the addition of water to replace losses due to evaporation, but that loss is no greater than for a lawn of similar size.

The pool should be located for maximum sun and privacy and shielded

from prevailing winds. Either keep it far enough away from the house so that it doesn't dominate the view, or design it as part of the view. There should be ample space for lounging,

Spa is separated from main pool by stone bridge. Dark blue plaster gives a mountain-lake effect.

Rather than remove old concrete decking, landscape architect Jack Smith added wood decking around this built-in spa.

Notice how the planting interweaves with the decking and boulders, and how the fences provide privacy. Landscape architects: Lang and Wood.

sun-bathing and entertaining, with easy access to dressing rooms and bathroom. Sprayed concrete construction methods allow flexibility of shape, but be careful. Choosing a shape in relation to the setting is much more important than choosing one for its own sake. A rectangular pool carefully placed within a rectangular area might be more pleasing than some jazzy, unrelated form selected from a pool company catalog.

Most activity takes place in the shallow area, even in families with expert swimmers, so this should be the greatest percentage of the pool space. Large, offset steps add interest and leave the main swimming area unobstructed so that even a 16-foot by 36-foot size with parallel ends is large enough for serious swimming.

An even smaller pool is sufficient for most families. It's better to try one on for size at a friend's house than build your own larger than necessary.

The widest decking should occur in relation to the shallow area and steps. In some cases it's even possible to entirely eliminate the walk area at the back side. Underwater seat/climb-outs can replace ladders and serve as convenient resting places. A spa will often induce non-swimmers to use the pool and one can be added for $2000 to $3000, much less than when it's built separately.

Diving is great fun and can be included in some form in almost every pool. A professional 16-foot long, one-meter board requires a 9-foot depth and a 20 by 40-foot pool. A 30-inch high, 10-foot long board is adequate for most divers and easier to fit into a smaller pool. Where space is limited, a 6-foot long jump-board or a raised decking area is more challenging than just diving off the edge.

POOL DECKS

Concrete is most frequently used for pool decking because it's practical and economical. The surface should be non-skid and well-drained, with expansion joints placed at frequent intervals. Color and texture such as salt-finish helps break glare and adds richness. Changes in level and cantilevered decking which eliminates coping are effective design elements.

In expansive soils, precautions must be taken to avoid cracking and shifting of the soil. Mastic or plastic expansion joints and a 2-inch deep sub-base of rock dust or decomposed granite, along with thorough soaking before pouring, is advisable. Special engineering of the pool structure is also necessary in expansive soils. This is usually termed an *adobe schedule.*

Other common decking materials include flagstone and brick. On hillsides, wood decking is frequently used. The main limitation is that they all cost much more than concrete. One solution is to use them in small areas for a welcome contrast to the concrete. For inland valley and dessert areas, a troweled-on topping that reduces surface temperature is a sole-saver. It's sold under various names and adds about 50 cents per square-foot to the basic concrete cost.

FILTERS

Filtering equipment should be placed as near as possible to the deep end of the pool for economy and maximum efficiency. By increasing the size of the piping, it can be moved to a less obtrusive location, at additional cost, of course. Every pool builder has a favorite manufacturer, but most agree that a filter of 36-square feet rating with a one horse-power motor is adequate for a 600 square foot pool. This equals 16 by 36 foot rectangle with offset steps. A separation tank eliminates the nuisance of backwash water and an overflow pipe will maintain proper water level despite heavy rains.

You can run the filter when the pool is in use, so noise is not a problem during sleeping hours. A spa aerating motor is another story. It needs to be placed fairly close to the spa and should be enclosed in a sound-proof chamber because it's quite a bit louder than a pool pump.

Pool maintenance is easier with a good filter system and with the skimmer located to catch debris from the prevailing summer breeze. Spacing three adjustable return lines for the 600 square-foot pool will improve water circulation and filtering efficiency. An automatic cleaning system will further reduce, but not eliminate, pool care at an installed cost of $600 and up.

HEATING AND LIGHTING

Solar heating is rapidly replacing gas for new installations. At approximately $1500, the cost is double that of gas—but you save in the long run because you won't be using any gas. Use of gas for pool heating is restricted in many areas anyway. You don't have to install the entire solar heating unit right away. Be sure to include piping and stub-outs so that it can be added later. Spas and hot tubs are normally raised to a higher temperature than is possible from solar heating alone. However, they're easy to cover when not in use which conserves heat and reduces maintenance.

A 500-watt light under the diving board is standard equipment. If the main view from the house or patio is directly towards the light, it can be shifted to the side of the pool to reduce glare. An ink-blue lens on the light also reduces glare and adds interest. A pull-box is usually located above grade outside the decking near the light. It should be placed in a shrub bed or be hidden. Additional lighting, such as in an attached spa, phone jacks and outlets for appliances should be planned for at this time to avoid later duplication.

PLANTING, WATER FEATURES AND FENCING

Planting around a pool should be clean and protected from chlorine water by raised beds or deck drains. Some planting near the water which casts a reflection on the surface is dramatic and it also helps relieve the flat plane of the water and decking. Building a raised planter directly at the pool edge is a good way of handling it. Stone or bark mulches adjacent to the paving are better than groundcovers and they eliminate mud and dust, require little care, and are not damaged by chlorine.

Waterfalls and fountains should be used with caution. They can be quite effective when related to the site and pool. A separate pump that can be turned off without interfering with pool operation is best. Slides are popular with children, but look terrible—so take your choice.

There's plenty of decking for sun-bathing around this Tucson pool designed by landscape architect Warren Jones. Pool form was emphasized by concrete decking layout with cool-to-the-feet topping.

Planting box raised to upper level is protected from chlorinated water. The tree is a blue Atlas cedar pruned in a bonsai fashion by the Leon Kings.

Poolside waterfall at the Tom Kennedy's home in Toluca Lake is backed by lush foliage and a Mediterranean fan palm.

Waterfall by Haruo Yamishiro seems to grow from the side of this swimming pool. White stains formed by alkaline or hard water will show less on light colored tile.

Balcony with open railing offered no privacy for sun-bathing.

Solid panels were added to block the wind and prying eyes. Plant in corner is *Syzgium Smithii*—one of the few named after a Smith.

Streetside view, it's impossible to see from below.

Most cities and counties have laws requiring non-climbable fencing 4-feet-6 inches or 5-feet high with self-closing gates, around any body of water more than 18 inches deep. This is usually interpreted to include spas and tubs. A door at the back of a garage that opens onto the pool area also requires a self-closing device. When small children are involved, consider placing this fencing around the pool itself rather than at the property lines. This will provide protection for family members as well as the public. Or, an openable or temporary fence can be included within the yard and removed when the children are older. With a little imagination, the interior safety fence can be turned into an asset rather than an eyesore. Wrought iron, expanded metal or welded wire can be attractive look-through barriers while still providing protection.

Check out solar heating companies carefully. Not many systems have been installed until recently and few people have had much experience with them. Ask to see a completed system in operation, the older the better, and talk with the owner. This is good advice not only for solar heating, but for any work you intend to contract for, whether it is a swimming pool, concrete, a sprinkler system or whatever.

SUN-BATHING

Sun-bathing is another activity that calls for privacy. Because it's often associated with a pool or spa, try to place some of the decking where it gets plenty of sun—without being in view of the neighbors. Of course you don't have to have water to sun-bathe. Walk around the house and try to pick a spot that is out of the wind and will get sun the time of day you want it. Be sure you won't block the sun when you build high fences or plant trees.

Roof-tops and balconies are always potential sunning areas. Sometimes a partial screen is all that's necessary for privacy and wind control. Use a few container plants to dress-up the area—and beware of helicopters.

If a pool is to be constructed at a later date, room should be left for access of heavy equipment. Also, it's best to do as little as possible in the entire area. Unless a very carefully considered master plan is drawn for the complete project, major changes and damages will occur when the pool is finally constructed. Water, electric and gas service lines may have to be stubbed-out to avoid costly breaking through pavement.

CAUTION

Pool contracting is a highly competitive business. Question *free* services. The ideal way is to have a plan *before* getting bids from several companies. Then carefully compare before signing any agreement. Clarify exactly what is included in the contract. Unforeseen extras can turn the low bidder into the high bidder. Many pool companies have gone bankrupt, leaving the homeowner with an unfinished pool. To make matters worse, you can be required to pay twice if the pool company doesn't pay *its* bills! Never pay for more than what has been installed. Secure material and labor releases for all work. A completion bond or payment through a bank or loan company are added protections worth investigating.

Irrigation Systems | 5

It's almost time to furnish your outdoor room with plants, but first you need to plan how to keep those plants healthy and alive. Low seasonal rainfall, water shortages and high labor costs make some kind of sprinkler system mandatory for almost every Western garden. Lawn, groundcovers and other plantings that require frequent watering are difficult to irrigate properly without a permanent installation. Watering with a hose is time-consuming and almost always wasteful. Portable sprinklers attached to the hose are better than nothing at all, especially if left connected for convenient use. Even with an underground system, some hand watering will still be necessary because installing sprinklers in every planting bed is normally prohibitive in cost.

SPRINKLERS

For large areas with well-drained soil and tolerant and compatible plant material, large diameter heads that water everything at once can often be used satisfactorily. Impact heads, commonly called *Rainbirds*®, and gear or cam-driven rotary heads with a radius from 25 to 40 feet are well-suited for lawns and slopes where the spray won't hit walls and windows. They usually cost less because fewer heads are required.

In most gardens, smaller stationary heads are preferred because of their more selective control. Here, lawns are usually put on separate circuits from ground covers and other areas having different watering requirements. Slopes and shaded areas should also be controlled separately. It wastes a lot of water if you have to turn on the sprinklers just because one spot in the full sun dries out.

The lawn around pop-up heads

Pop-up type impact head for about $20 rests flush with lawn when not in use. A mower can ride over with no problem and there's nothing to trip on.

Water pressure raises the head clear of the lawn when in use.

Impact head is fine in a ground cover but is a hazard and a chore to trim around in a lawn. Cost is less than $10.

This is an unsightly and dangerous way to trim around a stationary lawn head.

A better choice is to use a pop-up type lawn head which requires less trimming to keep grass clear of spray.

Stream-spray heads apply water like a gentle rain and reduce erosion around these Lilies-Of-The-Nile.

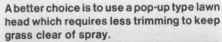

75

Putting your shrub heads on a separate valve from lawn sprinklers permits less frequent watering of shrub and ground cover areas.

These bubbler heads save water because they apply it directly to the plant and not to the bare ground in between.

A gate valve at this fruit tree bubbler permits precise control of the amount of water the tree receives.

needs less frequent trimming than lawn around stationary heads. Stream-spray heads, which throw out tiny streams of water from pin-point holes, are useful for steep banks where erosion is a problem, or where pressure is too low for conventional heads.

Because it's better not to water shrub beds as often as lawns, they should be watered by bubbler or low-spray heads. This type layout is relatively expensive because the heads have to be placed close together. Some small shrub areas can be watered with a hose. Other areas can be planted with drought tolerant plants with large watering basins. Thus, shrub heads could be termed desirable, but optional.

The actual design of a sprinkler system can be done by a landscape architect, irrigation consultant, sprinkler contractor or homeowner. Generally, the sprinkler contractor designs on the ground as he installs. Simple systems with adequate pressure, 50 pounds per square inch, psi, can be laid out by the homeowner with the aid of a sprinkler catalog and a little free advice. Pressures exceeding 100 psi call for a pressure regulator to protect piping and to prevent atomization of sprinkler spray.

Triangular pattern, half and quarter heads spraying away from paving and structures, and control valves located conveniently out of spray are desirable features. Ten stationary heads or three large diameter heads are normally run on a 3/4-inch control valve and a 1-inch supply line. Low pressure, grade changes and other complicating factors would indicate the need for professional advice on the layout.

PIPES

Galvanized steel piping used to be the standard material used for residential sprinkler systems. It is relatively cheap, readily available, strong and simple to install. It is also heavy to handle, subject to corrosion and requires special tools.

Plastic has taken over practically all sprinkler work. There is a wide range of different types to suit almost every situation. Rigid polyvinylchloride, (PVC) schedule 40 or class 315 for pressure lines, and class 200 for "downstream" of the valves, is recommended for residential installations. It is impervious to corrosion, lightweight and can be worked with common household tools. Material runs

slightly higher than galvanized steel, but installed costs are just about the same.

Plastic is strong, but handle it carefully. The only place it isn't advisable to use plastic is where it's exposed above grade, such as on a slope where you don't want to disturb the soil with a trench. In this case, galvanized steel is commonly used. Schedule 80 PVC is extra heavy and can be threaded for use as risers—or you can use galvanized steel risers instead.

Copper piping (type M) is quite serviceable, but is not used as much as it used to be. It costs more than either plastic or galvanized steel and it's difficult for a homeowner to install without previous experience and proper tools.

AUTOMATIC TIMERS

Automatic controllers that operate on a time clock are valuable for large properties, homeowners who take frequent trips, or those who just would not quite get around to watering otherwise. Properly monitored and frequently reset to conform with weather changes, they are real water savers. They're a life-saver in windy areas—you simply set the clock so that they come on when the wind isn't blowing,

INSTALLING PLASTIC PIPE

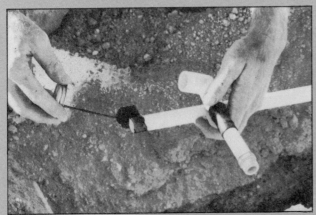

Coat the end of the pipe with plastic pipe cement.

Coat the inside of the plastic fitting.

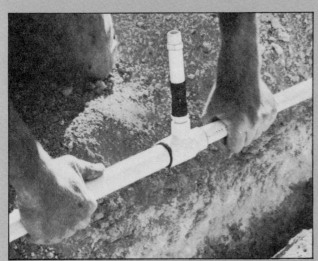

Slip the pipe into the fitting, making a quarter turn to spread the cement. Hold firmly for about a minute. Let joint cure overnight before turning on the water.

Flexible riser protects plastic pipe and fitting from breaking if head is moved.

Turn on water to flush out piping as sprinkler head is installed.

Existing manual valves can be converted to remote control by replacing the innards of the old valve with an electric solenoid type. The wires go to the automatic controller.

by cold and should be wrapped, or frost-proof types used.

IS AN AUTOMATIC SYSTEM TRULY AUTOMATIC?

Not in the sense that you can just hook it up and then forget it. What the controller does is activate the sprinklers at the hour and days you choose, for the desired length of time. Repeat cycles allow them to come on more than once each day. Sophisticated controllers allow separate circuits, called *stations*, to activate on different days. This way, the lawn can be watered several times a week while the shrubs and ground cover can be set to come on only once.

It is a mistake to set automatic controllers and then ignore them. The yard gets the same watering during a cool period as it does when it's hot and windy. Some people even neglect to allow for the rainy season. The sprinklers just go merrily on their way through the winter months and rainstorms. However, with reasonable attention, an automatic controller will save both water and gardening time.

The way to make sprinklers truly automatic is to eliminate the human element as much as possible by incorporating moisture-sensing devices. *tensiometers,* into the system. These probe-like devices are inserted in the root zone and measure the actual soil moisture. By connecting them into the controller circuit, the sprinklers cannot come on until water content drops below the desired setting. Thus, when the clock reaches a normal starting time and there is still sufficient water reserve in the soil, sprinklers will not come on. If the soil is drier next time around, *then* they'll be allowed to come on.

One master tensiometer located in a spot that tends to dry out first, usually in lawn or groundcover, will serve *fairly* well. For best results, a separate tensiometer for each station that takes into account differences in moisture requirements, slopes, sun/shade patterns and other factors, will be *much more* successful. However, at a cost of approximately $50, plus installation, for each unit, only one master may be economically feasible.

Another type of controller is regu-

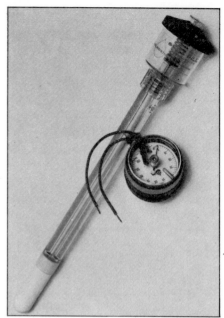

This is what a switching tensiometer looks like. The wire leads are connected to the automatic controller, and the switch turns on when the soil moisture falls below the desired setting. The ceramic sensing tip must be placed in the soil at the root zone you want monitored. Photo courtesy of Soilmoisture Equipment Corp., Santa Barbara, CA.

lated by a moisture sensor and needs no clock. The sprinklers automatically come on whenever the plants need it. This is okay, except for use areas such as lawns where it might be somewhat inconvenient for the sprinklers to turn on in the middle of a sun-bath or croquet game.

Moisture-sensing devices are not only expensive, they also need to be properly installed and require periodic maintainance. If you're the kind of person who likes to fiddle around with gadgets, they might be made-to-order for you. The average homeowner can still make good use of an automatic controller without permanent moisture sensors by frequently checking soil moisture with a portable sensing device or a soil sampler. Then it's a simple matter to manually omit a scheduled watering cycle if it isn't needed.

RESTRICTIONS

Most building departments require plumbing permits for the installation of any sprinkler system. Anti-siphon devices are required to prevent back-siphonage of irrigation water into the

usually in the very early morning when you'd hardly want to get up to do it.

Cost for including an automatic timer when installing a new system ranges from about $300 for the simplest 3-valve installation, to $600 and up for more elaborate ones of 6 valves or more. This is what a contractor would add to the price of a manual control system. Your material cost would be approximately one-half. Most existing systems can be converted to automatic quite simply by adapting existing valves and adding connecting wires from the new controller. The cost is slightly more than for a new installation. For the average garden, automatic controllers are not necessities and the initial budget often doesn't allow for the additional cost. For those whose main problem is forgetting to turn off the sprinklers, mechanical timers that automatically shut off the water can be used or added to existing valves. The cost for these is only about $25 per valve.

In severe winter climates where the ground freezes, some precautions are advisable to protect piping and equipment. Piping can be sloped slightly to a drain at the end of the line. When cold weather approaches, water should be drained from the lines after every sprinkling. Or, it may be easier to bury the piping deep enough to protect it from freezing. Some plastic valves can be easily damaged potable water supply. Some plumbing codes call for separate high-pressure supply lines direct from the water meter to the sprinklers. Plastic is allowed for this use by most agencies if schedule 40 is used and it's buried at least 18 inches deep.

For a house under construction, an oversize service line to the house is needed if many sprinklers are to be taken off it. When possible, it's advisable to increase the service line from the usual 1 inch to at least 1-1/2 inches, and to extend a 1-inch high-pressure spur to the back of the house. Leaving convenient tees for future sprinkler connections is much easier than having to cut the line. Hose bibbs that are part of the house plumbing system are usually unsatisfactory to connect permanent sprinklers to, and in most cases this is not allowed by code.

ESTIMATING COSTS

To make a rough cost estimate for a sprinkler system, figure material costs, including pipe and fittings, at $7.50 per shrub head, $10 per pop-up lawn head, $25 per large diameter head, $12.50 per manual control valve, 75 cents per lineal foot for 1-inch pressure lines. Double the prices for installed cost if you intend to have a contractor do it. Allow something extra for hard and rocky soil, high-pressure supply lines, long runs from valves to sprinklers and steep slopes.

DOING IT YOURSELF

Now that you know all about installation and the fact that you can save 50 percent on costs, perhaps you've decided that putting in the sprinklers yourself isn't such a bad idea after all. If so, here's a simple guide to follow.

Check with a pressure gauge during the day in warm weather to approximate the minimum water pressure, and again at night for the maximum. Some water companies will give you this information over the phone. Look back a few paragraphs to see what to do if the readings are below 50 psi or above 100 psi.

If you haven't already measured and made a plot plan of your yard as

Combination valve and anti-siphon device satisfies plumbing code requirements in most areas. These are hidden behind a dwarf Chinese holly, but easily reached from the walk.

described in Chapter 2, do it now. Or you can just pace it off and make a rough plot, and rely more on ground layout.

Refer to the example plan and draw a plan or rough sketch after deciding which areas you want covered and which ones should have separate valves. Select the type of heads best-suited for each area and lay them out in a triangular pattern. The spacing is generally determined by taking 60 percent of the diameter of throw. For example, a head listed as a 10-foot radius would be .6 x 20 foot diameter equals 12-foot spacing. There are two exceptions to this. Stream-spray heads are laid out in a square pattern and must throw from head-to-head. A 15-foot radius can have 15-foot spacing. The other exception is the group of slow flowing irrigators described on page 82 under Drip, Trickle, Bubble and Ooze.

Complete the plan by establishing your high-pressure supply line to the valves. A 1-inch line is adequate for normal loads. You should be able to conveniently reach the valves from a paved area and turn them on without getting wet. If you install an automatic controller, the remote control valves don't *have* to be out of the sprinkler spray—but they may need occasional

adjusting, so it's better if they are.

Before you start the actual work, show your plan to the building department and get a plumbing permit. They can advise you on what kind of backflow prevention you need and other requirements.

Stake out all the piping, valves and heads on the site. Adjust the stakes indicating head spacing until it appears they will give full and even coverage without spraying all over everything.

Make an estimate of the material, tools and equipment necessary to do the job, and purchase them so they'll be on hand when you need them. Include enough pipe, fittings and risers to allow for a few mistakes.

You can dig the trenches by hand if the ground is fairly soft and if it's an average-size yard. A power trencher can be rented for hard soils and large projects.

Install the high-pressure supply lines and the valves. Don't forget to turn off the water at the meter first. It's doubtful that you'll find a convenient 1-inch tee to connect to. If the service line is plastic, it's easy to cut into and install a tee. Galvanized steel or copper is more difficult. Look for a union to disconnect where the piping enters the house. If there isn't one, you may need assistance from a plumber. A gate valve that will enable you to shut off the sprinkler supply without disturbing the house can be included in the pipe just before the first valve. Putting in a hose bibb wherever there isn't one nearby on the house is worth the few extra dollars.

Install the piping and risers. Turn on the valve so that it flushes out the line and bubbles out the top as you put the heads on. This gets rid of most of the dirt that can cause clogging. Turn on each section and adjust the individual heads for best coverage and to minimize spray on paving and structure. If a head doesn't quite throw far enough, you can often insert a large nozzle and avoid having to increase piping or valve size.

This is a water service line where it enters the house. The hanging device is a pressure regulator. Anything to the right of it has too little pressure for conventional sprinklers, although it may be fine for drip types. The hose bibb piping at the left is too small to connect to. What you have to do is break into the line somewhere between the meter and the shut-off valve on the vertical pipe and connect your sprinklers from that point.

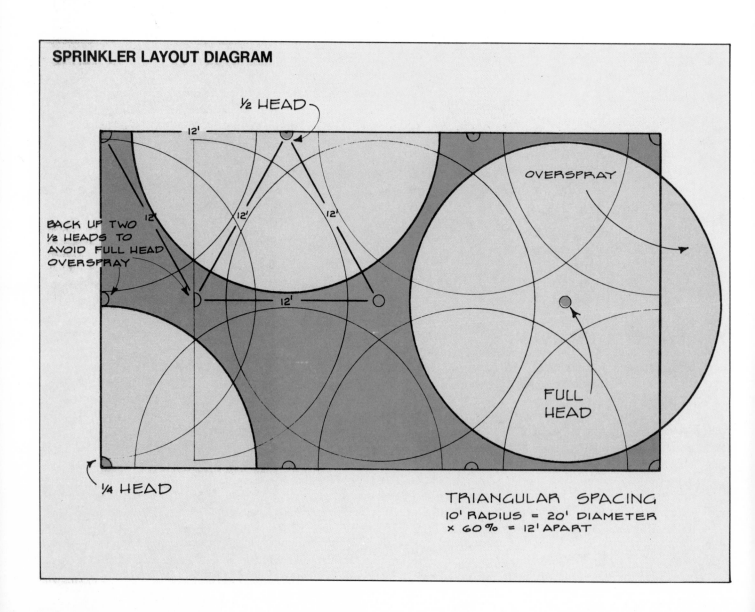

SPRINKLER LAYOUT DIAGRAM

½ HEAD

12'

12'   12'

OVERSPRAY

BACK UP TWO
½ HEADS TO
AVOID FULL HEAD
OVERSPRAY

12'

12'

FULL
HEAD

¼ HEAD

TRIANGULAR SPACING
10' RADIUS = 20' DIAMETER
× 60% = 12' APART

SPRINKLER PLAN

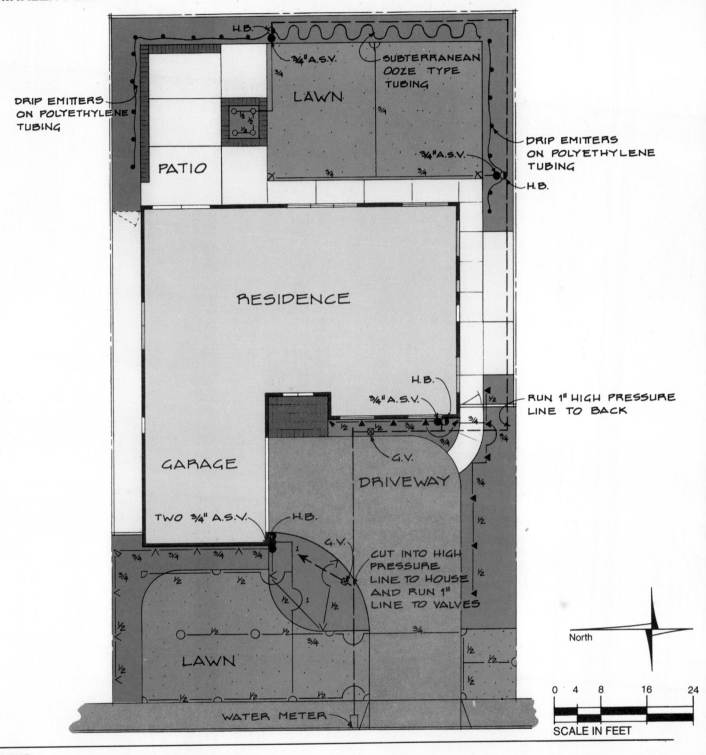

DRIP EMITTERS ON POLYETHYLENE TUBING

PATIO

LAWN

H.B.

¾" A.S.V.

SUBTERRANEAN OOZE TYPE TUBING

DRIP EMITTERS ON POLYETHYLENE TUBING

¾" A.S.V.

H.B.

RESIDENCE

H.B.

¾" A.S.V.

RUN 1" HIGH PRESSURE LINE TO BACK

G.V.

GARAGE

DRIVEWAY

TWO ¾" A.S.V.

H.B.

G.V.

CUT INTO HIGH PRESSURE LINE TO HOUSE AND RUN 1" LINE TO VALVES

LAWN

WATER METER

North

0	4	8	16	24

SCALE IN FEET

LEGEND

— — — PVC Class 315 Supply Line—12" Deep
——— PVC Class 200 Sprinkler Line—8" Deep
G.V. ⊠ Gate Valve
A.S.V. ● Anti-Syphon Control Valve
H.B. ◑ Hose Bibb
● Drip Emitter
⊣ Connection
⌣ No Connection

Low-Spray Shrub Heads—6' Radius Equals 8' Triangular Spacing
  ↗ 1/4 Head
  ▼ 1/2 Head

Shrub Heads—8' Radius Equals 10' Triangular Spacing
  △ 1/4 Head
  ∨ 1/2 Head
Lawn Heads—10' Radius Equals 12' Triangular Spacing
  ⊓ 1/4 Head
  ⌒ 1/2 Head
  ○ Full Head
Impact Heads—30' Radius Equals 12' Triangular Spacing
  ⊠ 1/4 Head
  ⌂ 1/2 Head
Bubbler Heads—12 Inch Radius
  ○ Full Head

DRIP, TRICKLE, BUBBLE AND OOZE

Drip and trickle systems usually employ 5/16-inch diameter flexible polyethylene tubing attached to a monitoring device, called an *emitter,* and running to the plant to be irrigated. Some emitters are plugged directly into rigid or flexible piping without the small tubing. The emitter allows a very low rate of water to pass through—usually 1 to 2 gallons per *hour.* The water soaks in slowly, minimizes run-off and evaporation, and the deep penetration encourages deep rooting.

Bubbler heads flow at a much higher rate—about 1 gallon per *minute* for most kinds. The water doesn't spray, so it's easy to confine it to where you want it. An earth basin or planter box works quite well. As with drip and trickle systems, water soaks in deeply when it's properly contained. Evaporation is less than with conventional spray heads.

Ooze systems are perforated flexible pipe that is installed approximately 4 to 6 inches below ground. It can be laid adjacent to shrubs and trees or in rows approximately 18 inches apart for lawn and groundcover. Depth and spacing depend on what kinds of plants are to be irrigated, soil type and whether the land is flat or sloping. Because no water flows on the surface, run-off and evaporation are virtually eliminated. The old-time soaker hose is similar to ooze piping, except it's used above ground. It's still a useful way to water large trees, planter boxes, narrow beds and rows of shrubs.

Bubbler heads are installed in the same manner as sprinklers. The only difference is that they are either placed one for each shrub or tree, or approximately 5 feet apart in a floodable planter box.

Drip, trickle and ooze system kits are the simplest to install. Most attach to a hose bibb and many don't even have to go underground. They come complete with directions and all the necessary equipment. You only have to decide what needs watering. Large systems can get tricky—it's best to get advice from the supplier.

Flexible, 1/2-inch diameter polyethylene piping at about 10 cents a foot is considerably cheaper than rigid PVC. This is a slip-on clamp to close off the end of a line.

Sub'Terrain® emitter plugs into 1/2-inch diameter polyethylene piping and small tubes are run to the tree. Most drip systems can be connected to a faucet or a hose. A backflow preventer, pressure regulator and filter are normally incorporated at the point of connection.

This sophisticated emitter has 6 outlets and is attached to rigid PVC piping for permanence.

Here 7/32-inch polyethylene tubing is run in shallow trenches to connect emitters to plant basins.

All that shows above ground is the tip of the tubing. Mulch of redwood shavings helps conserve moisture and cool the root zone.

Despite their meteoric rise to popularity, drip, trickle, bubble and ooze systems will not solve all irrigation problems. They're not suitable for all situations. Used in the right place and properly installed and operated, they are valid and valuable ways to water certain plants in your garden.

All these various types save water by reducing run-off and evaporation, and by applying it only where it's needed. This also minimizes weed growth during the dry season. They operate on low pressure and need smaller-size piping than conventional heads.

They do have disadvantages, however. They're subject to clogging and most types must have an effective filter. Pressure often needs to be reduced to fit the individual product requirement. Tubing laid on the surface is subject to injury and vandalism—an obvious solution is to bury it, except it's still vulnerable to a probing spade and burrowing animals.

Cost for bubblers is similar to standard shrub spray heads, except it usually takes more of them to cover the same area, which adds to the cost. Subterranean ooze systems are relatively expensive. It's difficult to find an installer anyway, so putting it in yourself is a way to cut the cost.

The logical place to use all of these methods is for individual trees and shrubs where you don't want to water the bare ground in between. Orchards, widely-spaced trees on a hillside and a row of screening or windbreak plants are good examples. Where you want to save as much water as possible for lawns and groundcover, the underground ooze types are worth consideration.

This drip kit attaches directly to hose bibb. It uses 5/16-inch polyethylene tubes connecting with even smaller emitter tubes at each strawberry plant.

This orchard emitter plugs directly into flexible piping at each avocado tree.

Roberts *Spot-Spitter* is attached to flexible polyethylene piping with smaller tubing and stuck into the ground at the base of the plant. A cross between a drip and regular head, it applies a small spray of water at a rate of 5 to 15 gallons per hour. It doesn't usually need a filter because the opening is large enough to avoid clogging.

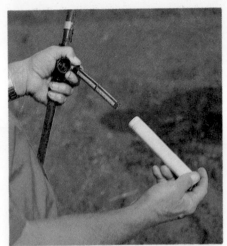

Filtering is essential for most emitters because of their very small openings. This one is easily removable for cleaning.

This type of ooze piping, called *Nu Way*®, has invisible pores that permit water to escape at a very slow rate. Installed underground, it can reduce water waste to practically nothing.

Transparent tubing by *Thirst Quencher Systems*® is practically invisible. You can control the flow at each plant with an adjusting screw.

Foolproof Plants | 6

Now it is time to furnish your outdoor room. The suggestions and lists in this chapter are designed to help you select the best plants for your needs and location. These lists contain the kind of plants that should be used for *basic* planting. Properly selected for a specific location, they will serve the intended purpose with a minimum of care and a low rate of failure.

There really isn't any such thing as a foolproof plant. Fortunately there are many rugged, reliable performers that come reasonably close. Obviously the lists couldn't possibly include *every* plant that meets these requirements. If you know an outstanding performer by all means use it if you wish. Likewise, if you are adventurous and like the challenge of growing temperamental or exotic plants, use them sparingly or hide them around the corner so that a possible dismal showing won't be a catastrophe.

GETTING THE MOST FROM YOUR PLANTS

In order to determine what plant to put where, you should first have an idea as to what you want it to do for you. Keep in mind that plants have many important functions in addition to their natural beauty. Here are some common uses.

Shade—Usually thought of primarily as a tree to sit under or park a car under. You can also air-condition your house by planting trees to block the sun from the roof, walls and glass areas. A deciduous tree allows winter sun to enter when it is appreciated most. Low-branching trees or tall shrubs can ward off devastating afternoon sun.

Privacy—If the space is quite narrow, a clipped hedge may be necessary. However, careful selection can change

There's a telephone pole behind that eucalyptus tree. It only took two years for the upright-growing *E. nicholii* to camouflage it.

Mixed planting of African daisy and cape weed controls erosion on this large slope and reduces fire hazard from the hillside covered with chaparral.

Thick growth of myoporum behind a concrete block wall gives privacy, breaks the wind and reduces traffic noise.

These plants were carefully combined by Landscape Architects Lang and Wood to both look well and grow well together.

There's a car in the shade of that carrot wood tree. Some trees drop sticky-stuff that can ruin a car's finish—check it out first.

This combination of native shrub and ground covers controls erosion and dust, and looks good with the rock outcroppings. Think carefully before you tear out native plants. They may be more useful than you think.

a hedge into a screen of natural growth that requires less care. If privacy from a specific point, such as a neighbor's window, is the problem, a well placed shrub or tree can often take care of it.

Screening—Mask a service area, blot out a bad view, or obliterate a telephone pole with planting. Why look at a trailer or a meter or a pile of firewood when they can be hidden with plants?

Wind Break—Most properties don't have room for several rows of large trees, but sometimes an undesirable prevailing or seasonal wind can be modified with heavy planting. Large shrubs or small trees that extend above a solid fence are effective in breaking a wind down into a gentle breeze.

Traffic Barrier—Tough plants can encourage dogs, children and adults to walk where you want them, rather than cutting across lawn and planting beds. If the situation is severe, don't hesitate to use prickly or thorny plants.

Carpet—Lawn or lawn substitutes can provide a soft, safe, cool area to play or sit and look good at the same time. Selection of the right kind of lawn is just as important as picking out a shade tree.

Erosion, Mud, Dust and Fire Control—If you live on a hillside, this may be your first concern. Ground covers and shrub covers also help cool the soil and the surrounding air along with breaking the glare.

Noise Reduction—The more planting to absorb the sound, the quieter your garden will be. However, to block out the noise from a busy street or highway would take a forest several hundred feet thick, so don't expect a single row to be of much help.

Food and Flowers—You can grow cut flowers, herbs and vegetables in the traditional patch; or you can mix some effectively with ornamental shrubs. Many fruits look good enough to deserve a place anywhere in the garden.

Once you've decided what a plant is supposed to do, then you can think of what size it should be and what exposure and other conditions it will be subjected to.

CLIMATE ZONES

There are more than twenty climate zones in the Western United States. Based on temperature alone they range from frost-free, sub-tropical belts along the Southern California coast to areas that are subject to snow and sustained freezing temperatures. To further complicate matters, there are often wide variations within a few square miles. A south-facing hillside lot can easily be as much as 10 degrees warmer in winter than one on the valley floor a stone's-throw away. There are even warm and cold pockets within an individual yard.

Most of the plants on the following lists should perform satisfactorily in all the climate zones unless noted otherwise. Exceptions are extreme conditions such as along the cool, foggy Northern coast, in the severest high desert and mountain areas, or within the salt spray at the ocean.

SAN FRANCISCO BAY AREA AND THE NORTHERN COAST

If you live in the unique area surrounding San Francisco and along the Northern coast, most of the plants noted to be on the *cool* side, along with many of the *least fussy* ones, will do fine for you. The heat lovers will find it a little too chilly. Local favorites such as rhododendron, azalea, fuchsia, mirror plant, *Pittosporum eugenioides,* hydrangea, mayten tree, David viburnum, Japanese pieris and *Skimmia japonica* are noticeably absent from the general lists. They're great plants for your specific region but they don't do nearly as well away from "home." They have been included in a special list on pages 112 and 113.

OREGON AND WASHINGTON

As you go farther north into Oregon and Washington you can use most of the plants on the San Francisco Bay Area and Northern Coast list along with many of the *cool* and *least fussy* ones. In addition, maple, beech, spruce, mountain ash, salal, *Chamaecyparis, Pachysandra,* Christmas rose and hosta are well adapted to the Pacific Northwest, but not generally found south of San Francisco. Once again, it's a good idea to check on what's growing successfully in your specific climate and to see what's being offered by local nurseries.

MOUNTAIN REGIONS

For those who garden at 6,000 feet or above, quite a few of the hardiest plants at the top of the general lists will survive a mountain climate. Ponderosa pine, dogwood, fir, quaking aspen, giant sequoia, Mugho pine, Irish yew, common laurel-cherry, mock orange, Japanese snowball, spirea, lilac and forsythia are also excellent plants for higher elevations. These are extreme conditions—check extra carefully before selecting a plant. If you don't find one growing nearby, better to use a "tried-and-true" than to take a chance.

EXPOSURE

There are few plants that will survive in all degrees of sunlight from deep shade to reflected sun. Most have a definite requirement that must be satisfied. For simplicity, the four basic wall exposures of your house are a good guide. The north side—N—is the coolest and shadiest. It only gets direct sun in the early morning and late afternoon for a short time during the longest summer days.

The east side—E—gets the morning sun, but is protected from the afternoon sun when temperatures are high. This is not exactly the same as the filtered sunlight of a lathhouse or under a tree, but similar.

The south side—S—gets the most sun and is comparable to full sun out in the open. However, with a normal 3-foot overhang, the house wall is shaded during the hottest months because the sun angle is higher. During the winter, the wall is exposed to the lower sun angle and the overhang affords some frost protection during cold nights.

The west side—W—is probably the most difficult exposure to select plants for. It's cool in the morning and hot in the afternoon. In desert and inland valleys, the reflected heat is enough to cook the leaves off many plants. Keeping an air space between the wall and plant is advisable.

Obviously, all plants aren't planted directly against a wall and all houses aren't oriented exactly north and south. So, another way to determine exposure is to equate N with full shade, E with partial shade, S with full sun and W with reflected sun. Nearby fences, neighbor's houses, trees and large shrubs and mountains may modify the amount of sun a plant will receive. Also, as your own trees reach maturity, a sunny spot may become a shady one.

Plants sometimes can adapt to more or less sunlight than is considered typical for the species. However, if E and N are indicated as the best exposures for a plant, this means it requires a shady situation. Trying to grow it against a west wall in a hot climate is doomed to failure. Likewise, a sun-loving plant listed as S and W will most likely dwindle away in the shade.

Caution: If a sun-loving plant is grown under partial shade conditions in the nursery, it may suffer if planted in the sun. Try to duplicate the exposure it has been accustomed to or plant during a cool season. Provide protection for tender-barked trees such as citrus and alder, in hot climates until there is enough foliage to shade the trunk. Try to avoid setting out any plant during a hot spell; cool, overcast days are best for planting.

SELECTING PLANTS

The plants on these lists are easy to grow and will give consistent results in your landscape. They will tolerate a wide range of conditions and thrive under normal garden situations when given reasonable care.

The general organization of the lists is by type and approximate size. There is a certain amount of overlapping. If you're looking for a low shrub, you might also refer to medium shrubs, shrub covers and small accents. Likewise, you might find a large tree to suit your needs also listed under medium trees or narrow-upright trees.

Arrangement is in order of tolerance to cold. If you live in a severe climate, start at the top of the list first. Tender plants, and most of those that thrive in a mild climate are at the bottom of the lists.

COMPATIBILITY

If you're consistent in your preferences, most of the plants you select will look fairly well together. If you like pines, you probably also like junipers, nandina and *podocarpus*. The resultant combination is harmonious. If you happen to like everything you may be tempted to use too many different kinds and end up with a hodge-podge of textures, forms and colors. A design based on simplicity, repetition and restraint is usually more pleasing than an overly complex one.

I've always been proud of this foliage combination. The dwarf red-leaf plum and bronze ajuga were "made for each other." The shiny, light green leaves of the dichondra lawn sets them off. Think a little about how plants will look together before you plant.

The texture of silvery-blue pathfinder juniper is similar to the dark green tamarix juniper at its base and the color contrast is striking. The purple-leaf plum in the background completes the successful composition.

Horticulturally, the plants on the lists are quite compatible when placed according to their exposure requirements. They should grow together satisfactorily when given similar care and watering. As you become intimately acquainted with their specific needs, you'll get to know that a certain one responds to more water, or that another needs an extra application of fertilizer once in a while.

You can assume the plants in the lists require normal watering unless stated otherwise. Once a plant is well-established and has a deep root system, it won't curl up and die if you miss a watering. Those especially able to withstand dryness are noted to be drought tolerant. They can often get along on rainfall alone, or with one or two deep soakings each summer. Drought tolerance is discussed in Chapter 13.

Outstanding features, special uses and important characteristics are included under *Remarks*. All plants are evergreen unless termed deciduous. Especially slow or fast growers are indicated—all others have moderate growth rates.

Now you're ready to use the lists of "old reliables" and pick those that appeal most to you.

FLOWERING TREES

A number of trees not only have a pleasing shape, but have the added bonus of flowers. Those shown here are shown in full on the pages indicated after their name.

Silk Tree, see page 97.

Purple-leaf Plum, see page 95.

Crape Myrtle, see page 95.

Kaffirboom Coral Tree, see page 99.

New Zealand Christmas Tree, see page 95.

MINIMUM TEMPERATURE

The first thing you need to know about a plant is whether or not it can survive the lowest temperatures likely to occur with some frequency in your area. If you're a newcomer, ask a knowledgeable local nurseryman or weather station expert what kind of temperatures can be expected at your site. The *approximate* sustained minimum temperature that a plant will tolerate is noted on the lists. Those unaffected by temperatures as low as zero degrees Fahrenheit, (−20°C.) are termed *hardy*.

COLOR CODES

In addition to low temperature, there are many other climate factors that affect how well a plant will perform. Wind, rainfall, humidity, fog and air quality are all important. Some plants need heat, others like it cool—for convenience, these two characteristics are noted by color bands on the lists.

If you find a particular plant works well for you, plants backed by the same color on the other lists are also likely to work well in your area. Keys to the color codes appear with each list.

USING THE LISTS

It might simplify matters to mark an "X" next to the plants that *aren't* recommended for your zone. For example, if you live in a cold, interior valley or desert that gets high summer temperatures and frost every winter, you can immediately eliminate those plants that can be injured by frost and prefer coolness. If your site is tempered by cooling ocean breezes in the summer, then the heat-lovers are not for you—*unless* you have a favored spot that collects the southern sun most of the day.

The best way to use the lists is first go to a local nursery to familiarize yourself with the plants that are available. Talk with the nurseryman and find out which plants are best suited for your specific area. Then take a drive and record those plants growing nearby that you can recognize

and like. Now, refer to the lists and make a tentative selection based on your planting design. Finally, before buying the plants, double check that they are all able to grow in your climate and they are placed in the proper exposure.

Use the lists properly and you can avoid almost all the gardening problems that you see around your neighborhood. There is no need for you to make common mistakes such as planting a wide, spreading shrub close to a sidewalk or a large shrub in front of a view window or a giant tree where it will rip up paving and drop leaves over an entire yard. The right plant in the right place—the first time—is what we're after.

Study the landscape plans at the end of Chapter 7 before deciding on your choices. Pay special attention to the plan based on the climate that's nearest your own. Obviously, you can't use all the plants shown on the plan—or even want to. But you should find at least several to your liking and be able to get the feel for proper use and spacing.

PLANT NAMES—Plants usually have two scientific or Latin names. They may look difficult, but you can avoid costly mistakes if you are careful about them. The first word is the *genus* name. The second name is the *species*. A third name, which is not always included, is the *variety* name. Each scientific name designates only one type of plant, while the same common name can be applied to many different plants. You should be sure that both or all three names of a plant are exactly what you want.

Botanists are constantly reclassifying plants and changing their names. Nurseries are understandably reluctant to switch from the old name to an unfamiliar one. For example, you may find *Fatsia japonica* still sold as *Aralia sieboldi*, *Syzygium paniculatum* as *Eugenia myrtifolia* and *Ligustrum lucidum* as *Ligustrum japonicum*. It's not necessarily "wrong." Just be careful that it's really the plant that you're looking for.

Color Key For Plant Lists

	Location & Climate	Remarks
	Interior valleys, deserts, south-facing slopes of mountain ranges.	Plants in this group perform best with heat. If you live where a sweater is necessary even in the summer, better forget it.
	California coast, low desert, favored warm slopes.	These plants are tender to temperatures only a few degrees below freezing. Don't plant them in cold deserts, interior valleys, or where frost occurs every winter.
	Northern and cool California coast and nearby areas.	These prefer it on the cool side. They are not as likely to be happy in southern interior valleys or deserts.
	All zones.	Least fussy of all. They should do well almost anywhere.

LOW SHRUBS—18 inches to 3 feet

For small planting areas, foreground planting and in front of low windows. Space 2 to 4 feet apart. Also see shrub covers.

Common Name *Scientific Name*	Best Exposure/Climate & Minimum Temperature	Remarks
Dwarf Red-leaf Barberry *Berberis thunbergii* *'Crimson Pygmy'*	S, W, E Good in desert. Hardy.	Outstanding red foliage in sun. Deciduous.
Gold Coast Juniper *Juniperus chinensis* *'Gold Coast'*	S, W, E Hardy.	Yellow-tipped foliage makes good color contrast. Compact, does not spread. Photo below.
Dwarf Pyracantha *Pyracantha in variety*	S, W, E Hardy.	Small leaves; red berries. 'Red Elf' and 'Tiny Tim' most common. Photo below.
Japanese Boxwood *Buxus microphylla* *japonica*	E, S, N, W Hardy.	Small, yellow-green leaves. Excellent clipped or natural form.
Lavender Cotton *Santolina* *chamaecyparissus*	S, W Good in desert. Drought tolerant. Hardy.	Whitish-gray leaves; yellow flowers. *S. virens* is similar but has bright green leaves. Do not overwater. Photo page 175.
Texas Ranger *Leucophyllum frutescens* *'Compacta'*	S, W, E Good in desert. Drought tolerant. 10°F, −12°C.	Small, silvery-gray leaves; rose-purple flowers. Do not overwater. Photo below.
Dwarf Myrtle *Myrtus communis* *'Compacta'*	S, W, E Likes heat. 10°F, −12°C.	Fine textured, dark green aromatic foliage.
Compact Heavenly Bamboo *Nandina domestica* *'Compacta'*	E, N More sun okay in cool climate. 10°F, −12°C.	Fern-like and lush in shade. Bronze and red foliage in sun.
Dwarf Chinese Holly *Ilex cornuta* *'Rotunda'*	E, N More sun okay in cool climate. 10°F, −12°C.	Prickly, holly foliage makes good barrier. No berries. Slow growth. Photo below.
Wheeler's Dwarf Tobira *Pittosporum tobira* *'Wheeler's Dwarf'*	E, N More sun okay in cool climate. 10°F, −12°C.	Shiny leaves, attractive texture. Tailored, elegant. Slow growth.
India Hawthorn *Raphiolepis indica*	E, S Best coastal, not for hot interior valley or desert. 15°F, −10°C.	Dark green leaves. Clean appearance. Named varieties available with white to deep pink flowers, compact to open growth. Photo below.

Gold Coast Juniper

Dwarf Chinese Holly

India Hawthorn

Texas Ranger

Dwarf Pyracantha

MEDIUM SHRUBS—3 to 5 feet

Consider these before using large shrubs that may require constant cutting back. Space 4 to 5 feet apart.

Common Name *Scientific Name*	Best Exposure/Climate & Minimum Temperature	Remarks
Japanese Barberry *Berberis thunbergii*	S, W, E Good in desert. Hardy.	Fall color; red berries in winter. Spiny, makes good barrier. Deciduous.
Evergreen Euonymus *Euonymus japonicus*	S, W Good in desert. Hardy.	Many variegated forms. Also *E. j. 'Micro-phylla'* to 2' high. Needs sun and air circulation to avoid mildew. Photo below.
Four-wing Saltbush *Atriplex canescens*	S, W Best in desert. Drought tolerant. Hardy.	Gray foliaged plant for adverse conditions. Do not overwater. Use *A. lentiformis breweri* in salt spray at ocean.
Rose *Rosa in variety*	S, W E okay in hot climate. Hardy.	Grandifloras and floribundas fit into land-scape better than hybrid teas. Deciduous.
Mint Julep Juniper *Juniperus chinensis 'Mint Julep'*	S, E, W Hardy.	Bright green; semi-upright; vase shape. Armstrong juniper has medium-green foliage, not as wide. Photo page 122.
Goucher Abelia *Abelia 'Edward Goucher'*	E, S, W 10°F, −12°C.	Arching habit; small lavender flowers. Evergreen but will drop leaves in temperatures below 20°F, −7°C.
Wax-leaf Privet *Ligustrum japonicum 'Texanum'*	S, E W okay in cool climate; N okay in desert. 10°F, −12°C.	Shiny, dark green foliage. Excellent hedge. Will get taller if left untrimmed. Photo below.
Dwarf Oleander *Nerium oleander 'Mrs. Roeding'*	S, W, E Likes heat. Drought tolerant. 10°F, −12°C.	Salmon flowers. Several other dwarfs available. All parts are poisonous. Photo below.
Dwarf Burford Holly *Ilex cornuta 'Burfordii Nana'*	E More sun okay in cool climate; N okay in desert. 10°F, −12°C.	Glossy leaves; red berries. neat and re-fined. Use regular Burford Holly where large shrub is desired. Photo below.
Variegated Tobira *Pittosporum tobira 'Variegata'*	E, N More sun okay in cool climate. 10°F, −12°C.	Green and white foliage. Fragrant, small, creamy-white flowers. *P. tobira* has dark green leaves, grows larger. Photo below.
Aralia *Fatsia japonica*	E, N Tolerates deep shade. Needs protection in desert. 20°F, −7°C.	Large, tropical, dark green leaves.

Dwarf Oleander

Wax-leaf Privet

Variegated Tobira

Evergreen Euonymus

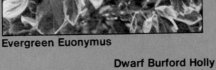
Dwarf Burford Holly

LARGE SHRUBS—6 to 15 feet

Place carefully with ultimate size in mind. Plant away from walls and paving. Space 6 to 10 feet apart. Regular pruning can limit growth.

Common Name *Scientific Name*	Best Exposure/Climate & Minimum Temperature	Remarks
Silverberry *Elaeagnus pungens*	*S, W, E* Good in desert. Drought tolerant. Hardy.	Grayish-green leaves with brownish overtones. Spiny stems, sprawling. Photo page 174.
Pyracantha *Pyracantha coccinea*	*S, W, E* Hardy.	Orange and red berried forms. Rangy and thorny. Good espalier. Photo page 141.
Blue Pfitzer Juniper *Juniperus chinensis pfitzeriana glauca*	*S, W, E* Hardy.	Blue-gray foliage makes good background. Upright, vase shape. Photo below.
Parney Cotoneaster *Cotoneaster parneyi*	*E, S, W* Hardy.	Red berries. Arching. Trainable as espalier or weave into chain link fence.
Oleander *Nerium oleander*	*S, W, E* Likes heat. Drought tolerant. 10°F, −12°C.	Pink, red, white flowers. Also grown as small tree. All parts are poisonous. Photo below.
Fraser Photinia *Photinia fraseri*	*E, S* *W* okay in cool climate. 10°F, −12°C.	Reddish spring and fall foliage; white flowers. Also small tree and espalier. Photo below.
Wilson Holly *Ilex altaclarensis 'Wilsonii'*	*E* More sun okay in cool climate. *N* okay in desert. 10°F, −12°C.	Large, shiny, dark green leaves with red berries. Polished, neat. Also small tree and espalier. Photo page 122.
Carolina Laurel Cherry *Prunus caroliniana*	*S, W, E* Takes desert, looks better on coast. 15°F, −10°C.	Shiny, light green leaves. Dense growth good as clipped hedge or natural screen. Also single or multi-trunk tree.
Purple Hop Bush *Dodonaea viscosa 'Purpurea'*	*S, W, E* Likes heat, but also good on coast. Drought tolerant. 15°F, −10°C.	Willowy, purplish leaves. Also green type, not as interesting. Photo page 67.
Sydney Golden Wattle *Acacia longifolia*	*S, W* Not for desert. Good on coast. 20°F, −7°C.	Bright green leaves; yellow flowers. Rapid growth to 15' x 15'. Good on a large slope. Many other shrub and tree species available.
Myoporum *Myoporum laetum*	*S, W, E* Not for desert or cold valley. Excellent on coast. 25°F, −4°C.	Dark green leaves. Dense, rapid growth to 15' x 15' and larger. Also small tree after trunk old enough for rigidity. Photo below.

Fraser Photinia

Myoporum

Blue Pfitzer Juniper

Oleander

UPRIGHT SHRUBS—for narrow places

Most shrubs grow about as wide as they do high. Here are some that can be kept narrow with a minimum of effort.

Common Name *Scientific Name*	Best Exposure/Climate & Minimum Temperature	Remarks
Wintergreen Barberry *Berberis julianae*	E, S, W Hardy.	Large, dark green leaves. Red fall color. Makes 4' to 6' thorny barrier. Semi-evergreen in cold desert.
Twisted Juniper *Juniperus chinensis torulosa*	S, W, E Best on coast, but tolerates heat well. Hardy.	Rich dark green near coast. Striking, irregular shape. Grows to 15' or more with age, but can be held below 10' with pruning. Photo below.
Laurestinus *Viburnum tinus*	S, E, W Best inland, subject to mildew on coast. 5°F, −15°C.	Dense, dark green foliage; pinkish flowers. Grows 5' to 8' high.
Heavenly Bamboo *Nandina domestica*	E, N More sun okay in cool climate. 10°F, −12°C.	Reddish, fern-like foliage. Multiple stems 3' to 5'; naturally narrow.
Yew Pine *Podocarpus macrophyllus*	E, N More sun okay in cool climate. 10°F, −12°C.	Long, narrow, dark green leaves. 6' to 10' tall; slowly becomes a tree if not pruned. Good against chain-link. Photo page 67.
Golden Bamboo *Phyllostachys aurea*	E, S, W 10°F, −12°C.	Light green leaves. Slow to start, then grows rapidly to 10' or more. Remove old canes to control height. Spreads if roots aren't contained. Photo below.
Desert Myrtle *Myrtus communis* *'Boetica'*	S, W, E Good in desert. Drought tolerant. 10°F, −12C.	Fragrant, dark green, leathery leaves. Rigid, upright growth to 6'. Develops character very early. Prefers well-drained soil. Photo below.
Holly-leaf Mahonia *Mahonia lomarifolia*	E, S Not for desert. 20°F, −7°C.	Spiny leaves, yellow flowers. Open, multiple stem, 5' to 8' tall. Photo below.
Common Eugenia *Syzygium paniculatum*	E, S, W 30°F, −1°C.	Small, shiny, bronzy-red leaves. Fast hedge 5' to 20' with frequent clipping. Becomes a graceful tree if allowed to grow naturally. Photo below.
Threadleaf Aralia *Dizygotheca elegantissima*	E, N Protected atrium. 30°F, −1°C.	Interesting purplish-green leaves, multiple stem silhouette. Cut back to renew and keep 5' to 6' high.

Twisted Juniper

Holly-leaf Mahonia

Desert Myrtle

Golden Bamboo

Common Eugenia

SMALL TREES—10 to 20 feet

Some are merely large shrubs trained into trees. Others will eventually grow more than 20 feet tall unless pruned. Use them where you want something taller than a shrub, but where space is limited.

Common Name *Scientific Name*	Climate/Culture & Minimum Temperature	Remarks
Purple-leaf Plum *Prunus cerasifera* *'Atropurpurea'*	Okay in lawn. Hardy.	Several varieties with purple foliage; white or pink flowers. Deciduous. Photo on facing page.
Peruvian Pepper *Schinus polygamus*	Good in desert. Drought tolerant. Okay in lawn. Hardy.	Fast grower, fairly narrow. Spiny branches make good screen if planted close together. Also multi-trunk.
Chinese Jujube *Zizyphus jujuba*	Good in desert. Drought tolerant. Okay in lawn. Hardy.	Slow growing, weeping form. Glossy, light-green leaves; date-like fruit. Also multi-trunk. Deciduous.
Japanese Black Pine *Pinus thunbergiana*	Hardy.	Can be kept small by pinching out new growth. Most attractive as irregular specimen. Photo on facing page.
Italian Buckthorn *Rhamnus alaternus*	Drought tolerant. Hardy.	Fast growing. Small, shiny leaves. Also multi-trunk or grown as dense hedge.
Glossy Privet *Ligustrum lucidum*	Drought tolerant. Hardy.	Large, dark green leaves. Sprouts from base, makes a good 10' to 20' screen or hedge. Also an upright shrub. Photo on facing page.
Shiny Xylosma *Xylosma congestum*	Drought tolerant. 15°F, −10°C.	Light green, shiny leaves with red tinge. Arching. Deciduous in cold deserts. Also large shrub and espalier. Photo on facing page.
Dwarf Southern Magnolia *Magnolia grandiflora* *'St. Mary'*	Likes heat. Okay in desert with moisture and out of wind. Excellent in lawn. 15°F, −10°C.	Slow growing. Large, glossy leaves; fragrant, white flowers. Usually multi-trunk, also espalier. *M. grandiflora* much larger.
Crape Myrtle *Lagerstroemia indica*	Likes heat. Frost will damage in cold desert. Mildews near coast. 15°F, −10°C.	Handsome white, pink, red or lavender flowers. Also multi-trunk. Deciduous. Photo on facing page.
African Sumac *Rhus lancea*	Likes heat, borderline for coldest deserts. Drought tolerant. 15°F, −10°C.	Graceful, with lacy foliage; rough, reddish bark. Also multi-trunk and espalier.
Pineapple Guava *Feijoa sellowiana*	Not for cold desert. Best fruit on coast. 20°F, −7°C.	Usually multi-trunk, similar to a small olive tree. Edible fruit, named varieties best.
Lemon Bottlebrush *Callistemon citrinus*	Not for cold desert. Needs iron. Drought tolerant. 25°F, −4°C.	Bright red flowers. Also shrub and espalier. Photo on facing page.
Bronze Loquat *Eriobotrya deflexa*	Not for desert or reflected heat. 25°F, −4°C.	Large leaves; new growth is bronze; white flowers. *E. japonica* is hardier, has edible fruit. Photo on facing page.
New Zealand Christmas Tree *Metrosideros excelsa*	Coastal only. Not for interior valley or desert. 30°F, −1°C.	Slow growth. Dark red flowers. Also multi-trunk. Photo on facing page.

Purple-leaf Plum, see also page 88.

Crape Myrtle, see also page 88.

Shiny Xylosma

Glossy Privet

Lemon Bottlebrush

Japanese Black Pine

New Zealand Christmas Tree, see also page 88.

Bronze Loquat

MEDIUM TREES—20 to 30 feet

In time, most will grow taller than 30 feet in a favorable climate. However, they can serve in a normal-sized yard for many years without taking over if properly pruned. Keep 10 feet or more away from house walls.

Common Name *Scientific Name*	Climate/Culture & Minimum Temperature	Remarks
Fruitless Mulberry *Morus alba 'Stribling'*	Drought tolerant. Okay in lawn. Hardy.	Large, glossy, dark green leaves. Fast grower, classic shade tree umbrella. Heavy shade and surface roots make it hard to garden under. Deciduous. Photo on facing page.
Silk Tree *Albizia julibrissin*	Drought tolerant. Okay in lawn. Hardy.	Light green, ferny foliage; pink flowers. Slow to start, then fast. Low, spreading shape. Also multi-trunk. Deciduous. Photo on facing page.
Italian Stone Pine *Pinus pinea*	Good on coast or desert. Drought tolerant. Okay in lawn. Hardy.	Bushy globe when young, becomes broad and very large with age. Photo on facing page.
White Birch *Betula verrucosa*	Takes cold and some heat, but not good in deserts. Best in lawn with ample water. Hardy.	Lacy foliage; upright-weeping habit. White trunk is outstanding feature. Good in clumps and groves. Deciduous. *B. nigra,* River Birch, has pinkish bark, takes heat better. Photo on facing page.
Jerusalem Thorn *Parkinsonia aculeata*	Excellent in warm desert. Drought tolerant. 15°F, −10°C.	Sparse foliage; yellow flowers. Not tailored. Usually low-branching. Deciduous. Photo page 169.
Olive *Olea europaea*	Takes extreme heat, borderline coldest deserts. Drought tolerant. 15°F, −10°C.	Willowy, olive-green foliage. Gnarled trunk and branches show best when thinned out for sculptural form. Olives stain pavement badly. Photo on facing page.
Evergreen Pear *Pyrus kawakami*	Not for cold deserts. Better a few miles away from ocean. Okay in lawn. 20°F, −7°C.	White flowers in mid-winter. Drops leaves for short period in cold. Also multi-trunk and large espalier. Photo on facing page.
Fern Pine *Podocarpus gracilior*	New growth can be damaged by frost. Not for cold desert or extreme heat. Tolerates partial shade. 25°F, −4°C.	Fine texture with graceful pendulous branches. Often thin and straggly in container. Needs staking when young. Also large espalier. Photo on facing page.
Brazilian Pepper *Schinus terebinthifolius*	Borderline interior valley, not for cold desert. 25°F, −4°C.	Drops small leaves and berries, has surface roots. Prune to emphasize structure. Also multi-trunk.
Carrot Wood *Cupaniopsis anacardioides*	Not for interior valley or cold desert. Okay in lawn. 30°F, −1°C.	Fairly open, neat appearing. Slow to develop. Also multi-trunk. Photo page 86.
Indian Laurel Fig *Ficus retusa*	Not for interior valley or cold desert. Okay in lawn. 30°F, −1°C.	Medium-sized, bright green leaves with drooping branches. Pruning reveals clean, gray trunk and branches. Also multi-trunk. Variety *nitida* is more upright, can be clipped. Photo on facing page.

Fruitless Mulberry

Silk Tree, see also page 88.

Evergreen Pear

White Birch

Olive Tree

Italian Stone Pine

Indian Laurel Fig

Fern Pine

LARGE TREES—30 feet and over

Use these trees with caution. They require considerable room and can drop enormous quantities of leaves when mature. Keep 15 feet or more away from house walls.

Common Name *Scientific Name*	Climate/Culture & Minimum Temperature	Remarks
Mojave Hybrid Cottonwood *Populus fremontii* *'Mojave Hybrid'*	Will grow anywhere; excellent for desert. Okay in lawn. Hardy.	Medium-sized, light green leaves turn yellow in fall. Very fast, broad-upright growth, 40' to 60' tall. Roots are invasive. Deciduous. *P. candicans*, Balm of Gilead, is similar. Photo on facing page.
Aleppo Pine *Pinus halepensis*	Excellent in desert. Drought tolerant. Okay in lawn. Hardy.	Light olive-green needles. Irregular shape to 30' and more. Varieties. *'Brutia'* and *'Eldarica'* are darker green and symmetrical.
London Plane Tree *Platanus acerifolia*	Okay in lawn. Hardy.	Large, lobed leaves; whitish-tan bark. Fast, broad-upright growth, 40' to 60' tall. Deciduous.
Weeping Willow *Salix babylonica*	Needs moisture. Okay in lawn. Hardy.	Narrow leaves, graceful weeping habit. Needs pruning-up for clearance beneath. Fast grower to 30' and more. Roots are invasive. Deciduous for short period. Photo on facing page.
Modesto Ash *Fraxinus velutina* *'Modesto'*	Drought tolerant. Okay in lawn. Hardy.	Light green leaves turn yellow in fall. Round form to 40' tall. Deciduous.
California Sycamore *Platanus racemosa*	Needs moisture. Okay in lawn. Hardy.	Large, lobed leaves; whitish-tan mottled bark. Fast growth to 40' and more. Best as irregular, leaning clump. Deciduous for short period. Arizona sycamore, *P. wrightii*, is similar. Photo on facing page.
Deodar Cedar *Cedrus deodara*	Okay in all but low desert. Hardy.	Bluish, gray-green needles. Fast growth to 50' broad pyramid with sweeping branches. Can be kept narrower by planting in groups 10' apart and pruning. *C. atlantica Glauca* is silvery-blue, can be trained into irregular form and kept 10' tall.
White Alder *Alnus rhombifolia*	Not for desert. Needs water. Okay in lawn. Hardy.	Very fast growth to 50' broad pyramid. Deciduous, but leafs out early spring. Photo on facing page.
Red Gum *Eucalyptus camaldulensis*	One of the hardiest eucalypts. Okay in all but the coldest desert. Drought tolerant. Okay in lawn. 15°F, −10°C.	Long, slender leaves; whitish-tan mottled bark. Very fast, broad-upright growth to 80' tall. Many other species available.
Evergreen Elm *Ulmus parvifolia*	Okay in all but coldest desert. Okay in lawn. 20°F, −7°C.	Small, shiny leaves. Fast growing, weeping umbrella to 30' and more. Deciduous in cold areas. Upright forms available. Photo on facing page.
California Pepper *Schinus molle*	Not for cold desert. Drought tolerant. 20°F, −7°C.	Narrow, light green leaves; pinkish berries. Fast growing, weeping form to 30' and more. Thin out to reveal tan, shaggy bark. Roots are invasive, leaves and berries drop continually—nothing grows beneath. Photo on facing page.
Evergreen Ash *Fraxinus uhdei*	Not for cold desert. Okay in lawn. 25°F, −4°C.	Dark green, lush foliage. Fast growth to 30', then more slowly to eventual broad-upright form reaching 50' and more. Will lose leaves for short period in cold. Also multi-trunk. Surface roots. Photo on facing page.
Kaffirboom Coral Tree *Erythrina caffra*	Coastal only. 30°F, −1°C.	Large leaves; red-orange flowers. Fast growth to 30' with equal spread. Drops leaves in January during blooming period. *E. coralloides* and *E. humeana* are smaller. Surface roots. Photo on facing page.

Cottonwood

California Pepper

White Alder

Weeping Willow

Evergreen Ash

Kaffirboom Coral Tree, see also page 88.

California Sycamore

Evergreen Elm

NARROW-UPRIGHT TREES—for grouping and rows

Although some of these trees get very tall, they can be used in almost any garden because they don't spread very wide. Planting in groups or groves 10 to 20 feet apart will further limit lateral growth. Many make good windbreaks and privacy screens when planted in rows 6 to 10 feet apart.

Common Name *Scientific Name*	Climate/Culture & Minimum Temperature	Remarks
Lombardy Poplar *Populus nigra 'Italica'*	Hardy.	Medium-sized, light green leaves turn yellow in fall. Very fast columnar growth to 40' and more. Suckers and roots are invasive. Deciduous.
Blue Italian Cypress *Cupressus sempervirens 'Glauca'*	Hardy.	Dark, blue-green foliage. Narrow column to 40' and more. Can be sheared to keep smaller. Bold skyline silhouette. Photo on facing page.
Smooth Arizona Cypress *Cupressus glabra*	Best in cold desert. Drought tolerant. Hardy.	Blue-gray-green foliage; red bark. Good windbreak and screen. Several varieties available.
Leyland Cypress *Cupressocyparis leylandii*	Drought tolerant. Hardy.	Very fast growth to 20' to 30' tall. Fat, pyramidal form. Good windbreak and screen. Photo on facing page.
Maidenhair Tree *Ginkgo biloba*	Not for desert. Okay in lawn. Hardy.	Odd shaped, light green leaves. Slow growth, eventually 50' tall. Narrow-upright in youth, old trees more spreading. Yellow fall color. Deciduous. Photo page 18.
American Sweet Gum *Liquidambar styraciflua*	Not for desert. Needs moisture and iron. Excellent in lawn. Hardy.	Maple-like leaves. Variable red, yellow, purple fall color. Variety 'Palo Alto' has consistent color. Narrow, pyramidal form to 40' and more. Deciduous. Photo on facing page.
Coast Redwood *Sequoia sempervirens*	Not for desert. Okay in lawn. 10°F, −12°C.	Dark green foliage; narrow pyramidal form. Fast growth to 50' and more, and more. Photo on facing page.
River She-oak *Casuarina cunninghamiana*	Good on coast or desert. Drought tolerant. Okay in lawn. 15°F, −10°C.	Pine-like, fast growth to 50' tall. Other species available but most sold in nurseries are *C. cunninghamiana* no matter how labeled. Invasive roots. Photo below.
Canary Island Pine *Pinus canariensis*	Not for desert. Okay in lawn. 20°F, −7°C.	Long, lush needles. Narrow, pyramidal form to 40' and more. Scraggly in nursery container, fills in after a few years in ground. Photo on facing page.
Giant Timber Bamboo *Bambusa oldhami*	Not for cold desert. 20°F, −7°C.	Very fast growth to 40' tall, once established. Slowly spreading clump. Drops lots of leaf sheaths. Large screen.
Cajeput Tree *Melaleuca quinquenervia*	Not for interior valley or cold desert. Dryish or with moisture. 25°F, −4°C.	Growth to 25' and more, with hanging branches; white flowers. Striking white bark gives birch-like effect. Also multi-trunk. Photo on facing page.
Lemon-Scented Gum *Eucalyptus citriodora*	Not for interior valley or cold desert. 30°F, −1°C.	Long, sickle-shaped, fragrant leaves. Open, graceful form with smooth white trunk. Very fast growth to 50' tall. Photo on facing page.

Cajeput Tree

American Sweet Gum

Blue Italian Cypress

Leyland Cypress

Canary Island Pine

Coast Redwood

River She-Oak

Lemon-Scented Gum

101

GROUND COVERS

These are usually purchased as rooted cuttings, 50 to 100 per flat. Some, like baby's tears, Korean grass and lippia, fill the flat like sod and can be planted solidly or in 2-inch squares, 6 to 12 inches apart. Plant small ground covers 12 inches apart. Plant larger types 18 to 24 inches apart.

Common Name *Scientific Name*	Exposure/Climate & Minimum Temperature	Height	Remarks
Common Winter Creeper *Euonymus fortunei radicans*	S, E, W Good in desert. Drought tolerant. Hardy.	18" to 24"	Small, dark green leaves. Purple and variegated leaf forms available. Rapid, sprawling.
English Ivy *Hedera helix*	E, N More sun okay in cool climate. Hardy.	12" to 18"	Medium-sized, dark green leaves. Will cling to masonry, hang over a wall, cover chain-link. Slow to start. Cut back to renew. Photo below.
Carpet Bugle *Ajuga reptans*	N, E More sun okay in cool climate. Hardy.	3" to 6"	Medium-small, dark green leaves; blue flowers. Bronze leaf variety popular. Will bear some traffic. Needs good drainage. Mow to renew.
Periwinkle *Vinca major*	E, N More sun okay in cool climate. Drought tolerant, but best with water. Hardy.	12" to 18"	Medium-small dark green leaves; blue flowers. Arching, informal habit. Will trail over a wall. Cut back to renew. *V. minor* is smaller and lower, not as good in heat. Photo below.
Hahn's Ivy *Hedera helix 'Hahni'*	E, N More sun okay in cool climate. Hardy.	6" to 12"	Light green leaves, slightly smaller than English ivy. Will cling to masonry, hang over wall. Slow to start. Many similar varieties. Cut back to renew.
Lippia *Phyla nodiflora*	S, W, E Likes heat. Poor winter appearance in cold. Drought tolerant. Hardy.	Flat to 6"	Small, gray-green leaves. Small flowers attract bees. Can be walked on. Mow to renew. Photo below.
Spring Cinquefoil *Potentilla verna*	E, S W is okay in cool climate. Poor winter appearance in cold. Hardy.	6" to 12"	Small, bright green leaves; yellow flowers. Rapid growth with water and fertilization. Will bear some traffic. Mow to renew. Photo below.

English Ivy

Korean Grass

Spring Cinquefoil

Periwinkle

Lippia

Common Name / *Scientific Name*	Exposure/Climate & Minimum Temperature	Height	Remarks
Korean Grass / *Zoysia tenuifolia*	S, E, W / Good on coast. Turns brown in frost. 10°F, −12°C.	Flat	Moss-like, dark green, bumpy. Can be walked on. Plant during hot months only. Photo on facing page.
Algerian Ivy / *Hedera canariensis*	E, S, N, W / Not for cold desert. Will sunburn in extreme heat. 20°F, −7°C.	18" to 24"	Large, shiny, green or variegated leaves. Fast growth and invasive. Best for large areas and slopes. Will cling to masonry, hang over a wall, cover chain link. Cut back to renew. Photo below.
White Ice Plant / *Delosperma alba*	S, W, E / Good on coast. Not for cold desert. Best with moderate water. 20°F, −7°C.	6" to 12"	Small, bright green leaves with triangular cross section; white flowers. Not dry looking. Photo below.
Gazania / *Gazania splendens*	S, W / Not for cold desert. Drought tolerant. 20°F, −7°C.	6" to 12"	Bright, 2" daisy-like flowers in white, yellow, orange and red. Not long-lived. Best as filler in flat areas. *G. uniflora* has silvery-gray leaves.
Cape Weed / *Arctotheca calendula*	S, W / Good on coast. Not for cold desert. Drought tolerant. 20°F, −7°C.	6" to 12"	Gray-green, lobed leaves; large yellow daisy flowers. Rampant and coarse. Good for large areas and slopes. Photo below.
Trailing African Daisy / *Osteospermum fruticosum*	S, W / Excellent on coast, not for cold desert. Drought tolerant. 20°F, −7°C.	12" to 18"	Brilliant, white to purple 2" flowers. Rapid and vigorous. Best for large areas and slopes. Do not overwater. Photo below.
Baby's Tears / *Soleirolia soleirolii*	N / No hot sun or frost. 30°F, −1°C.	Flat	Tiny, light green leaves. Moss-like. No traffic. Needs moisture. Photo below.

Algerian Ivy with Lavender Lantana. See page 104 for Lantana.

Cape Weed

Baby's Tears

Trailing African Daisy

White Ice Plant

SHRUB COVERS—12 to 24 inches

Similar to ground covers except woodier and usually slower to cover. More likely to discourage traffic. Makes an interesting transition between flat areas and taller shrubs. Usually planted from one-gallon cans—some are available in flats but will take longer to cover.

Common Name *Scientific Name*	Best Exposure/Climate & Minimum Temperature	Remarks
Tamarix Juniper *Juniperus sabina* *tamariscifolia*	S, E, W Hardy.	Dark bluish-green; symmetrical 12" to 18" high. Space 4' to 5' apart. Most common shrub cover juniper. Photo page 87.
Prostrata Juniper *Juniperus horizontalis*	S, E, W Hardy.	Gray-green foliage on stiff, horizontal branches. 12" to 18" high. Space 4' to 5' apart. Many varieties.
Japanese Garden Juniper *Juniperus procumbens* *'Nana'*	S, E, W Avoid extreme heat. Hardy.	Fine-textured, blue-green needles, slow, tight growth to 12" high. Space 3' to 4' apart. Photo below.
Bearberry Cotoneaster *Cotoneaster dammeri*	S, W, E Hardy.	Shiny, light green leaves; small white flowers; red berries. Creeping to 6" high. Space 4' to 5' apart. Photo below.
Prostrate Rosemary *Rosmarinus officinalis* *'Prostratus'*	S, W, E Drought tolerant. Hardy.	Narrow, dark green leaves with gray below; tiny blue flowers. Aromatic leaves used in cooking. Flat to 18" high. Attracts bees. Space 2' to 3' apart.
Santa Cruz Pyracantha *Pyracantha 'Santa Cruz'*	S, W, E Hardy.	Dark green leaves; white flowers; red berries. 24" or higher. Space 3' to 4' apart.
Shore Juniper *Juniperus conferta*	S, E, W Best on coast. Not for interior valley or desert. Hardy.	Light green foliage, trailing to 12" high. Space 4' to 5' apart. Good in sandy soil.
Dwarf Coyote Brush *Baccharis pilularis*	S, W, E Good both on coast and desert. Drought tolerant. 5°F, −15°C.	Small, light green leaves. 12" to 18" high. 'Twin Peaks' variety more compact. Space 3' to 4' apart. Photo below.
Star Jasmine *Trachelospermum* *jasminioides*	E, S W okay in cool climate. Appreciates part shade in hot climate. 10°F, −12°C.	Shiny, dark green leaves; white, fragrant flowers. 18" to 24" high. Also a well-mannered vine. Space 2' to 3' apart. Photo below.
Lavender Lantana *Lantana montevidensis*	S, W, E Not for cold desert. Drought tolerant. 20°F, −7°C.	Dark green leaves; lavender flowers most of the year. Many hybrids in yellow, orange and pink—but not as hardy. Trailing to 12" high. Space 4' to 5' apart. Photo page 174.
Sprenger Asparagus *Asparagus sprengeri*	E, S, W Not for cold valley or desert. 25°F, −4°C.	Light green ferny foliage. 18" high, trailing habit. Makes good pot or hanging basket. Space 2' to 3' apart. Photo page 145.
Tuttle Natal Plum *Carissa grandiflora* *'Tuttle'*	S, E, W, N Good on coast. Not for cold valley or desert. 30°F, −1°C.	Shiny, dark green leaves; white, fragrant flowers; red, edible fruit. Neat and tailored 18" to 24" high. Space 3' to 4' apart. Photo below.

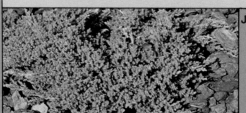

Japanese Garden Juniper

Tuttle Natal Plum

Dwarf Coyote Brush

Bearberry Cotoneaster

Star Jasmine

VINES

Perhaps the most difficult to use of all types of plants, they can also be the most striking. Provide adequate support to suit the specific method of climbing. Allow extra time for training and trimming. Also see shrub lists for those suitable for espalier.

Common Name *Scientific Name*	Best Exposure/Climate & Minimum Temperature	Remarks
Chinese Wisteria *Wisteria sinensis*	E, S, W Best with regular watering and iron. Hardy.	Heavy trunk and branches need sturdy support. 12" long, hanging flower clusters, violet-blue or white. Large, but trainable. Deciduous. Japanese wisteria is similar. Photo below.
Boston Ivy *Parthenocissus tricuspidata*	E, N More sun in cool climate. Hardy.	Large leaves turn orange to red in fall. Clings to masonry. Deciduous. *P. quinquefolia*, Virginia Creeper, similar.
Hall's Honeysuckle *Lonicera japonica halliana*	S, W, E Drought tolerant. Hardy.	Small, fragrant whitish-yellow flowers. Rapid growth, can take over. Good on chain-link. Also deep ground cover. Photo page 62.
Climbing Rose *Rosa* in variety	S, W, E Hardy.	Needs pruning and support. Deciduous. Photo below.
Grape *Vitis* in variety	S, W, E Match variety to climate zone. Drought tolerant. Hardy.	Excellent for pergola. Fruit messy if not picked. Deciduous.
Carolina Jessamine *Gelsemium sempervirens*	S, W, E 10°F, −12°C.	Shiny, light green leaves; fragrant yellow flowers. Top needs occasional cutting back. All parts are poisonous. Photo below and page 62.
Creeping Fig *Ficus pumila minima*	E best S okay in cool climates. 10°F, −12°C.	Leaves will stay small for years. Clings to masonry with no additional help. Do not plant on wood. Slow to start, later grows fast to a large size.
Violet Trumpet Vine *Clytostoma Callistegioides*	E, S Not for cold desert. 15°F, −7°C.	Shiny dark green leaves; 3" long violet flowers. Will climb with only a little help. Easily controlled. Photo below.
Blood-red Trumpet Vine *Phaedranthus buccinatorius*	S, W, E Not for cold valley or desert. 30°F, −1°C.	Lush foliage; large, red, trumpet-shaped flowers with yellow throat. Rapid grower. Will get quite large. Photo below.
Bougainvillea *Bougainvillea* in variety	S, W, E Likes heat. Not for cold valley or desert. Drought tolerant with age. 30°F, −1°C.	Dazzling colors: white, yellow, orange, red, magenta, mixed. Thorny branches need support. Rapid grower. Most will get quite large. Transplant with great care. Photo page 62.

Blood-red Trumpet Vine

Climbing Rose

Chinese Wisteria

Carolina Jessamine

Violet Trumpet Vine

SMALL ACCENTS

To liven up an entrance, break the monotony of a ground cover and add a little sparkle where it's needed. Almost any plant that has a striking form, contrasting texture, brightly colored foliage or outstanding flowers can serve as an accent. These smaller types are usually more effective when planted in clumps or groups.

Common Name *Scientific Name*	Best Exposure/Climate & Minimum Temperature	Remarks
Fountain Grass *Pennisetum setaceum*	*S, W* Drought tolerant, moisture okay. Dormant in frost. Hardy.	Fast growing perennial grass to 3' high. Pinkish plumes look like miniature pampas grass. Seedlings can be a nuisance. Photo on facing page.
Blue Fescue *Festuca ovina 'Glauca'*	*S, W, E* Hardy.	Fine, blue-gray tufts of foliage to 8" high. Cut back to renew.
Evergreen Daylily *Hemerocallis aurantiaca*	*S, W, E* Hardy.	Light green, strap-shaped leaves arching to 3' high. Large, orange flowers. Many hybrids available in yellow, orange and red tones—not all are evergreen. Photo on facing page.
Mondo Grass *Ophiopogon japonicus*	*N, E* More sun okay in cool climate. Not for desert. 10°F, −12°C.	Thin, dark green leaves forming arching clumps 12" high. Also used as ground cover, but quite slow to spread. Photo on facing page.
Fortnight Lily *Moraea iridioides*	*S, W, E* 15°F, −10°C.	Stiff, sword-shaped leaves to 3' high. White iris-like flowers with orange-brown-purple markings. Photo on facing page.
Dwarf Aloe *Aloe nobilis*	*S, E, W* All but cold desert. Drought tolerant. 15°F, −10°C.	Fleshy, dark green, toothed leaves forming rosettes to 12" high. Stalks of red flowers in summer. Most other species have grayish leaves, appear desert-like. Photo on facing page.
Giant Liriope *Liriope gigantea*	*N, E* More sun okay in cool climate. Not for desert. 15°F, −10°C.	Dark green, strap-shaped leaves gracefully arching to 3'. Small violet flowers. *L. muscari* similar, not as tall. Photo on facing page.
Dwarf Sword Fern *Nephrolepis cordifolia compacta*	*N, E* 20°F, −7°C.	Light green fronds 18" to 24" high. Will naturalize in favorable location. Likes moisture. Photo on facing page.
Lily-of-the-Nile *Agapanthus africanus*	*E* More sun okay in cool climate. Not for cold desert. 20°F, −7°C.	Wide, dark green strap-shaped leaves, arching to 24" high. Blue or white flower heads on tall stalks. *A. 'Peter Pan'* only grows 12" high. Photo on facing page and 74.
Society Garlic *Tulbaghia violacea*	*S, E, W* Not for cold desert. 25°F, −4°C.	Narrow, strap-shaped leaves to 12" high. Lavender flowers. Crushed leaves have strong odor. Photo on facing page.
Sea Lavender *Limonium perezii*	*S, E, W* Not for interior valley or cold desert. Excellent on coast. Drought tolerant. 25°F, −4°C.	Large leaves, 18" high. Tiny, purple flowers in large clusters, preserve well. Remove old plants and allow seedlings to replace. Photo on page 174.
Richmond Begonia *Begonia richmondensis*	*N* More sun okay in cool climate. Tender to frost. 30°F, −1°C.	Shiny, reddish leaves; light and dark pink flowers. Shrubby to 24" high. Likes moisture with good drainage. Photo on facing page.

Fortnight Lily

Fountain Grass

Evergreen Daylily

Richmond Begonia and Lily-of-the-Nile

Mondo Grass

Dwarf Sword Fern

Society Garlic

Dwarf Aloe

Giant Liriope

MEDIUM AND LARGE ACCENTS

Give these enough space so the form can be displayed to best advantage. Plant in groups or as a single specimen.

Common Name *Scientific Name*	Best Exposure/Climate & Minimum Temperature	Remarks
Pampas Grass *Cortaderia selloana*	S, W, E Grows in heat or cool coast. Drought tolerant. Hardy.	Narrow, sharp-edged leaves. Grows rapidly to 10' and more. Striking, whitish plumes on 5' stalks. Can be planted 6' apart as a windbreak. Overwhelming; difficult to cut back, self-seeding—can become a pest. Photo page 174.
Curveleaf Yucca *Yucca recurvifolia*	S, W, E Drought tolerant. Hardy.	Blue-gray-green, strap-shaped leaves with sharp spine on tip. Leaves curve gracefully downward. Single or multi-head or short trunks to 6' tall, or saw off to keep lower. White flower clusters on 3' stalks. Photo on facing page.
New Zealand Flax *Phormium tenax*	S, W, E Grows in heat or cool coast. Hardy.	Sword-shaped, flexible leaves to 6' tall. Bronze and variegated forms common.
Ocotillo *Fouquieria splendens*	S, W Desert only. Drought tolerant. Hardy.	Clusters of spiny stalks 8' to 15' high. Temporary, tiny leaves, bright red flowers. Avoid illegal plants taken without permit. Do not overwater. Needs good drainage.
Soft-tip Yucca *Yucca gloriosa*	S, W, E 10°F, −12°C.	Bright green, sword-shaped leaves with "soft" spine on top—will not pierce the skin. Eventually forms a multi-trunk tree 15' or taller with stout trunk. Photo on facing page.
Sago Palm *Cycas revoluta*	N, E More sun okay in cool climate. 15°F, −10°C.	Dark green, palm-like leaves. Very slow growth, will stay 3' or less for many years. Photo on facing page.
Century Plant *Agave americana*	S, W, E All but cold desert. Drought tolerant. 15°F, −10°C.	Stiff, fleshy, blue-green, sword-shaped leaves with toothed margin and sharp tip. Up to 6' high and as wide. Variegated form also common. Several smaller types grown in desert. Photo on facing page.
Golden Barrel Cactus *Echinocactus grusonii*	S, W All but cold desert. Drought tolerant. 15°F, −10°C.	Cylindrical form with gold spines. Slow growth to 3' tall. Needs good drainage. Several other species hardy in cold desert. Avoid illegal plants taken without permit.
Prickly Pear *Opuntia ficus-indica*	S, W, E Not for cold desert. Drought tolerant. 15°F, −10°C.	Large, flat, thick "leaves." Sprawling habit to 10' and more. Yellow flowers; red edible fruit. Tiny bristles make it an impenetrable barrier. Smaller forms available.
Bird-of-Paradise *Strelitzia reginae*	S, W, E Can take partial shade in warm desert. Not for cold desert. 25°F, −4°C.	Large, blue-green leaves on stalks form 4' high clumps. Striking orange and blue flowers. Good in large container. Photo on facing page.
Tree Aloe *Aloe arborescens*	S, W, E Not for interior valley or cold desert. 25°F, −4°C.	Large, spiny-gray-green leaves to 10' or more. Red-orange flower stalks in winter. Photo on facing page.
Soft Agave *Agave attenuata*	E, S Leaves sunburn in hot sun. Not for interior valley or desert. 30°F, −1°C.	Wide, fleshy, gray-green leaves in rosettes to several feet across. Recurving flower stalks reach 10' long and look bizarre.

Curveleaf Yucca

Bird-of-Paradise

Sago Palm

Tree Aloe

Soft-tip Yucca

Century Plant

Ocotillo

PALMS

No other group of plants typifies the Western United States more than this widely varied family. Large or small, sun or shade, coastal or inland, there's a palm for almost every conceivable location. They appreciate warm soil and establish best when planted during summer.

Common Name *Scientific Name*	Climate Zone/Culture & Minimum Temperature	Remarks
Mediterranean Fan Palm *Chamaerops humilis*	Hardiest of all. Good both on coast and in desert. Drought tolerant, but responds to water. 10°F, −12°C.	Bluish-gray-green fan-shaped leaves. slow grower. Can be used as shrubby accent. Develops multiple trunks with age. Good scale for average garden. Photo on facing page.
Fortune Windmill Palm *Trachycarpus fortunei*	All but coldest desert. Good on coast and in desert. Likes moisture. 10°F, −12°C.	Dark green fan-shaped leaves; hairy, brown trunk. Narrow growth to 15' to 20' high. Good scale for average garden. Photo on facing page.
Pindo Palm *Butia capitata*	All but coldest desert. Drought tolerant. 15°F, −10°C.	Gray, arching, feather-like fronds; thick trunk. Eventually grows to 15', but quite slow—can be used with 6' height in mind. Photo page 70.
Date Palm *Phoenix dactylifera*	Excellent warm desert. Okay on coast. Not cold desert. 15°F, −10°C.	Long, gray-green, feather-like fronds. Narrow trunk to 30' and more with 20' head. Stiff appearing. Edible fruit. Photo on facing page.
California Fan Palm *Washingtonia filifera*	All but coldest desert. 15°F, −10°C.	Large, fan-shaped leaves; thick trunk. Fairly fast growth to 30' high. Scale too large for most gardens. Photo on facing page.
Canary Island Date Palm *Phoenix canariensis*	Good on coast or inland, but not cold desert. 20°F, −7°C.	Similar to date palm except fronds are greener and recurving, trunk stouter. Scale too large for most gardens. Photo on facing page.
Guadalupe Palm *Erythea edulis*	All but cold desert. 20°F, −7°C.	Bright green, fan-shaped leaves. Trunk is slow to develop, eventually reaches 25', but okay for average garden. *E. armata* is similar, has bluish-gray leaves, stouter trunk. Photo page 131.
Mexican Fan Palm *Washingtonia robusta*	Not quite as hardy as California Fan Palm. Not for cold desert. 20°F, −7°C.	Large, fan-shaped leaves; narrow trunk. Fast growth to 50'. Soon gets too tall for most gardens—but widely planted anyway. Photo on facing page.
Chinese Fountain Palm *Livistona chinensis*	Not for cold valley or desert. Tolerates considerable shade. 25°F, −4°C.	Large, dark green, fan-shaped leaves. Slow to develop a trunk, can be used as a lush foliage shrub.
Queen Palm *Arecastrum romanzoffianum*	Not for cold valley or desert. Protect from wind. Likes moisture. 25°F, −4°C.	Arching, long, feather-like fronds. Fairly fast growth to 20' and more. Handsome when well grown. Photo on facing page.
King Palm *Archontophoenix cunninghamiana*	Protect from wind. Partial shade and moisture best. 30°F, −1°C.	Arching, long, lush, feather-like fronds; clean, green trunk at head. Fairly fast growth to 20' and more. Aristocratic.
Pigmy Date Palm *Phoenix roebelinii*	Protect from wind. Partial shade and moisture best. 30°F, −1°C.	Gracefully arching, feather-like fronds 3' long; narrow trunk. Takes years to reach 5' tall—okay for small area.
Kentia Palm, Paradise Palm *Howeia forsteriana*	Protect from sun and wind. Tolerates deep shade. 30°F, −1°C.	Lush, dark green, arching, feather-fronds. Grows to 6' or more. Excellent container and indoor plant.

Fortune Windmill Palm

Mediterranean Fan Palm

Date Palm

Canary Island Date Palm

California Fan Palm

Queen Palm

Mexican Fan Palm

111

SAN FRANCISCO BAY AREA AND NORTHERN COAST

These plants thrive on coolness, high humidity and frequent fog. Stray too far inland or down south and many of them require partial shade and frequent watering, and some *still* may not do well. Frost is of minor importance along the coast so the list starts with the smallest plant and ends with trees.

Common Name *Scientific Name*	Best Exposure/Climate & Minimum Temperature	Remarks
Ice Plant *Carpobrotus chilensis*	*W, S, E* Excellent on beach, right down to high tide line. Entire coast from north to Baja. Drought tolerant. 20°F, −7°C.	Ground cover. Water-laden leaves with triangular cross section. Purplish flowers, coarse texture. Too heavy for steep slopes. *C. edulis* is similar with yellow and rose flowers. Sandy soil best. Photo below.
Aaron's Beard *Hypericum calycinum*	*E* All areas, but really shines in north. Appreciates partial shade and plenty of water if used inland. Hardy.	Ground cover. Light green leaves; bright yellow flowers. Spreads underground. Can be sheared back to renew. Photo below.
Australian Fuchsia *Correa pulchella*	*S, W* Common northern plant. Sun-lover that should grow well in south—but doesn't. 20°F, −7°C.	Low shrub. Gray-green leaves; pink, tubular flowers. Sprawling—good for planter boxes and slopes. Needs well-drained soil, not too much water.
David Viburnum *Viburnum davidii*	*E, N* Just doesn't perform well in south. Most viburnum species are better in the north, but many also do well in warmer climates. Hardy.	Small shrub. Dark green, pleated leaves; blue berries. Needs acid soil. One of the most beautiful foliage plants.
Hybrid Fuchsia *Fuchsia hybrida*	*E* Will grow in south if given coolness and humidity. Filtered shade best for most varieties. Dies back from frost, but re-grows in spring.	Small to medium shrub. Wide range of colorful flowers. Some varieties make excellent hanging baskets. Others can be espaliered. Needs frequent watering. Photo below.
Skimmia *Skimmia japonica*	*E* One of the best plants for coastal Oregon, Washington and Northern California. Difficult anywhere else. Hardy.	Small to medium shrub. Large, glossy leaves; red berries. Slow, compact growth. Acid soil.
Oliver's Snapweed *Impatiens oliveri*	*E* Withstands salt spray and wind along ocean. More sun okay, but appreciates partial shade. Dies back from frost, but re-grows in spring.	Medium shrub. Succulent stems; many pinkish flowers. A great filler plant used in masses. Easy to grow. Photo below.
Japanese Pieris *Pieris japonica*	*E, N* Not for south at all. Protect from wind and hot sun. Hardy.	Beautiful bronzy new foliage; tiny, white flowers similar to lily-of-the-valley. Aristocratic and refined. Needs acid soil and good care.

Ice Plant

Aaron's Beard

Oliver's Snapweed

Hybrid Fuchsia

Primrose Tree

Common Name *Scientific Name*	Best Exposure/Climate & Minimum Temperature	Remarks
Bigleaf Hydrangea *Hydrangea macrophylla*	E More sun okay where cool. Will survive in almost all zones, but doesn't do nearly as well away from north coast. Hardy.	Medium to large shrub. Large leaves; large blue, white, pink or red flowers, depending on variety and soil acidity. Deciduous. Needs lots of water.
Mirror Plant *Coprosma repens*	E, S Will grow along coast all the way to Baja, but best in north. Full sun okay where cool. 20°F, −7°C.	Large shrub. Very shiny leaves. Sprawly form, difficult to manage. Can be clipped or trained as an espalier. Variegated and dwarf forms available. Responds to plenty of water. Sandy soil best. Photo below.
Escallonia *Escallonia* species	E Grows all along coast, but most at home in north. Full sun and wind okay at ocean. Needs partial shade in hotter areas. 20°F, −7°C.	Small to large shrubs. Small, shiny leaves; white, pink or red flowers. Neat looking. Somewhat drought tolerant, but better with water.
Rhododendron *Rhododendron* species	E More sun okay where cool. Some can be grown with reasonable success inland and in south. By far the best ones are grown in the north. Hardy.	Small to large shrubs. Wide group of plants characterized by large leaves and outstanding flowers. Azaleas belong to the same genus and require similar conditions—except Southern indica azaleas can be grown in warm climates. Needs well-drained acid soil and plenty of water. Photo below.
Pittosporums *Pittosporum eugenioides,* *P. crassifolium*	S, W Much better in north than south. *P. crassifolium* excellent at the beach. 20°F, −7°C.	Large shrubs, hedges or small trees. *P. eugenioides* has yellow-green leaves. *P. crassifolium,* shown below, has gray-green leaves.
Pink Melaleuca *Melaleuca nesophila*	S, W Loves all beaches, thrives in salt-spray. Can also be grown inland. 20°F, −7°C.	Large shrub or small tree. Small, gray-green leaves; round, pink flowers. Irregular branches; tannish-gray bark. Excellent screen or pruned as a character tree.
Boxleaf Azara *Azara microphylla*	E, N Difficult to grow away from cool, northern coast. 20°F, −7°C.	Small tree. Narrow, light green leaves. Delicate, open growth. Requires intelligent pruning. Good espalier. Needs good drainage with adequate moisture.
Washington Hawthorn *Crataegus phaenopyrum*	Full sun. Grows anywhere in the north. Tolerates cold. Hardy.	Small tree. Shiny leaves with good fall color. White flowers; red fruits. Deciduous.
Flowering Crabapple *Malus* species	Full Sun. Okay away from the coast, but best in north. Hardy.	Small tree. White, pink or red flowrs. Some have edible fruit. Deciduous.
Mayten Tree *Maytenus boaria*	Full sun. Will grow in south, but not as reliable. 20°F, −7°C.	Small tree with graceful weeping form. Small shiny leaves. Well-behaved. Good in a lawn. Needs lots of water with good drainage. Also multi-trunk.
Primrose Tree *Lagunaria patersoni*	Full sun. At its best all along the coast. Also takes heat. 25°F, −4°C.	Medium tree. Gray-green leaves; rose-pink flowers. Pyramidal shape. Photo on facing page.

Mayten Tree

Mirror Plant

Rhododendron

Pittosporum crassifolium

Foolproof Planting | 7

Here is where all your selections from the plant lists are put to use. But selecting plants is not enough. Once you've developed a planting plan similar to the ones at the end of this chapter, you must then provide a proper environment for the plants if they are going to perform well.

PLANTING SEASON

What is the best time of year for planting? In mild winter climates, planting can actually be done any day of the year. However, fall is the best season for most plants in all but the coldest zones. Root growth continues while the soil is still warm, watering is less critical and winter rains lend a hand. The plant will be well-established by the following spring and will respond with a burst of growth as the weather warms up.

If you missed the fall season, late spring is the second-best planting time for most plants. In areas subject to frost, borderline tender plants such as citrus, avocados, bougainvillea and hibiscus should be planted in late spring. This gives them a chance to become established before being subjected to the next winter's cold.

Heat-loving palms and bamboos prefer warm soil for root growth. They're usually happier when planted from June to October. Bermuda, zoysia and St. Augustine grasses, and dichondra also belong in this category.

Deciduous shade and fruit trees, roses, berries and deciduous shrubs are often sold bare-root. They normally are available in January and February and should be planted at that time, preferably before leaf buds have begun to open.

SOIL PREPARATION

Topsoil is often stripped away in large-scale grading operations and most Western soils need to be improved before any planting is done. In extreme cases, it may even be advisable to replace the existing soil with imported topsoil. Generally, though, the addition of organic material and fertilizer is not only less expensive, but also more satisfactory. Soil tests are usually unnecessary except when large areas of questionable soil are to be planted or when growth problems do not respond to standard treatment. Weeds are a good indicator. If you have a

Steer manure should be mixed with red-wood shavings to avoid an excess of salt.

good crop, desirable plants should grow just as well.

For lawn and relatively flat ground cover areas, a good basic application is a mix of 3 cubic yards of organic material, 250 pounds of organic fertilizer, such as processed sewage sludge, and 20 pounds of chemical fertilizer for each 1,000 square feet of ground. Rototill or dig the mix 6 inches deep by hand. For very poor soils, such as subsoil or pure sand, the amount of organic material should be increased. At a cost of less than 10 cents per square foot for all materials, this treatment will loosen clay soils, increase the water holding capacity of sandy soils and provide humus, nitrogen and phosphorus.

The organic material can be nitrolized redwood sawdust, peat moss, rice hulls, mushroom compost, steer manure, grape vineyard residue, walnut shells, leaf mold or a similar product. They each have advantages and disadvantages. Nitrolized redwood sawdust, peat moss and rice hulls are very good, but are the most expensive. Mushroom compost and steer manure have a fairly high salt content and don't last as long. Leaf mold can be a source of oak-root fungus infection. A compost of shredded leaves and twigs with added nitrogen is great, but you'll have to do the composting yourself. Purchasing the organic material by the truckload is advisable for quantities of more than 3 cubic yards. For example, nitrolized redwood sawdust priced at $2.50 for a 2 cubic foot sack would take 40 sacks to cover 1,000 square feet at the 3 cubic yard rate. This adds up to $100. If you can find a bulk source at $10 to $20 per cubic yard, it's well worth giving up the convenience of buying it in a sack.

This basic preparation will be satisfactory in most cases. However, modifications and other treatments may be called for under certain conditions. If an alkaline clay soil is tightly compacted, rototilling a 6-inch layer of agricultural gypsum, which requires about 300 pounds per 1,000 square feet, followed by heavy watering will improve the workability. The organic material and fertilizer is added after the soil has dried out enough to permit cultivation. Include 10 pounds of soil sulphur per 1,000 square feet to help counteract alkalinity, and make a more favorable condition for plants such as camellias, azaleas, ivy, bluegrass, dichondra and most conifers.

Sandy beach and desert soils may contain an excess of salts harmful to plant growth. By applying copious amounts of water, these salts can be carried down past the root zone in a process called *leaching*. When excess salts are found in a soil that does not drain readily, such as adobe, drainage can sometimes be improved by the addition of organic material, gypsum and sulphur as described above. Then leaching can be accomplished. If this doesn't work, underground drain lines can be installed or tolerant plants selected.

If soil depth is limited by an impermeable layer such as rock, caliche or hardpan, this should be broken through by drilling or excavating to permit root penetration. A minimum of 12 inches of soil is desirable for lawn and ground cover, 24 to 36 inches for shrubs, and 36 to 60 inches for trees. Raised planting beds and containers are called for when it's impractical to provide these minimum depths.

Ground covers on steep banks and shrubs and trees are normally treated individually by incorporating materials directly in the planting hole rather than in the entire area. So don't worry about having a minimum depth of soil throughout the entire yard. You only need it at each individual planting hole.

PLANTING

There are many formulas for planting. The "fish-with-the-corn-seed" of the American Indians was reportedly quite successful, but a trifle impractical today. Old-time gardeners have mysterious ingredients that they insist are essential for proper growth. In fact, nearly everyone has a favorite planting method—and most of them work. Even though every variety of plant has specific individual needs, these needs are not always critical and most plants will do reasonably well if basic requirements are met. The planting directions in this chapter have proven to be satisfactory for almost all plants. They are simple, economical and practically foolproof.

The key to success is blending of the excavated soil with the added organic material. Roots grow more easily into the surrounding soil, and drainage is better via capillary action when the existing soil and the backfill around the new plant are similar. Otherwise, an "underground pot" is created and roots and water tend to stay confined with the planting hole.

Drainage is the crucial factor. Here is a simple test. Dig the plant hole and fill it with water. If the water is still there several hours later, additional precautions are recommended, assuming the soil wasn't thoroughly wet when you dug the hole. Use a post hole auger or large drill to drill or dig two or more *chimneys* several feet deep in the bottom of the hole. *Don't* fill them with sand or gravel. Believe it or not, this will actually impede water flow because of the change in soil texture. Instead, fill the chimneys with the prepared backfill as shown in the illustration. With proper watering techniques, drainage will be adequate unless excess water accumulates everytime it rains or the sprinklers are turned on. In this case, you'll need to correct the overall drainage situation before planting. Very few plants thrive in a swamp.

The size of the plant at the time of planting is closely related to the problem of growth-rate and spacing. If the budget permits, relatively large plant material can be used and properly spaced. Slower growing plants can be chosen without having to wait years for their development. However, most landscape budgets don't allow this. Large individual plants not only cost more, so does the labor for planting them.

Also, there is much to be said for plants in smaller sizes because many transplant better when young. The price chart on page 117 shows sizes and costs of various classes of plants normally used.

Citrus, avocado, rhododendrons and some conifers are commonly sold balled-in-burlap, called *b/b*, at a price somewhat higher than a similar plant grown in a container. Roses, deciduous shade trees and fruit trees are available bare-root during the winter at a price considerably less than for a container-grown plant.

It's fun to shop for bargains, but in purchasing plants at supermarkets and discount house "nurseries," the advice and reliability of an experienced nurseryman is usually lost. Beware of overgrown "specials" with root problems. Conversely, beware of undersize plants not yet grown into the can-size offered. Sometimes 1-gallon plants are sold in 5-gallon cans at 5-gallon prices. To avoid mix-ups in identification, be sure of the plant you want or look for the wholesaler's tag. If you know what you're after, a $1.39 one-gallon plant

Overgrown elephant food plant in 1 gallon can is a real bargain. Roots are loosened prior to planting.

on sale may be just as good as one selling for $2.00.

But how can you know what you are after? Generally, a good plant will appear healthy, young and vigorous. As you examine more plants, you will begin to notice differences in color and form which indicate health and vigor. Shrubs should have a nice shape. Trees should have a stout trunk and sturdy framework.

Stick your finger down into the soil to feel if there are roots circling directly around the main stem or trunk. Sometimes when a seedling is transferred to a new pot, its roots are directed in a circle. This can seriously limit growth and could eventually choke the plant. This is more important than if the container appears to be "root-bound." Actually, most plants are okay if the container is full of roots, as long as they're not kinked, circling or girdling. Loosen the outside roots and spread them out when planting and they'll soon grow into the surrounding soil.

Be careful, though. Some rapid-growers such as eucalyptus and acacia, most California and Arizona natives, bottlebush, raphiolepis and many gray-leaved plants are touchy about being grown in a container. Check their roots carefully and base your selection on health and vigor rather than size.

Plant Prices			
		Approximate Price	
Class of Plant	**Usual Size**	Retail	Installed
Perennial	1 quart	$ 1.00	$ 2.00
Most shrubs and vines	1 gallon	$ 2.25	$ 4.00
Special shrubs	5 gallon	$ 8.00	$ 15.00
Most trees	5 gallon	$ 10.00	$ 20.00
Special trees	15 gallon	$ 45.00	$ 60.00
Specimen trees	24-inch box	$175.00	$200.00
Ground cover	flat	$ 8.00	$ 13.00

STEPS IN PLANTING

● Excavate the pit for the plant to approximately twice the diameter of the plant's root ball.

● Check the drainage as described on the previous page. If the drainage is poor, dig chimneys.

● Mix soil for backfill. A mixture of 1/4 organic material, 1/4 processed sewage sludge and 1/2 soil excavated from the plant pit works well.

● Backfill the bottom of the pit so the plant will be at the same level with the ground level as it was in the nursery can. Tamp the backfill firmly to prevent settling.

● Remove the plant from its container taking care not to break the root ball. You can loosen any roots that look bound, but be careful not to damage the root system.

● Set the plant in position. Fill the pit with soil mixture and tamp soil firmly around the root ball. Place

fertilizer pills next to the root ball according to the manufacturer's directions. Use the 5-gram size for ground cover plants and the 21-gram size for shrubs, vines and trees.

● If you are planting a tree, carefully remove the wooden tree stake. If the tree is incapable of supporting itself, drive two redwood 2x2s, lodgepole pine stakes, or 1-inch diameter steel pipes at the outside edges of the plant pit. Secure the tree loosely to permit movement in the wind.

● Build an earth watering basin at the outside edge of the plant pit. Install a mulch of organic material, bark chunks or stone approximately 2 inches thick.

● Soak the plant by filling the basin several times. Apply transplanting hormone, Hormex® or Superthrive®, in basin water to reduce transplanting shock and to stimulate root growth.

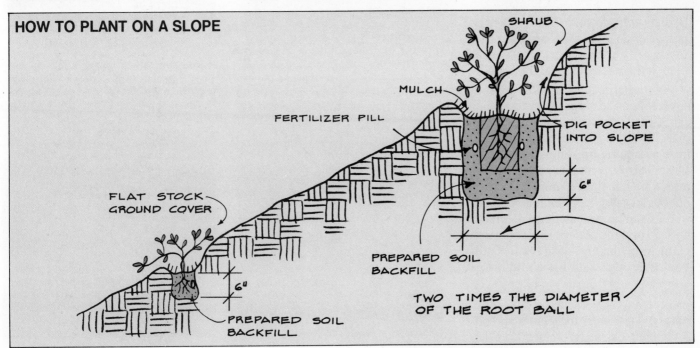

HOW TO PLANT ON A SLOPE

SHRUB

MULCH

FERTILIZER PILL

DIG POCKET INTO SLOPE

6"

FLAT STOCK GROUND COVER

PREPARED SOIL BACKFILL

6"

PREPARED SOIL BACKFILL

TWO TIMES THE DIAMETER OF THE ROOT BALL

SLOPE PLANTING

Slope planting is often a major problem for homeowners in hillside areas. Besides the initial expense and continual maintenance that would tax the abilities of a mountain goat, erosion and earth slippage can cause serious damage and even lead to lawsuits. The following procedure should be carefully adapted to your specific site:

● Check with your building department before starting any work. Regulations are usually very strict in areas subject to slides or fires.

● Cover slopes with polyethylene as a temporary measure if damage from rains seems likely to occur before planting can be installed.

● Install sprinklers for areas difficult to water by hand. Avoid excess water both on the bank and the flat surface above because it might saturate the soil and cause major slippage.

● Water the slope to germinate weed seeds. Spray with a knock-down weed-killer as discussed in Chapter 13, or remove by hoeing. Repeat this process if weed growth comes back.

● Install jute mesh now if it is to be used. This fiber matting will help eliminate surface erosion until the groundcover is established. Material cost is about 8 cents per square foot.

● Plant shrubs and trees in drifts and groves. Oleander, lemon bottlebrush, Sydney golden wattle, California pepper, Aleppo pine, pfitzer juniper and toyon are good choices. Don't overplant if there is a potential fire hazard.

● Plant a permanent, reliable ground cover. Ivy (all types), periwinkle, cape weed, croceum and white iceplant, dwarf coyote brush and prostrate rosemary are some of the best. Dig an ample plant pit approximately 6 by 6 by 6 inches. Carefully spread out the roots of the plant and backfill with 50 percent excavated soil mixed with an organic material. Water each plant immediately—don't wait until you're through with the entire area.

● Sow sweet alyssum, white clover or creeping red fescue to cover the bare ground until the plants spread and meet. This is recommended if the slope is steep and if jute mesh is not used.

● Keep weeds under control. Hand weeding is okay, especially if the area is small, but never strip completely bare during the rainy season. Immediately after planting, *before* weeds have germinated, you can apply a pre-emergent weedicide such as trifluralin, diphenamid or EPTC—but not if using sweet alyssum, white clover or creeping red fescue or hydroseeding. *After* weeds have germinated, you can carefully spray young grasses with dalapon and broad-leaved weeds with a knock-down weedicide. Take care not to get any on the ground cover plants. Check labels carefully for plant susceptibility.

● Water regularly, keeping young plants moist until roots have a chance to develop. Because you can't apply very much water at one time without causing erosion, this means watering several times a day. Fertilize at monthly intervals for quick coverage. Liquid fertilizer is easy to apply to new plantings.

● Consider hydro-seeding application instead of conventional ground cover for large banks. Cost is approx-7 to 10 cents per square foot for a minimum area of 5,000 square feet. Mixes containing narrow-leaf birdsfoot trefoil, creeping red fescue, Australian saltbush, clover, alyssum and various flowers are fairly permanent when properly irrigated.

Jute mesh is held in place with large "staples." Ground cover is then planted in small openings.

Hydroseeding large slopes is much easier than planting each individual plant by hand. Shrubs and trees can be planted from containers before hydroseeding, or included in the seed mix. Upright gazania and creeping red fescue are the dominant plants on this slope.

Rather than take a chance on serious erosion, this hillside is covered with plastic until a permanent slopecover can be planted.

PLANTING TREES

Follow the basic steps suggested on page 120 for planting. If you buy your tree wrapped in burlap, loosen the twine or wire and open the burlap at the top of the root ball before you fill the hole.

If you purchase a bare-root tree, make sure the roots are plump and fresh. If they are dry, soaking them in water overnight before planting should help. After you place the tree in its pit, work the soil around the roots and tamp it down carefully. Then stake the tree and soak the roots using a water basin. After this initial soaking, be careful not to overwater. Bare-root trees are dormant and need less water. When the weather warms, you can begin watering regularly.

Staking is an important part of tree planting. It's often overlooked until windstorms break branches or blow trees over. Ideally, a nursery tree will have a stout trunk, called *heavy caliper*, and will require no support at all. Low-branching and pyramidal trees such as olive, coral trees, liquidambar and pines can often get by without staking. Trees with *small caliper*, flexible trunks and a heavy head of foliage are usually grown with a stake at the nursery and cannot stand without help.

Remove the nursery stake and tie the trunk loosely between two sturdy stakes to allow it to flex with the wind and gain strength. This is kind of like exercise for the tree. Rigid constraint keeps the tree a cripple, dependent on the stakes like crutches. When a big blow comes, the entire head of the tree can snap off if it has nowhere to bend. Rubber or plastic ties should be used so that the bark isn't chafed or the limbs cut into by thin wires. Thinning the foliage allows wind to pass through, reducing the sail effect.

As your tree develops, you should enlarge its watering basin. The area next to the trunk should be kept relatively dry to prevent disease, but the outside diameter of the basin should be at least as wide as the *drip line* of the tree, the point where most rain rolls off the tree's leaves. Enlarging the basin beyond the drip line will encourage root growth, as will deep watering. Roots will only grow where there is water. Too small a basin will inhibit growth and shallow watering will produce shallow roots. In either case, the tree will not grow as strong as it should.

HOW TO PLANT A TREE

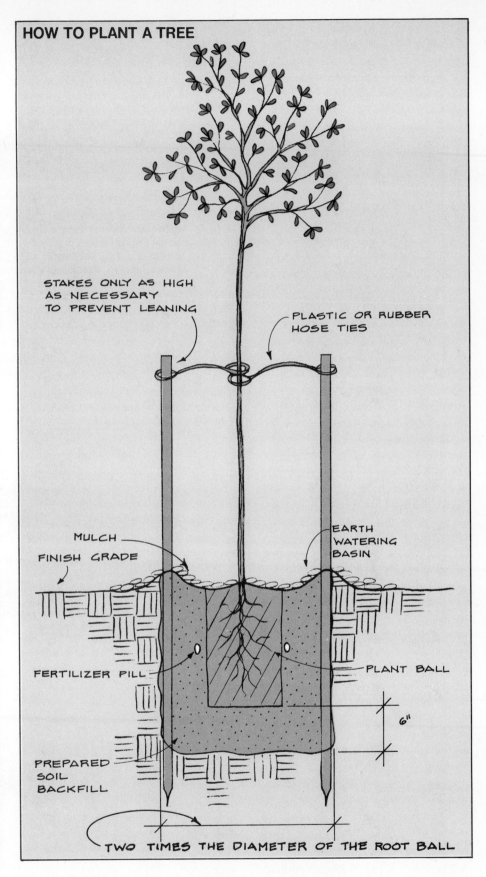

STAKES ONLY AS HIGH AS NECESSARY TO PREVENT LEANING

PLASTIC OR RUBBER HOSE TIES

MULCH

FINISH GRADE

EARTH WATERING BASIN

FERTILIZER PILL

PLANT BALL

PREPARED SOIL BACKFILL

6"

TWO TIMES THE DIAMETER OF THE ROOT BALL

HOW TO PLANT A TREE

Holes are dug after tree locations have been laid out. Mix approximately 25 percent organic material 25 percent processed sewage sludge and 50 percent excavated soil for the backfill mix. Fill bottom to receive plant ball and tamp *firmly*.

Metal can should be cut on all four sides. Plastic containers are tapered and plant can be gently tapped out if well-rooted. Handle the root ball with care. If it breaks, apply transplanting hormones and you may help it recover from the shock.

Set plant to grade. Backfill part way and put fertilizer pills in place before filling the rest of the way.

Firm the soil against the root ball so there are no air spaces.

Stake as necessary. This Leyland cypress practically supports itself, so a temporary single stake was used. Fill basin with water several times to make sure entire root area is saturated.

Make a large earth basin and fill with a 2-inch deep mulch of organic material.

HOW TO STAKE TREES

Loop the hose around the trunk and fasten the wire to a stake, leaving some room for movement. It is usually best to stake a young tree from both sides.

You can make your own tree ties by cutting old plastic hose into 12-inch lengths. Then thread them onto heavy gauge wire.

This young eucalyptus tree is properly staked. It can move in the wind and gain strength naturally.

HOW TO PLANT A SHRUB

MULCH

EARTH WATERING BASIN

FINISH GRADE

FERTILIZER PILL

6"

PREPARED SOIL BACKFILL

DRAINAGE CHIMNEYS

TWO TIMES THE DIAMETER OF THE ROOT BALL

WEED CONTROL

The best time to control weeds is *before* any planting is done. This is especially important in ground cover and lawn areas where weeding is difficult. Existing weeds and those germinated when the soil is soaked are fairly easy to eliminate. Keeping the area moist for several weeks will usually bring up a good crop. Most broad-leaved weeds and grasses can be hoed off or rototilled into the soil without regrowing from the roots. Perennial broad-leaf weeds such as oxalis and wild morning glory, a low sprawling plant with attractive white flowers, should be sprayed with a 2,4-D mix. Johnson, Bermuda and other deep-rooted perennial grasses should be sprayed with dalapon, also called Dowpon®, several weeks before cultivating. Two applications are sometimes necessary.

Eliminating existing weeds is only part of the problem. Most soils will still contain many weed seeds in addition to those already germinated by soaking. For extreme situations I suggest using either of these two temporary soil sterilants. They will kill the weed seeds without affecting future planting.

NURSERY CONTAINER SIZES

One quart chrysanthemum and one gallon dwarf sword fern.

Five-gallon *Mint Julep* juniper and wax-leaf privet. The concrete blocks are 6 inches high.

Seven-gallon Wilson holly.
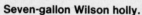

Fifteen-gallon evergreen ash.

Evergreen pear in a 24-inch box.

● *Cyanamid®*, calcium cyanamide, is applied at the rate of 50 pounds per 1,000 square feet raked in 1 inch deep, kept moist for two weeks and allowed to dry out for another two weeks before planting. Material cost is about 2 cents per square foot. A bonus feature is that nitrogen is left in the soil.

● *Vapam®* is applied at the rate of 2-1/2 gallons per 1,000 square feet in a water solution and allowed to dry out for three weeks before planting. Cost is also about 2 cents per square foot. It also gives some control of nematodes and soil diseases.

Both should be applied after all other soil preparation has been completed. Keep them outside the dripline area of existing trees and shrubs. Treated areas should be planted as soon as the waiting period is over to avoid reinfestation. Effectiveness is highest in warm weather, often disappointing in extremely cold or hot weather.

Various products containing diphenamid such as Enide® or Dymid® can be used for dichondra lawns. Applied at the same time as when sowing the seed, this chemical will give good control of most weeds without harming the germinating dichondra. Rate of application and cost varies with the specific formulation.

Important: Be sure to read labels carefully and follow the manufacturer's directions when applying any chemicals to the landscape.

USING PLANTING PLANS

On the following four pages you will find planting plans based on the plans in Chapter 2. They will give you some hints for plant selection. Follow the steps below and use the plant lists in Chapter 6 to select the best plants for you.

First give some thought as to what purpose you want a plant to serve. Next decide on the general category, size and placement. Then determine if the plant is adapted to your climate and whether it will have the proper exposure. Now zero back in on the use and function once again. If a medium tree is needed for quick, dense shade, fruitless mulberry would be a better choice than fern pine. If you want a large shrub that can be kept from getting too wide, Carolina laurel cherry would win hands down over myoporum.

In many situations the choice is not critical. Often a low shrub could be almost any noted on the list as suited for the climate and exposure. This is where you can begin to combine plants for a pleasing composition of color, form and texture. Perhaps you can throw in a bit of seasonal interest with a tree that develops fall color or a few flowering shrubs. Also, you can group them according to their watering needs so that a lone, thirsty redwood doesn't end up on a dry hillside covered with ice plant.

Don't sacrifice utility for the sake of color. There's no need for every plant in your garden to be a heavy bloomer. Actually, many of the plants in the foolproof lists are both reliable *and* flowering. If you want more color, consider using annuals, bulbs and perennials in addition to the basic planting.

What's fascinating about planting design is that the requirements are challenging, the possibilities unlimited and the rewards tremendous.

Notice the flowers. A small touch can make a world of difference. Photo: Kirk Aiken.

Try to think of the total effect as you select and place your plants. Careful selection can give you splendid results.

PLANTING PLAN—Interior Lot

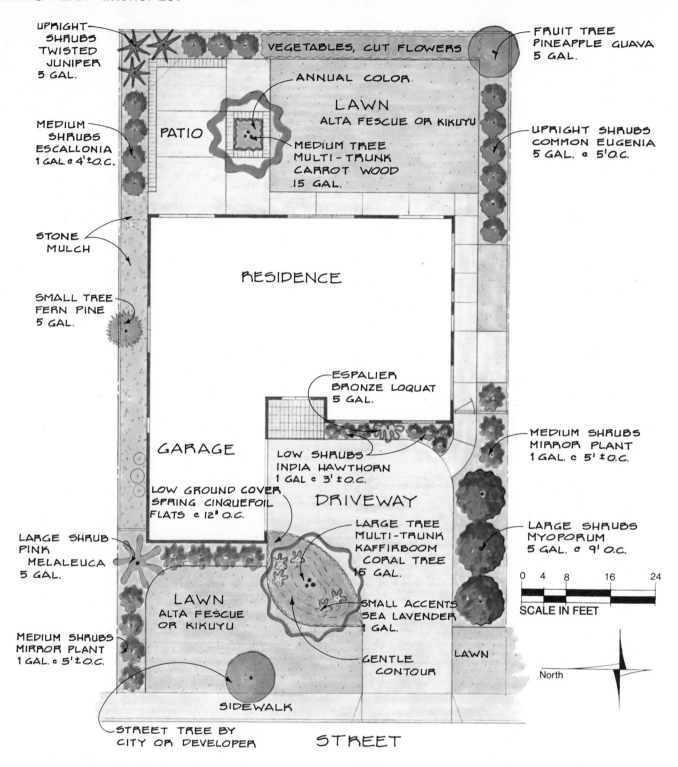

UPRIGHT SHRUBS TWISTED JUNIPER 5 GAL.

VEGETABLES, CUT FLOWERS

FRUIT TREE PINEAPPLE GUAVA 5 GAL.

ANNUAL COLOR

LAWN ALTA FESCUE OR KIKUYU

PATIO

MEDIUM SHRUBS ESCALLONIA 1 GAL. @ 4'± O.C.

MEDIUM TREE MULTI-TRUNK CARROT WOOD 15 GAL.

UPRIGHT SHRUBS COMMON EUGENIA 5 GAL. @ 5' O.C.

STONE MULCH

RESIDENCE

SMALL TREE FERN PINE 5 GAL.

ESPALIER BRONZE LOQUAT 5 GAL.

GARAGE

MEDIUM SHRUBS MIRROR PLANT 1 GAL. @ 5'± O.C.

LOW SHRUBS INDIA HAWTHORN 1 GAL. @ 3'± O.C.

LOW GROUND COVER SPRING CINQUEFOIL FLATS @ 12" O.C.

DRIVEWAY

LARGE TREE MULTI-TRUNK KAFFIRBOOM CORAL TREE 15 GAL.

LARGE SHRUBS MYOPORUM 5 GAL. @ 9' O.C.

LARGE SHRUB PINK MELALEUCA 5 GAL.

LAWN ALTA FESCUE OR KIKUYU

SMALL ACCENTS SEA LAVENDER 1 GAL.

MEDIUM SHRUBS MIRROR PLANT 1 GAL. @ 5'± O.C.

GENTLE CONTOUR

LAWN

0 4 8 16 24
SCALE IN FEET

North

SIDEWALK

STREET TREE BY CITY OR DEVELOPER

STREET

Cool, Coastal Climate

- Frequent fog and overcast skies.
- Extreme heat is rare. Evenings are chilly.
- Frost is uncommon and then usually light and of short duration.
- Prevailing westerly winds, but away from salt spray of ocean.

Planting Considerations

- Plants are mostly those noted on the lists as preferring coolness or coastal conditions.
- *Contemporary* style calls for neat-appearing plants arranged in an orderly way.
- Small container sizes are used to stay within the modest budget.
- Alta fescue or Kikuya grass withstands anticipated heavy use and is well adapted to the climate.

PLANTING PLAN—Corner Lot

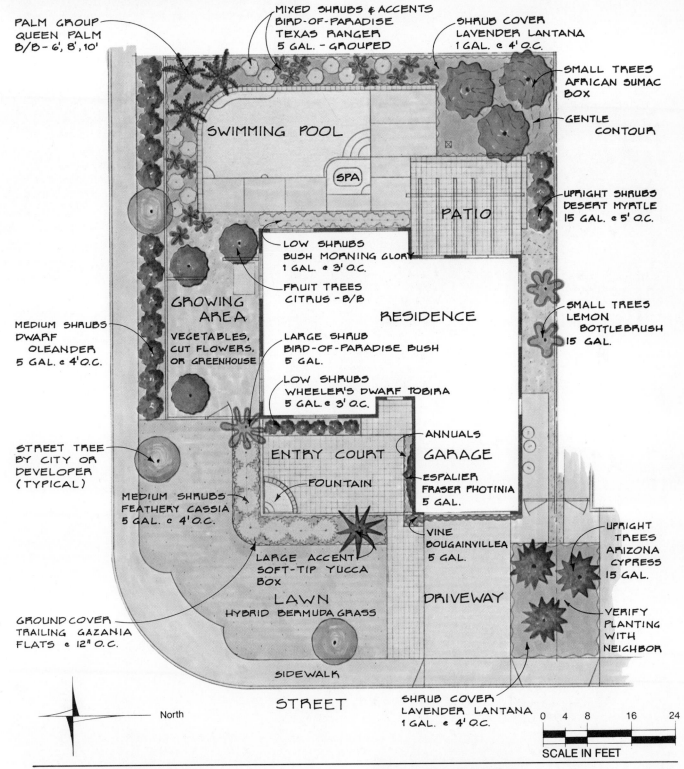

PALM GROUP
QUEEN PALM
B/B – 6', 8', 10'

MIXED SHRUBS & ACCENTS
BIRD-OF-PARADISE
TEXAS RANGER
5 GAL. - GROUPED

SHRUB COVER
LAVENDER LANTANA
1 GAL. @ 4' O.C.

SMALL TREES
AFRICAN SUMAC
BOX

GENTLE CONTOUR

SWIMMING POOL

SPA

PATIO

UPRIGHT SHRUBS
DESERT MYRTLE
15 GAL. @ 5' O.C.

LOW SHRUBS
BUSH MORNING GLORY
1 GAL. @ 3' O.C.

FRUIT TREES
CITRUS – B/B

RESIDENCE

GROWING AREA

VEGETABLES,
CUT FLOWERS,
OR GREENHOUSE

SMALL TREES
LEMON BOTTLEBRUSH
15 GAL.

MEDIUM SHRUBS
DWARF
OLEANDER
5 GAL. @ 4' O.C.

LARGE SHRUB
BIRD-OF-PARADISE BUSH
5 GAL.

LOW SHRUBS
WHEELER'S DWARF TOBIRA
5 GAL. @ 3' O.C.

ANNUALS

STREET TREE
BY CITY OR
DEVELOPER
(TYPICAL)

ENTRY COURT

GARAGE

ESPALIER
FRASER PHOTINIA
5 GAL.

FOUNTAIN

MEDIUM SHRUBS
FEATHERY CASSIA
5 GAL. @ 4' O.C.

VINE
BOUGAINVILLEA
5 GAL.

UPRIGHT
TREES
ARIZONA
CYPRESS
15 GAL.

LARGE ACCENT
SOFT-TIP YUCCA
BOX

LAWN
HYBRID BERMUDA GRASS

DRIVEWAY

VERIFY
PLANTING
WITH
NEIGHBOR

GROUND COVER
TRAILING GAZANIA
FLATS @ 12" O.C.

SIDEWALK

North

STREET

SHRUB COVER
LAVENDER LANTANA
1 GAL. @ 4' O.C.

0   4   8   16   24

SCALE IN FEET

Warm, Sub-Tropical Climate
- Many days of sunshine with high light intensity.
- Hot summers, temperatures exceeding 100°F, 40°C, common.
- Evenings warm.
- Occasional light frost.
- Some seasonal winds, but not strong.

Planting Considerations.
- Plants that prefer coolness are avoided. Heat-lovers are given first preference.
- Palms, silhouette, color accents and drought tolerant plants carry out the *Spanish-Mediterranean* theme.
- Ample budget allows for 5-gallon and larger shrubs and several specimen size trees.
- Hybrid Bermudagrass will be green almost all year, thrives in high summer heat.

PLANTING PLAN—Cul-de-sac Lot

Moderate Climate

- Hot summers, but only a few days over 100°F, 40°C.
- Usually light frost in winter, temperatures below 25°F, −4°C, uncommon.
- Evenings cool and pleasant.
- Occasional high winds.

Planting Considerations

- Plants tender to frost and preferring coolness are excluded from selections.
- Most plants have a casual quality and are placed in clumps and groups for a *Natural* feeling.
- Modest size plants fit in with the average budget.
- Mixed lawn will withstand considerable wear and be reasonably presentable all year without special care.

North

0   4   8   16   24

SCALE IN FEET

UPRIGHT TREES
CANARY ISLAND PINE
5 & 15 GAL.

LARGE SHRUBS
GLOSSY PRIVET
5 GAL. @ 5' ± O.C.

GAME COURT

ANNUALS

LAWN
COMMON BERMUDAGRASS
DICHONDRA, AND FINE
BLADED PERENNIAL RYE MIX

STONE
MULCH

UPRIGHT TREES
SILK OAK
5 & 15 GAL.

MEDIUM SHRUBS
VARIEGATED TOBIRA
5 GAL.

LOW SHRUBS
COMPACT NANDINA
1 GAL.

MEDIUM SHRUBS
GOUCHER ABELIA
5 GAL. @ 4' O.C.

MEDIUM SHRUBS
MINT JULEP JUNIPER
5 GAL. @ 4' ± O.C.

SMALL TREES
LEMON
BOTTLEBRUSH
5 GAL.

RESIDENCE

GROUND COVER
PERIWINKLE
FLATS @ 18" O.C.

LOW GROUND COVER
LIPPIA
FLATS @ 12" O.C.

MEDIUM TREE
MULTI-TRUNK
SILK TREE
15 GAL.

NARROW SHRUBS
NANDINA
5 GAL.

DRIVEWAY

PATIO

GARAGE

UPRIGHT SHRUBS
TWISTED JUNIPER
5 GAL.

SHRUB COVER
PROSTRATE
ROSEMARY
FLATS @ 24" O.C.

PARKING

STONE MULCH

MEDIUM ACCENTS
@ BOULDERS
DAYLILY
1 GAL.

MEDIUM SHRUBS
WAX-LEAF PRIVET
5 GAL. @ 3' ± O.C.

UPRIGHT TREES
CANARY ISLAND PINE
5 & 15 GAL.

VINE ON WALL
CAROLINA JESSAMINE
1 GAL.

PLANTING PLAN—Condo Lot

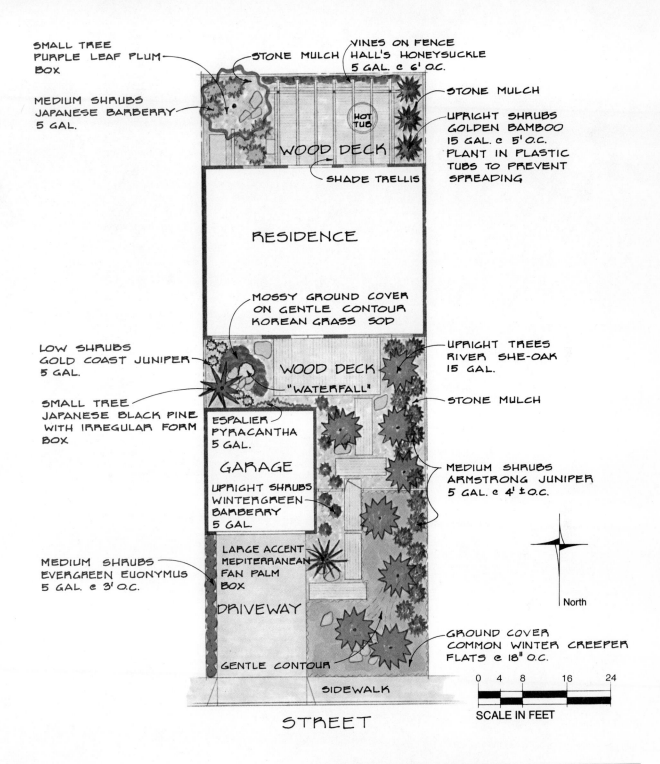

SMALL TREE
PURPLE LEAF PLUM
BOX

MEDIUM SHRUBS
JAPANESE BARBERRY
5 GAL.

STONE MULCH

VINES ON FENCE
HALL'S HONEYSUCKLE
5 GAL. @ 6' O.C.

STONE MULCH

HOT TUB

WOOD DECK

UPRIGHT SHRUBS
GOLDEN BAMBOO
15 GAL. @ 5' O.C.
PLANT IN PLASTIC
TUBS TO PREVENT
SPREADING

SHADE TRELLIS

RESIDENCE

MOSSY GROUND COVER
ON GENTLE CONTOUR
KOREAN GRASS SOD

LOW SHRUBS
GOLD COAST JUNIPER
5 GAL.

WOOD DECK

"WATERFALL"

UPRIGHT TREES
RIVER SHE-OAK
15 GAL.

STONE MULCH

SMALL TREE
JAPANESE BLACK PINE
WITH IRREGULAR FORM
BOX

ESPALIER
PYRACANTHA
5 GAL.

GARAGE

UPRIGHT SHRUBS
WINTERGREEN
BARBERRY
5 GAL.

MEDIUM SHRUBS
ARMSTRONG JUNIPER
5 GAL. @ 4' ± O.C.

MEDIUM SHRUBS
EVERGREEN EUONYMUS
5 GAL. @ 3' O.C.

LARGE ACCENT
MEDITERRANEAN
FAN PALM
BOX

DRIVEWAY

North

GENTLE CONTOUR

GROUND COVER
COMMON WINTER CREEPER
FLATS @ 18" O.C.

SIDEWALK

STREET

0 4 8 16 24
SCALE IN FEET

Severe Climate

- Very hot summers.
- Temperature to 25°F, −4°C, and below every winter.
- Wide temperature variation common within 24-hour period.
- Strong seasonal winds.

Planting Considerations

- Hardiest plants from the top of the lists are utilized throughout.
- Conifers, bamboo, irregular forms and mossy ground cover enhance the *Oriental* motif.
- Feature plants are of specimen size and key shrubs are 15 gallon in accordance with the ample budget.
- Low maintenance is achieved by use of rugged plants and elimination of lawn.

Unless you live in Oregon or Washington, the Western United States is not an ideal climate for lawns. Rainfall is insufficient to support most types of grass without considerable irrigation. Soils and water are usually alkaline and salts accumulate through repeated sprinkling to the detriment of most grasses. In addition, common Bermudagrass continually invades other more desirable grasses.

Many homeowners are unwilling to give the time, effort and expense necessary to maintain the "classic" bluegrass lawn. The logical alternatives are to choose a substitute that is easier to maintain, to reduce the size of the lawn, or to eliminate it entirely. However, there is nothing quite as rewarding as a lawn of some type and there is sufficient choice available to fit almost any need.

BLUEGRASSES

Bluegrasses are being constantly improved and can be grown reasonably well in most areas except where there is extreme heat. I recommend *Fylking* and *Baron* varieties. For best performance, they demand proper soil preparation, frequent watering, regular fertilization and careful weed, insect and disease control. Blending fine-bladed perennial rye with the bluegrass reduces some of the risk. It's less susceptible to fungus and insect attack, more wear-resistant and generally less demanding. I recommend *Pennfine* and *Manhattan* varieties. Texture is compatible with bluegrass, so appearance is unaffected. Fall and spring are best installation times for both bluegrass and fine-bladed perennial rye. Average installed cost starts at 15 cents per

Mottled trunk of native sycamore tree frames verdant expanse of bluegrass-mix lawn. Bluegrass is the most popular variety of grass, but it requires constant care and lots of water to look this good.

"Lawn is more care than it's worth. Ground cover will solve all my maintenance problems."

True. Once a permanent ground cover is fully-grown, it's much less work than lawn. Drought tolerant types will also require less water. But, it can be quite a task to get a ground cover established. The appearance is totally different and it's use is limited. A backyard lawn to romp on is the best solution for most gardens. That doesn't necessarily mean high maintenance or high water consumption.

Lawn substitutes are usually no easier than lawn to maintain. They just look different. Dichondra, Korean grass, creeping red fescue and lippia are some good choices. Don't believe photos of large expanses of Irish moss, pachysandra, mondo grass and ajuga unless you live in the San Francisco Bay area or a similar climate. These lawn substitutes usually don't thrive in the heat typical of most of the West.

square foot. Mowing height is 1-1/2 to 2 inches.

FESCUES

Service mixes vary with the nursery or seed company, but are usually predominantly meadow or alta fescue. They stand wear and hot weather well, but are coarse in appearance. These tall fescues tend to bunch when planted with other grasses, so they should comprise at least 60% of a mixture.

Alta fescue makes a good turf when sown by itself at 10 pounds per 1,000 square feet. Cool weather is best for planting, but they can be planted anytime if kept thoroughly moist during germination. Tall fescues thrive in most soils, require less water than bluegrass and take relatively little care. Cost is slightly less than finer mixes. Mowing height is 1-1/2 to 2-1/2 inches.

The pleasing curve of this beautiful lawn is framed by sweet alyssum and geraniums.

There's nothing quite like a rolling lawn. This is *Tifgreen* hybrid Bermudagrass. It requires first-class maintenance to look first class, but unlike bluegrass, it will survive even if totally neglected. Landscape Architects: Ken Smith and Dave Geller.

BERMUDAGRASSES

Common Bermudagrass has been almost entirely replaced with various hybrids of superior qualities. *Tifgreen* is one of the best for home use. It has a fine texture, is tolerant of heat, drought, poor soil, alkalinity, salt and heavy traffic. But it's normally installed by spreading sections of living stems called *stolons,* because the seeds are sterile. This makes the cost approximately twice that of seeded lawns. It turns brown in cold winter areas, does poorly in shade, has a high nitrogen requirement, suffers from smog damage and lawn moths like it. Three bushels of stolons cover 1,000 square feet. They are best installed from April to September when enough heat is available for rapid growth. If winter stolonizing is attempted, overseeding with 5 pounds of creeping red fescue per 1000 square feet provides temporary cover until the Bermuda begins to grow when the weather warms up. Hybrid Bermudas should be cut short and often, to 1 inch or less. This helps keep thatch build-up to a minimum. *Tifdwarf* is a slow, low-growing variety that requires less mowing, but is not as vigorous and is difficult to keep free of weeds. *Santa Ana* is similar to Tifgreen and has built-in smog resistance.

DICHONDRA

Dichondra is an excellent lawn

Small, heart-shaped dichondra leaves indicate that it isn't a grass at all. However, it serves well as a lawn under the right conditions. The *quarter* is from Thailand.

substitute with good color throughout the year in warm areas. It gets a little brown when temperatures get below 25°F and is borderline in zones that commonly see less than 20°F. A good use is as a low ground cover in small areas where lawn cutting would be a nuisance.

Soil should be enriched and sulphur incorporated for best growing conditions. Seed sown at the rate of 2 to 3 pounds per 1,000 square feet during the summer months will provide solid cover in 30 to 60 days. It needs quite a bit of water, 3 times a week under average conditions, and should

Main drawback of Bermudagrass is the winter dormancy period in all but the warmest areas. Overseeding or spraying with lawn dye are common practices for maintaining a year-round green.

be fertilized 3 or 4 times a year. Control must be provided for snails, flea beetles, cutworms and fungus diseases. It's also susceptible to nematodes. It needs little mowing and shouldn't be cut shorter than 1 inch. Most weeds can be controlled with diphenamid. Enide® or Dymid® are commercial names.

Zoysia looks similar to Bermudagrass and is just as tough. It loves heat.

St. Augustinegrass thrives in this tropical Ensenada garden. The blue Guadalupe palm, *Erythea armata,* makes a striking contrast against the bright green grass.

Bermudagrass, spotted spurge and oxalis can be real problems once they get started, so constant vigilance is necessary. Dichondra will tolerate partial shade and can stand more traffic than is generally believed. Still, constant wear and rough usage will make it appear shabby. You can add 5 to 10 percent dichondra seed to service or even "fine" mixes if the different texture is not objectionable. Installation, including initial weed control, is approximately 20 cents per square foot. Applying diphenamid along with the seed does not seem to affect the dichondra and will eliminate many weeds as they germinate.

OTHER GRASSES

St. Augustinegrass makes a thick, coarse turf that is excellent for chilren's play areas and can tolerate coniderable shade. It builds up rather fast and requires a sharp, heavy-duty mower.

Zoysiagrass is similar to hybrid Bermuda in appearance and performance, except it needs a little more water, has a higher shade tolerance, grows and establishes more slowly and has a longer dormant period

where temperatures drop below freezing.

Kikuyugrass is seldom planted purposely, it just comes in and takes over. It is coarse and invasive but, where it's already existing in the neighborhood, such as along the Southern California coast, it might be just as well to go along and plant it to start with. Get some sprigs or runners and they'll take off rapidly. This may very well be the grass of the future for the West. Tough enough to play football on, it can survive on rainfall alone if need be, and requires no special care.

Bentgrasses grow well in cool areas such as San Francisco Bay region and northward. They're difficult to grow in hot climates and are not usually attempted unless professional care is available, such as for golf greens. Some fine-bladed lawn mixes contain some bentgrass. Don't worry about it. If it grows, okay. If not, the others are better adapted, anyway.

COVER CROPS

Dutch whiteclover and narrowleaf birdsfoot trefoil are two *legumes* that

make excellent cover crops to hold down dust, eliminate mud and control erosion until a permanent lawn or ground cover can be installed. Plant them on slopes and all the way up to the house if you want. Sow 5 pounds per 1,000 square feet, rake in lightly and keep moist until established. The plants are beneficial to the soil and can be rototilled-in after they have served their purpose. With adequate watering, they'll persist indefinitely for a casual, meadow-like effect. Creeping red fescue can be used the same way, left unmowed for a billowing effect. Unfortunately, all three of these plants require frequent watering to look presentable.

INSTALLING YOUR LAWN

Installing a lawn isn't as much fun as planting shrubs and trees, but it can be satisfying and you can save a fair amount of money if it's done properly. Soil preparation and weed control are the same whether the lawn is seeded, stolonized or sodded, and are described in Chapter 7. Once they're completed and sprinklers have been installed, then your're ready to begin. You should also check page

Dutch whiteclover grows readily from seed and makes a good temporary lawn or slopecover.

Unmowed narrowleaf birdsfoot trefoil does a good job on this slope. It makes a serviceable lawn when mowed.

Creeping red fescue comes into its own when treated as an unmowed ground cover. Sow at 3 pounds per 1,000 square feet from October to April. It suffers from dryness and extreme heat—the most successful plantings are in cool, coastal areas.

with high salt content, such as manure.

● Roll with a water-filled lawn roller.

● Water to thoroughly saturate the mulch and keep moist continually until germinated. This may mean 4 or 5 times a day in hot weather for the first week. Turn the water on for short periods to avoid washing away the seed.

STOLONIZING

Stolonizing is an identical process except, instead of sowing seed, you distribute the stolons evenly and press them into firm contact with the soil with a special ridged roller before applying the mulch. Don't allow the stolons to dry out. For large areas it's best to water as soon as you complete a small area rather than wait until you're all finished.

SODDING

Sodding, quite common in the East, has become increasingly popular in the Western states. Bluegrasses, bluegrass/fine-bladed perennial rye blends, bentgrasses, dichondra, St. Augustine and hybrid Bermudas are generally

49 for grading and drainage information. Most nurseries will lend or rent mechanical seeders and rollers if you buy the materials from them.

SEEDING

● Drag the area with a 4-foot-long 2x4 with approximately 50 pounds of weight added on top. This helps avoid low spots. The soil should be somewhat moist, but not muddy.

● Prepare the seed bed by raking lightly. Rocks over 1/2 inch in diameter should be removed.

● Sow the seed at the rate prescribed on the package. Pick a non-windy time and use a mechanical seeder for even distribution. Rake the seed in very lightly, so that it's covered no more than 1/4 inch deep.

● Top-dress or cover the seed bed lightly with organic material approximately 1/4 inch deep. This equals 1/2 cubic yard per 1,000 square feet. A 50-50 mixture of nitrolized redwood dust and processed sewage sludge is good. Don't use material available in sod form at costs from 30 to 50 cents per square foot installed. Price varies with site conditions, quantity and variety used. Besides the obvious advantage of immediate effect, crucial maintenance and protection of young seedlings and most weed growth is eliminated. You can use a sod lawn much sooner than a seeded one, but give it at least 30 days to become well-rooted before subjecting it to heavy use. Many nurseries carry sod on weekends or can order it for for you. For large areas, you can often order direct from the sod farm and save a little on the cost.

To install sod, drag the area and rake lightly as you would for seed. Then lay the sod evenly and with tight joints. You can roll it lightly before watering, but don't take too long or it will dry out. No top-dressing is used. Don't walk on the sod for at least a week because you'll have to keep it pretty wet until the roots start to grow.

BUT YOU'VE ALREADY GOT A LAWN

What can you do to improve an existing lawn that looks poor, but isn't bad enough to tear out?

● First, mow it short to approximately 1/2 inch. Rake deeply to expose some soil. If existing thatch is thick, verti-cut it with a rented machine and remove all the debris.

● Soak thoroughly for several days.

● Aerate by removing cores of soil with a hand or power aerator.

● Remove any weeds that come up. If there are a great many broad-leaved weeds, apply a 2,4-D mixture of Trimec® or Trex-San®, and wait a week for it to do the job.

● There is probably common Bermudagrass over the old lawn. You can't get rid of it without starting all over, why not live with it? In fact you can include some Bermuda seed in the mix if your're looking for a really tough lawn. Be careful, though. Common Bermudagrass pollen is highly allergenic to some people. Frequent mowing is necessary to prevent formation of seed heads.

● Replant according to the previous directions. Fine-bladed perennial rye,

Sodding costs about twice as much as a seeded lawn, but saves a lot of hassle. This dichondra will be rolled for better root contact and to level the surface.

sown at the rate of 8 pounds per 1,000 square feet is an excellent grass for overseeding a shabby lawn in all but the hottest climates. Applying 20 pounds of ammonium phosphate per 1000 square feet along with the seed will give it a boost.

Dichondra, hybrid Bermuda, St. Augustine and zoysia are frequently plugged-in to both new and existing lawns. Total takeover of an existing lawn is doubtful unless conditions are most favorable to the plugged-in material.

HOW ABOUT TREES

It's often desirable to plant trees in a lawn for shade and appearance. Select a type that will tolerate lawn watering and will not cast dense shade or develop surface roots. Be sure the tree isn't planted in a low spot or it doesn't settle after planting. If your soil drains poorly, it is a good idea to plant the tree on a gentle rise or contour to avoid continual wet roots. However, relatively shallow watering encourages surface rooting. Use a root feeder or soil soaker once in a while to provide deep moisture.

Some of the trees most compatible with lawns include purple-leaf plum, magnolia, silk tree, evergreen pear, white birch, liquidambar, carrot wood, sycamore and canary pine. See the plant lists in Chapter 6 for additional information.

White birch trees not only thrive in a lawn, but the lawn thrives too.

Instant Landscaping | 9

There are several advantages in starting out with small plants. They're easier to install, they cost less, and they often establish themselves better than larger ones. After five years the 98-cent special will probably be as big as if you'd started with a $27.50 specimen. But—there are situations where an instant effect is worth paying the premium.

The average length of stay in a house is less than five years—most families move out just about the time the planting starts to look nice. It's frustrating to see all your expense, hard work and loving care benefit the new owners rather than yourself. Even if you don't sell within five years, there is little use and enjoyment of an unshaded patio, an un-private back yard, and a bleak and barren landscape.

We don't all have the budget to emulate the exterior decorating of model homes and commercial buildings, but we *can* borrow some of the techniques that transform a blank area into a full-grown garden overnight.

A common mistake is to rely entirely on plants. Use a solid fence instead of a hedge if immediate privacy is desirable. A shade trellis cools a patio the day it's finished—you don't have to wait years for a tree to grow. Planter boxes, low walls, benches and other landscape construction help make up for small plants.

TREES

Full-grown, or *specimen trees* as they are often called, are the backbone of instant landscaping. The 24-inch boxed tree, costing $200 to $250 installed is far from a full-grown tree, but it's a step in the right direction.

The size will vary greatly with the type and age. A slow-growing Italian stone pine or magnolia is usually less than 10-feet tall in a 24-inch box. A fast-growing white alder or London plane tree can be as tall as 16 feet.

If you really want to shoot the works, box sizes increase in 6-inch increments, along with the size and the cost of the tree. An 18-foot tree will most likely come in a 36- or 42-inch box and will cost somewhere around $500 to $600 planted. Don't plan on installing a boxed tree by yourself. Even a 24-inch size weighs over 700 pounds. A 42-inch boxed tree weighs approximately two tons and requires clear access for a big truck with a winch.

Brownish-tan boulders were selected to complement the redwood bark. Black pine is from a 15-gallon container which cost about $40 to $50 retail.

What about full-grown olives, date palms and other *bargains*? Certain trees do transplant more easily in large sizes than others and are available from orchards being phased-out, or from tree farms. If handled with reasonable care, they can usually survive the shock of being moved without a box and you end up with a large tree for a relatively low price. The catch is that the guarantee against frequent failure is often non-existent or difficult to enforce. A developer who buys 50 bargain trees still has a good deal if 5 die. If you're putting your money into just one tree and it dies, that's a mighty poor percentage. Unless you have a clear understanding with a reputable company, it's usually wiser to pay more for an established boxed tree that has a lower rate of failure and carries a legitimate guarantee.

Instead of buying larger sizes to start with, you can select rapid-growing plants such as white alder, glossy privet or Leyland cypress for a *delayed* instant effect. This is logical for a shade tree or a screen or a windbreak. There's no point in waiting 10 years for results. However, many fast growers are relatively short-lived and soon outgrow their location, necessitating excessive pruning or even removal. Use them with caution and allow plenty of room.

Another bargain is to buy large bare-root deciduous trees such as London plane tree, fruitless mulberry or Modesto ash.

The timing must be right because the season is limited to two months or less when the trees are dormant. Also, only a few nurseries carry bare-root trees in large sizes. Otherwise, it's the least expensive way to get good-size trees the first season.

THE ART OF INSTANT LANDSCAPING

Monday morning: Bare dirt without even a weed.

First, the walks were poured and sprinklers installed. Organic material was spread and then contractor John Rooney rototilled it into the soil.

Next, plant holes were dug. A heavy steel digging bar is helpful in hard soils.

It took two strong men to handle this boxed Fortune windmill palm. It weighed over 500 pounds.

Sod arrives in rolls like carpet.

Sod should be laid as fast as possible so it can be watered before it starts to dry out. Edges need to be trimmed to fit, so it takes several men to get the job finished quickly enough.

Friday afternoon: The finished yard after adding a few well-placed trees and shrubs, and lots of sod lawn. Bare ground was covered with bark chunks. Other areas were covered with stone mulch, dichondra sod or flowers.

SHRUBS

Rather than buy all 5-gallon or larger shrubs, concentrate on a few of the most important ones. Some larger plants near the front door or patio can help tremendously. One $50 plant in the right place can impart a lushness as soon as it's planted. Balance the budget by using one-gallon sizes for the less important places.

GROUND COVERS

Most ground covers take one or more seasons before they actually cover the ground. They sure don't qualify for an instant effect. With some ground covers, such as spring cinquefoil and Hahn's ivy, you can speed things up by planting as closely together as 9 inches, and by making sure they get proper care. A better way is to cover the bare areas with a bark or stone mulch. This will eliminate mud and dust, besides looking good right away.

LAWNS

Installing a lawn from sod is another technique often used when immediate results are desired. The advantage over seed is definitely short-term. Within six months, a seeded lawn should look just as good. However, sod does eliminate the crucial germination period when watering may be required three, four or five times a day. It also reduces erosion and weeds to a minimum and can be walked on in a few weeks rather than several months from seed. The biggest reward of all comes if you frankly want to impress your friends and neighbors. It'll blow their minds to see your bare dirt transformed into a green carpet within a few hours.

When you take into account the labor for watering, weeding, reseeding bare spots and cleaning-up nuisance erosion, sod doesn't cost that much more than seed. Soil preparation and grading is identical for both. Contractor's price for seeding 1,000 square feet is $100 to $150. Laying sod would be $250 to $300. The extra cost is often worth it for a small lawn. Of course, the cost difference does become significant when you want to cover large areas.

Dichondra sod was laid around this bronze loquat tree rather than wait at least a year for a ground cover to grow.

It takes a crane and several men to handle a boulder as large as this one.

OTHER TOUCHES

Boulders, driftwood, sculptures and similar features can help dramatize a new landscape. Earth sculpture or contouring is another effective, relatively low-cost method often employed in model home landscaping. If you have excess soil, it might even save money to use it for contours rather than having it hauled away.

Container plants can be used to put foliage at just the right spot. Yew pine, twisted juniper, Wilson holly, aralia and camellia are good subjects for large pots or wooden tubs. In many cases they can be seen from both inside and outside the house. Hanging baskets such as Sprenger asparagus, airplane plant and creeping Charlie are especially effective since they are usually at eye level.

A few spots of color finish things off. These flowers were planted closely together from 4-inch pots. The zigzag walk is much more interesting than the usual straight version.

Most lots don't have free boulders, but you can buy them at a building supply yard that specializes in landscape materials.

LIGHTING

Don't overlook nighttime viewing. This is when most entertaining occurs and when you want things to look special. A few well-placed lights that emphasize the biggest plants and outstanding features can make a newly planted yard appear much better than it really is.

Garden lighting can be divided into two main classifications: practical lighting for use, safety and security, and ornamental lighting for beauty and interest. Whenever possible, the two types should be combined so that the lighting is both useful and beautiful.

The need for practical lighting is fairly easy to determine. Steps, walks, house numbers, driveways, patios, swimming pools, game courts and other areas likely to be used at night obviously need illumination. Purely ornamental lighting is more open to personal preference and can even be left out entirely.

Up-lighting is where the light is at ground level and shoots upwards. This is effective at the base of the object to be featured. Usually the light is placed in front of the object to be highlighted. Sometimes the light can be in back, such as with a specimen tree, and an interesting silhouette created. The main problem with up-lighting is in placing the light so that it will not be seen directly, and only shines on the object to be illuminated.

Down-lighting is any type of lighting that is directed downwards. It can be above, below or at eye level. The larger the area to be covered, the higher the light must be. However, the problem of glare is again encountered as soon as eye level is reached. This can be solved with placement, shields or filters.

Outdoor fixtures must be waterproof, except low-voltage types, and should be of rugged construction. A hidden light source need not be a beautiful fixture, but where the fixture itself is seen, it should have a scale and design appropriate to the setting. Costs range from $10 to over $100, depending on size, type and quality. Junction boxes, as required by electrical codes, are distracting and should

Partially sunken floodlight unobtrusively up-lights a pine tree. The hood and grille help reduce glare.

This light not only provides up-lighting for nearby shrubs, it also serves as a safety light marking the edge of the brick walk.

Wood lamp was designed and installed with the railroad ties around it. Plastic was used instead of glass because it costs less and is easier to handle. The light source is a low-voltage floodlight.

Low-voltage wood light by Sylvan Designs Inc. Cost: approximately $15.

This driveway light is both practical and attractive. The bold scale of the heavy timbers is just right for the house.

This 18 watt, low-voltage floodlight highlights the shape of this tree without glare and creates a mellow mood.

Landscape architect Jon Myhre built this lamp so it could stand alone like a sculpture during the daytime and function as a light at night.

Waterproof 120-watt transformer is plugged into an exterior outlet. No permit or electrician required.

be hidden if possible, or replaced with an approved underground type.

Placement of garden lighting is best done at night, after construction and planting have been completed. Some experts advise working with extension cords, shifting fixtures until the desired effect is achieved. The difficulty with this method is that trenches for conduit then have to be dug through the existing planting and some damage is likely to occur. One way of avoiding this is to install waterproof outlets before planting and use plug-in type fixtures on short cords. Another way is to use a low-voltage system which is easy to move around.

All electrical work, except low-voltage lighting, requires a permit and inspection. Because of the danger involved, and the tools and experience that are necessary, all but the low-voltage types are best installed by an electrical contractor. Or, it's possible for the homeowner to do the trench digging and other unskilled labor and have the contractor do the electrical hook-up. If you're running 110-volt lines, you might as well include some waterproof outlets and stub-outs for any future work.

Costs vary considerably for installation of garden lighting and individual fixtures. Outlet boxes for 110-volt lighting cost about $25 apiece, conduit at least $1.50 per lineal foot, plus switches, fixtures, and connection charge. This is assuming the work will be done by a contractor. A rough way to estimate is to allow $50 per outlet, plus the actual fixture price.

Long conduit runs, breaking through walls and difficult access would be added to the basic figure.

LOW-VOLTAGE LIGHTING

By now, you can probably see the handwriting on the wall. Except where high-wattage is needed, such as for a game court or security floodlighting, low-voltage lighting has many advantages over 110-volt, and is probably the way you should go. Eight, 18-watt low-voltage lights use less energy than one 150-watt floodlight. Since the candlepower is also lower, the effect is more subtle. They're safe to handle and don't require a building permit.

No special tools or skills are required to install low-voltage lights. The wires can be buried directly in the same trench as sprinkler piping, hung on a wall or fence or laid on the surface. Because they require no conduit, placement is easily changed for best effect. They can be added to an existing planting with a minimum of disturbance and an existing circuit can usually be used without danger of overloading. Floodlights can be installed flush with the ground or even partially buried.

The cost is significantly lower than 110-volt lighting. Kits consisting of six lights, a waterproof transformer and 100 feet of wire are priced at under $100. A wide range of fixtures are available in addition to floodlights, such as hanging lights, path lights and wood lanterns.

It's handy to be able to switch on lights from inside the house. If you already have an exterior outlet that's switched from inside, just plug the transformer in and you're all set. For an exterior outlet that's not switched, you can get a transformer with a built-in timer for an extra $10 or so. Another way is to drill a hole through the garage wall and install the transformer inside with a switch, or just plug it in when you want to turn on the lights.

The typical 120-watt transformer will handle six 18-watt lights. If you want more than six, use two transformers. Also available are 200-watt and 300-watt transformers for 11 and 16 lights, respectively.

Small Spaces |10

Most of the ideas and information in this book apply whether you have a rambling ranch or a normal size city lot or a condominium with a tiny plot of land. Because you'll want to include as many amenities as possible even if your outdoor space is limited to a miniscule area, it will take extremely careful planning.

When an area is very small, such as an atrium or enclosed court, the first decision is whether or not it's only to look at or if it can also be used for dining, entertaining and lounging. If you have two such areas, sometimes one can be devoted entirely to planting and the other to outdoor activities. If there's only one, then the major portion of it may have to be paved and planting space severely limited.

Container plants, espaliers, vines and hanging baskets are good ways of getting the maximum amount of greenery in a small space. Dwarf shrubs such as Wheeler's dwarf tobira, compact nandina, dwarf burford holly and red elf pyracantha are valuable for small beds. Narrow, upright shrubs and trees are also likely candidates for a walled-in patio, as discussed in Chapter 6.

Heat is often intensified and sun-shade patterns change drastically with the seasons in an area enclosed by high walls. North-facing areas may never receive any direct sunlight. A southern exposure can be a real problem. Plants must be chosen carefully and moved or protected to survive. Check the exposure column on the plant lists in Chapter 6 to make sure a shade plant doesn't end up cooking against a sunny wall.

This small atrium was treated as a pleasant scene, not an outdoor activity area. The tropical tree is *Tupidanthus calyptratus* with a carpeting of baby's tears and bark mulch. Design: Ken Smith.

Sometimes you can have both paving and planting. Notice how the boulders, wood lamps and plants have a miniature scale to make this enclosed courtyard appear larger. A relatively uncommon totara tree, *Podocarpus totara,* from New Zealand carries out the miniature effect.

Fern pine is easily trainable against a wall. An informal treatment like this one is usually more pleasing than a precisely trimmed pattern.

Snip off a few branches once in a while and pyracantha will grow flat against a fence or wall.

This carefully scaled Japanese composition makes the most of a small area.

With only an 18-inch wide planting area it's difficult to soften an expanse of wall. This giant Burmese honeysuckle shows what can be done with a vine.

An empty deck is like an unfurnished room.

Add a couple of benches and a few container plants, plus a cat, and it becomes inviting.

Just because the front yard of this mobile home is only 6 feet wide doesn't mean it isn't important to the owner. Upright-growing twisted junipers are a good choice to shade the front windows and soften the structure.

This narrow planting area appears larger because of the receding gray color of the fence and foliage of the blue Atlas cedars. Notice how the pine tree background is "borrowed" from the neighbors.

Marigolds are grown in a redwood planter box along the edge of a garage-top balcony. They add color and provide privacy from the driveway below.

Balconies and small decks are the most restrictive of all. Planting has to be limited to containers and hanging baskets. Pots that hang on the outside of a railing save precious interior space. Built-in planter boxes may look better than a row of pots, but unless carefully constructed they always seem to leak and warp. And they can be very heavy. One way to avoid the problem is to build a simple sturdy box just the right size for the pots to fit inside. This also makes it easy to remove the plants for washing-off and leaching, and for replacement if they dwindle and fail.

The water is recirculated to spew out of a bamboo pipe to make a splashing sound on the rocks.

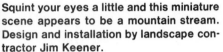

Squint your eyes a little and this miniature scene appears to be a mountain stream. Design and installation by landscape contractor Jim Keener.

Webbed chairs don't overpower this small patio.

SETTING THE SCENE

Scale of design is an elusive and intriguing consideration. Some Japanese gardens are able to suggest distant mountains and infinite space in a confined area. One device is to accentuate perspective by placing large-textured, bright green plants near the viewer and fine-textured grayish and purple plants at the far wall. This assumes you'll always be viewing it from the same spot. Otherwise, it could backfire and make the space appear smaller than it really is when seen from the other end.

Plants that are miniature versions of larger plants help achieve a spacious quality. A large shrub such as a pineapple guava or an old xylosma pruned-out to look like a multi-trunk tree can sometimes fool the eye. A grove of golden bamboo thinned-out to widely spaced canes can appear to be a forest. Companion plants should have small leaves, such as nandina, tobira and juniper, so as not to break the spell. One century plant or banana tree would blow the whole deal. Small boulders, 2x4 wood decking on edge, tiny pebbles and a mossy groundcover complete the scene—and that's what it truly is.

SPECIAL TOUCHES

Back to reality and practicality. Built-in seating and storage is one way to make the most of a limited space. Avoid heavy-framed wood furniture. The thinness of wrought iron is more appropriate. Even a glass table-top helps the illusion. If there's a chance for a see-through fence panel without sacrificing privacy, this is the ideal place for it. Wrought iron gates give security along with an airy quality.

Small water features can be used in any size garden, but are especially appropriate for miniature ones. A recirculating fountain operating on a 1/30 horsepower submersible pump requires very little water and power to operate. The sound of the water is more apt to be heard in an enclosed space and the visual effect is greatly appreciated at close range.

The same applies to works of art.

There was only room for a miniature mountain spring in this small garden. It's enough to introduce the sound of water and hint of a far-away place.

This tiny, submersible recirculating pump is only 1/30 horsepower and uses little energy. Reservoir is a 24-inch diameter fiberglass plant container sunken into the ground.

Flow is controlled by an adjustable clamp on the 1/2-inch polyethylene return line from the pump to the top of the spring.

A narrow-upright firewheel tree, *Stenocarpus sinuatus,* frames the dining-room view of a ceramic wall. Water sheets down from the top and glistens at night when illuminated by a hidden light.

Bas-reliefs are made to order for garden walls. This one is an assembled clay piece by Nancy Smith.

Artifacts are fun when casually placed in a garden, ready to delight an observant visitor. We purchased this metate from Pueblo Indians in Arizona. It adds interest to our garden and allows us to share an experience with friends.

Sculpture in full-round, mobiles, murals and bas-reliefs are quite often more at home in a small area than out in the open. This doesn't mean that a large artwork has no place in a normal-size garden. It's just that smaller ones are more within the average budget and are better protected from vandalism, theft and the elements within a secured space.

Driftwood, mineral rocks, artifacts and other collected items that have a special meaning to the owner are also fun to include in a mini-garden.

Good workmanship is crucial in a tiny area. Flaws show up like cigarette burns in white carpeting. Because smaller quantities are involved, everything can be done more carefully without taking forever. It's difficult to find contractors to install very small jobs. There's little profit involved, and lots of hassle. This is where a capable do-it-yourselfer can

build a masterpiece.

CONTAINER PLANTS

Container plants are valuable for relieving expanses of paving and for introducing foliage and color where planting directly in the ground would be impractical or impossible. Patios, atriums, courts, porches and balconies are places where a few carefully selected and well-placed plants in appropriate containers can extend

A protected patio is a good spot for a hanging basket like this common airplane or spider plant. A few baskets like this add close-up lushness.

Protruding beams are a natural for hanging baskets. Sprenger asparagus looks delicate and ferny, but is about as tough as they come.

Many hanging plants offer a bonus of flowers like this *Crassula multicava.*

Ninety-nine cent chrysanthemums are set inside pots for a temporary front door display. They'll be planted in the garden after blooming.

Ceramist Kirk Aiken didn't have *Crassula arborescens* in mind when he threw this pot, but they go so well together that it sure looks like he did. One-gallon can slips inside the pot, can be easily removed.

the feeling of a garden into an otherwise barren area. Exotic plants will often thrive within protective walls when they wouldn't have a chance out in the open. Plant collections such as bonsai, epiphyllums, cacti and succulents, herbs and cymbidiums are also best grown in containers where they can receive proper care and be appreciated at close range.

Almost any plant can be grown in a container, at least for a short period of time. However, there are certain plants that adapt much better to this type of culture and can be considered as being reasonably permanent. Some of the best include: twisted juniper, yew pine, jade plant, camellia, strawberry guava, aralia, kentia palm, Kaffir lily, black pine, Wilson holly and cycad. Airplane plant, fuchsia, *Periwinkle,* sasanqua camellia, creeping Charlie and sprenger asparagus are excellent hanging basket plants.

Another approach is to use the container as a holder and set the plant inside, leaving it in its nursery container. Bulbs, annuals, perennials

and flowering shrubs can be used in this way as a kind of living bouquet. Slip a one-quart plastic pot or one-gallon can into a slightly larger ceramic pot or wood tub and simply replace it when it's through blooming. Five-gallon size shrubs and trees with seasonal features can be used in a similar manner.

Ample root room in the container is critical for most plants. Kentia palm, bamboos, bonsai, Kaffir lily and many palms and succulents are exceptions. A 16-inch size is sufficient if you're starting out with a five-gallon size plant, and it's not too

heavy to move around. Larger shrubs and small trees in 15-gallon size need a 24-inch or larger container. They're quite heavy, so don't count on shifting them around very often.

Soil mix should be a packaged type or made up from 50 percent organic material and 50 percent sandy loam, with added nutrients and minerals. Commercial, lightweight mixes are fine for small plants, but larger shrubs and trees benefit from some sandy loam soil for better root anchoring. Drainage holes are essential, but staining of paving should be avoided by leaching out several times before moving into place. Saucers are available for all but the largest pots. Cut a piece of heavy plastic to put under wood containers that have any rustable metal.

The container should not only be the proper size but also be appropriate to the setting. For example, red clay looks well with stucco and tile, wood tubs with wood-siding and shake roofs. They don't have to be all the same kind, but too many different types of containers in a small area can be disturbing. Often, a simple pot will show a plant to better advantage than one that attracts attention to itself. There are a wide variety of containers available, including clay, wood, concrete and plastic. Cost ranges from about $5 for small mass-produced clay pots and redwood tubs to $50 and more for larger and fancier ones. Half-barrels with a diameter of 24 inches sell for $10 to $15 and are real bargains.

ESPALIERS

When you have a big, blank wall and only 12 inches of planting space, consider an espalier to alleviate the bareness. The term *espalier* seems to have an intimidating effect on many people. Perhaps they're picturing a perfectly trained specimen in the classic European style. Actually, an espalier can also be a plant casually flattened to grow against a wall or fence. In most cases, this is more appropriate in terms of design, and it's much easier to take care of.

Pre-trained plants on a trellis are available from most nurseries. The price is high—about $25 for a 5-gallon size. You can develop your own by selecting a somewhat one-sided plant and doing a little pruning. Some kind of support is necessary for most plants. A trellis, plastic-coated wires, pegs or nails can be used. When using a trellis, get one large enough or easily expandable to allow for future growth. Holding the plant away from the wall 6 inches or so allows air circulation and lessens the possibility of damage from reflected heat.

Here are some of the best-suited plants for both formal and informal

This wall needed something and there was less than 6 inches of soil depth for planting. The answer was a bleached barrel that matches the bark color of a *Melaleuca elliptica.*

espaliering. Most vines can also be used in this manner. Refer to the plant lists in Chapter 6 for climate, exposure and additional information. As with most of the other plant lists in the book, the plants most resistant to cold are first, and those least resistant, are at the end.

MAINTENANCE

Overall maintenance is greater and more exacting for container plants than for the same ones growing in the ground. Watering is critical. The water supply can be quickly exhausted during a hot day. When it's gone there isn't any more. Larger containers have more root room and more reserve. Small clay pots and hanging baskets are the most demanding. Setting one pot inside another and filling the space between with sphagnum moss cuts water loss considerably. A little soil in the mix described above also helps retain moisture better than a lightweight, very fast draining mix. Conversely, over-saturation easily occurs in pots with no drainage. Harmful salts accumulate and must be leached-out periodically by heavy watering. Light, frequent fertilization is necessary to replace nutrients lost through this leaching. Root-pruning and repotting are also sometimes necessary as the plant out-grows the container.

Plant List for Espaliers

Rose
Pyracantha
Deciduous fruit trees
Parney cotoneaster
Bronze loquat
Shiny xylosma
Twisted juniper
Fraser photinia
Burford & Wilson hollies
Dwarf Southern magnolia
African sumac
Lemon bottlebrush
Evergreen pear
Fern pine
Citrus

You can purchase espaliered plants like this Fraser photinia in containers and place them exactly where you want them.

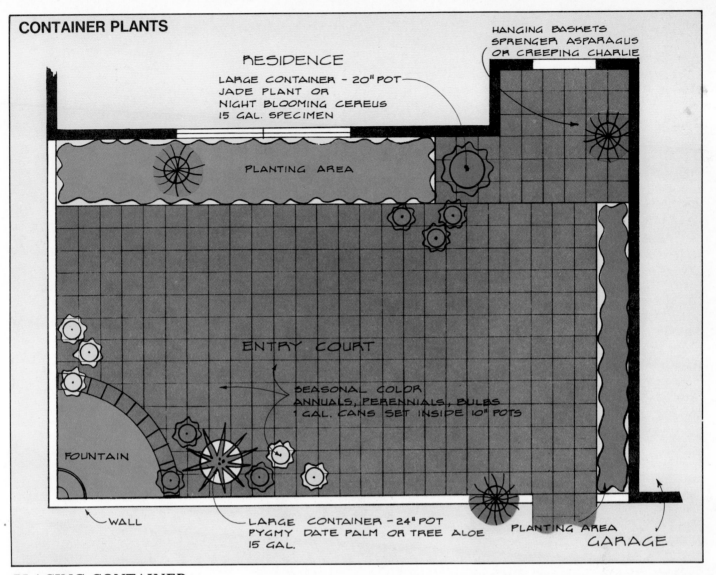

CONTAINER PLANTS

HANGING BASKETS
SPRENGER ASPARAGUS
OR CREEPING CHARLIE

RESIDENCE
LARGE CONTAINER - 20" POT
JADE PLANT OR
NIGHT BLOOMING CEREUS
15 GAL. SPECIMEN

PLANTING AREA

ENTRY COURT

SEASONAL COLOR
ANNUALS, PERENNIALS, BULBS
1 GAL. CANS SET INSIDE 10" POTS

FOUNTAIN

WALL

LARGE CONTAINER - 24" POT
PYGMY DATE PALM OR TREE ALOE
15 GAL.

PLANTING AREA
GARAGE

PLACING CONTAINER PLANTS

Selection and placement of container plants is tricky, but you don't have to do it perfectly the first time. Experiment a little and have some fun. They can be easily moved, changed or even discarded.

The walled entry court of our corner lot from Chapter 2 is ideal for container plants and used here as an example. In this case, red clay pots are selected as appropriate for the Spanish-Mediterranean style house and garden. Several 15-gallon specimens are placed at the front door and by the fountain as focal points. The cluster of flowering plants can be replaced when they are through blooming to provide constant color. Hanging baskets at the entry, on top of the wall at the gate and in front of the bedroom windows add eye-level foliage.

Container plants can be replaced to take advantage of seasonal blooms, as with these poinsettias. Grouping container plants is usually more effective visually than setting out small containers singly.

147

Grow Your Own

This small back yard is devoted entirely to vegetables. Midwinter crops in mild, coastal California include lettuce, carrots, turnips, cauliflower, pod peas, chard and a leftover tomato protected by plastic.

There are many reasons to include edible plants in your garden. Home-grown fruits and vegetables seem to taste better and be more nutritious. With food prices so high, you can more than recover the cash outlay for plants, seeds, fertilizer, sprays and water. Difficult to obtain and off-season items can often be grown if you give them a little extra attention. Increasingly precious fertilizer and water can be put to productive use, rather than only ornamental purposes. It's a good way to introduce children to the wonders of gardening—they'll even eat their "veggies" when they've had a hand in growing them. Besides all this, many edible plants are good-looking. And nothing can beat the pleasure of picking a delicious morsel from your own yard.

When surplus crops become a problem, try setting up a trading arrangement with your food-growing friends and neighbors. If you have too many tomatoes and peaches while there are loads of plums and squash right next door, both parties will welcome a little variety. Cold storage, freezing and canning are also ways to make best use of a bumper crop. With vegetables, spacing out planting times can help avoid an oversupply. After a few seasons, you get to know how much of what kind to plant.

Esthetics and food production are compatible. Some vegetables are every bit as attractive as shrubs and flowers. Here are a few that you could consider substituting for traditional planting: Rhubarb, artichoke, flowering kale, New Zealand spinach, rhubarb chard and Jerusalem artichoke are both ornamental and edible. You can use rhubarb and artichokes in place of shrubs. The others

A member of the sunflower family, Jerusalem artichoke puts on a nice display of flowers before dying back in the fall.

Some people cook the potato-like tubers, but a tastier use is raw as a crunchy substitute for water chestnuts.

Melons need plenty of sun. These baby yellow watermelons are not usually found in stores.

Bright green lettuce can be sown in a flower bed or between shrubs for a quick and delicious display. Red-leaved forms are also available.

are seasonal but will still outlast the span of most annuals. For a fern-like effect, try sowing some carrots in between other plants. The various types of lettuce give a fast showing of bright-green and reddish leaves.

GROWING VEGETABLES

Most vegetables are easy to grow. Meet the following requirements and success is practically assured.

Location—Select a location that gets sun most of the day. Obviously, cool, coastal gardens will need more sun than hot, desert areas. Corn, tomatoes, melons, eggplant, cucumbers and other heat-lovers require lots of sun. Reasonably good crops of chard, beets, carrots, lettuce, radishes, turnips and other cool-season types can be grown if they receive half-day sun.

Soil—Incorporate plenty of organic material at least 12 inches deep. Six cubic yards for every 1,000 square feet is fine for average soils. Most Western soils are deficient in nitrogen and can also stand some readily available phosphorus. Adding 20 pounds of ammonium phosphate per 1,000 square feet along with the organic material is usually sufficient. Chapter 7 gives more general information on soil preparararion.

Vegetables—Choose the right crop and variety for your specific climate and plant during the proper season. The back of the seed package will tell you a little, but you can get more

Organic material is dug deeply into this hill being prepared for summer squash.

A sheet of polyethylene extended the production of this tomato for more than a month into the fall.

specific information from agricultural extension publications and regionalized books on home vegetable gardening.

Watering—Develop good watering practices tailored to the individual crop. Germinating seeds must not be allowed to dry out. Many vegetables become bitter if growth is slowed by lack of water. Conversely, too much water can result in too much growth

or it can kill some plants.

Insects and Diseases—Watch carefully for insects and diseases. Many diseases can be avoided by planting resistant varieties. Pay a little more for the seeds of plants—it's worth it. The same insect control principles covered in Chapter 13 apply to vegetables. Remember that you're not only going to look at vegetables; you will be eating them too.

Vegetables are a natural for drip irrigation. However, those with dissimilar watering needs should be on separate valves.

This small, pie-shaped corner contains plum, pear, apricot and peach trees. Annual pruning keeps them from overgrowing the limited space.

HERBS

Many herbs are valuable landscape subjects in addition to their culinary qualities. Rosemary, lavender, mint and thyme are especially useful. Gray-foliaged lavender is an interesting contrast to green shrubs. Prostrate rosemary and creeping thyme are excellent drough-tolerant ground covers. Give mint plenty of water and cut it back once in a while, and it makes an attractive filler. Incidental-ly, strawberries also make a fairly good ground cover. Hybrid #25 has high-quality fruit and fills in more solidly than regular commercial varieties.

FRUITS

Any garden can accommodate fruit trees of some kind. For maximum success, use the specific variety best-suited to your climate zone. Your local nurseryman usually carries the types that have proven most reliable in your locality. If you're planning a small orchard, you might want to also check with your local farm advisor. In general, citrus, avocado and other tender types are limited to relatively frost-free areas. Most deciduous fruits do better in cold deserts and interior valleys where they receive adequate winter chilling. If you want to grow them in a mild climate, ask for special varieties such as *Winter Banana apple, Newcastle apricot, Bonita peach* or *Panamint nectarine.*

Where there is plenty of space, standard-size trees will produce larger crops and they can also serve for shade or background. Avocado, apricot, plum, apple and pear fall into this category. In well-drained soils, they all happen to be reasonably tolerant of normal garden watering. Apricots and pears will even do fairly well in a lawn.

Most other fruit trees are in the small category—at least for many years. Peach, nectarine, fig, persimmon and citrus can be tucked into a 10 by 10-foot space and kept there with normal pruning. These trees are not recommended for lawns or frequent watering. They'll all do better with orchard-type irrigation.

Less common fruits that are sometimes grown include pomegranate, pineapple and strawberry guava, loquat, jujube and sapote. The value of

Mint is not a bad looking ground cover for a small area if you cut it back once in a while. For some reason the growth habit, texture and color seem to combine pleasantly with the sprawling *Aloe striatula* in the background.

Citrus can be an attractive landscape plant in a mild climate. This orange tree is placed at the top of a slope where it won't be drowned by normal garden watering.

GROW YOUR OWN IN CONTAINERS

This 18 inch tall container will be large enough for this dwarf nectarine for 3 to 5 years. Then it should be replanted.

You eat the entire kumquat, skin and all. It's tart, but interesting. It's an excellent container plant and has colorful fruit most of the year.

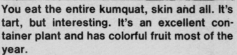

Celtuce, rhubarb chard and tomato grow happily in 5-gallon containers and make an attractive and edible display. They need watering almost every day in hot weather.

Kale not only tastes good, but has a fascinating texture. It grows very well in a container.

growing these is they are seldom sold in the market. The only way to get the fruit is from a friend or by growing it yourself. If you live in a favored subtropical zone, you might even be able to sneak in a banana, mango, papaya or cherimoya.

What if you don't have a 10 by 10-foot space? Figs, apples, persimmons, pears, citrus and loquats need only a narrow bed when espaliered on a wall or fence. Peaches, nectarines, apples, pears, avocados and citrus are readily available in dwarf form—with full-size fruit. These can be grown in a space as small as 5 by 5 feet. If you have no soil at all, almost any patio or balcony can accommodate a dwarf fruit tree in a large container such as a half-barrel. Surprisingly good vegetable crops can be raised entirely in containers.

Don't overlook food-bearing vines. You can have both grapes and summer shade by planting them on an overhead structure. The exotic kiwi can be used the same way. Chayote is an interesting perennial vine that produces large quantities of squash-like fruit. It dies back during winter in all but the mildest climates, and

The loquat is a small tree that will fit into most gardens. Once you get used to the fruit, chances are you'll love it.

resumes growth as soon as the weather warms in the spring. Berries can be trained against a fence or wall. Just be sure to wear heavy gloves and long sleeves for protection from thorns.

If you inherit a mature fruit tree already growing on your property, try not to drastically change the watering schedule. Most orchard trees receive infrequent, deep waterings rather than the typical several-times-a-week for home landscapes. Don't plant lawn or other moisture-needing plants within the *drip-line*, the area covered by its branches. Overwatering at the *crown* of an old fruit tree, where its trunk grows out of the soil, is usually fatal.

FOLIAGE

Eucalyptus leaves are only edible to koala bears, but they can be considered a type of ornamental crop. The silvery-gray, shish kebab foliage of *E. pulverulenta* and *E. cinerea* are expensive florist items that you can easily grow yourself in all but the coldest areas of the West. Be careful of the common name, silver dollar, because it's also used for *E. polyanthemos* that has the similar leaves—except they're not skewered.

Hindu laurel *(Cocculus laurifolius),* fern asparagus *(Asparagus setaceus),* papyrus *(Cyperus papyrus)* bronze and common loquat, and leather fern *(Polystichum capense)* are some other excellent plants for arrangement greenery.

FLOWERS

With the price of cut flowers as high as they are, about the only way to have a fresh bouquet very often is to grow them yourself. The possibilities are limited only by climate and the amount of time you want to devote to them. I've had good success with roses, calla lilies, gladiolas, snapdragons, stocks, sea lavender, daffodils, poinsettias, chrysanthemums, ranunculas and marigolds. Plant some of these and you can brighten-up the house with blooms any season of the year. Care is similar to that described for vegetables. In fact, there's no reason why you can't combine them in the same plot.

The *Boysen* is actually a type of blackberry. Along with *Logan, Olallie* and *Young,* it's one of the best producers for warm areas of the West. Raspberries are easier in cooler areas. Blueberries require acid soil and are best in Northern climes.

If you grow chayote, allow plenty of room and be prepared to give some away.

This eucalyptus is probably silver mountain gum, but most everyone calls it *silver dollar tree*. Tuck it in a dry corner and cut it back occasionally, and you'll have loads of branches for fresh and dry arrangements.

These orange trees were here when the house was built. Rather than continue the lawn under them, I used drought tolerant plants with stone mulch to avoid overwatering.

Most orchids require a greenhouse and exacting care. Cymbidiums can be grown in a mild climate with minimum protection and effort.

Remodeling A Garden | 12

Ask any landscape architect. It's much easier to start with a new house and bare land than to redo an existing garden. The basic decision is what to save and what to tear out. Let's consider paving and construction first.

PAVING

Wherever possible, it's sensible to try to save existing paving. Not only is it a big job to break up paving and haul it away, but you end up paying double for removal *and* replacement.

Inspect existing paving to make sure it drains properly and to see if it has any structural cracks or tilting and settling. By structural cracks I mean anything wider than 1/4 inch. If the paving appears sound, but doesn't look as good as it should, perhaps it can be *improved* rather than replaced. Where part of the paving is good, you can rent a concrete saw and cut out the bad portion.

If a paved area is too small or a walk too narrow, add to it rather than starting over. Match it as closely as possible to help avoid a patchy appearance. A safer way is to choose a contrasting material and make the addition a design feature.

Acid stain can often transform dull, drab concrete into an attractive surface with a minimum of expense and effort. This method is especially effective in solving the problem of glare. For stain to take properly, it needs to soak in. The concrete must be clean and free of paint, wax, oil and grease. Trisodium phosphate or a dilution of one part muriatic acid to 20 parts water can be used to remove whatever you can't scrub off with a broom and hose. The cleaner the concrete, the better the results will be. The stain is brushed on in two coats. Allow time for the first coat to

dry before applying the second. In most cases, the stain soaks in unevenly for a pleasing, mottled effect. Don't expect it to be solid or to cover chips, cracks and other imperfections. Material cost is approximately 20 cents per square foot.

Another way to upgrade existing paving is to use it as a base to lay new paving over. The trick here is to make

A crack as large as this may mean the concrete isn't structurally sound and should be replaced. The coin is a quarter.

sure that the extra thickness doesn't create a drainage problem or a dangerous small step. New concrete poured over the old should be at least 3 inches thick. Thinner layers tend to crack. Roughening the old surface and painting it with concrete glue will help form a bond. Usually the price will be similar to new work, but you still save the removal cost.

A concrete stain was used to give a brownish-rust color that ties in with the new wood landing. Stain has a chemical reaction with cement and, unlike paint, is permanent.

A power saw slices right through concrete so that undesirable sections can be removed.

Take an existing yard, add some paving and a shade trellis, furnish it with lush plants and then enjoy the results.

ADDING CONCRETE

Adding concrete follows the same procedure as shown in Chapter 3. Here Billy Becher lends a hand while his father installs forms for an addition to a narrow front walk.

To give this walkway a texture, 3/4-inch lomita stone is sprinkled on the surface.

The stones are pressed into the wet concrete until barely covered.

As soon as the concrete starts to harden, it's swept lightly with a broom to expose the lomita stone.

The crucial decision is when to start washing the surface with a light stream of water. This concrete is just about "ripe."

The exposed pebbles make a subtle contrast with the plain concrete of the old paving.

You can lay 1/2-inch thick bricks in a mortar base over an existing concrete patio. Mortar joints are filled-in later.

Tile is best laid on a concrete base anyway, which makes it ideal for upgrading an old slab.

Common bricks or flagstone laid on a 1 inch sand or mortar bed on top of old paving will also raise the level approximately 3 inches. If this is too much, split-bricks or patio tiles can be set in mortar or mastic to keep the added thickness down to as little as 1 inch. Cost is quite often less than new work because there isn't any grading and excavating.

Pressure-treated or redwood planks are easily laid over existing concrete. They can be nailed to wood *sleepers* attached to the concrete with a cartridge-fired stud gun or with counter sunk carriage bolts set in expansion plugs. Or the planks can be laid directly in concrete glue. This works great on a small porch or landing where a single plank can be used without splicing. Figure approximately $1.00 per square foot for 2-inch planking. You'll probably have to do the work yourself. Finding a carpenter for a small job that's different is unlikely.

It's easy to seal-coat asphalt that looks shabby. Just sweep sand into the cracks and then broom on the emulsion. Material cost is about 10 cents per square foot. If the surface is really shot, you can sometimes have a paving company add a 1-inch layer of new asphalt on top of the old for much less than tearing it all out and starting over.

Here, 2x4 *sleepers* are glued to a concrete landing and redwood 2x4s nailed in place.

CONSTRUCTION

Approach the question of whether or not to keep walls, fences, shade trellises and other garden construction the same way as you approach paving. If it's structurally unsound or downright unsafe, remove it. Otherwise look for ways to improve it. You can use the same acid stain suggested for concrete on concrete block walls. Or you can use a cement-based paint or plaster. Wood fences can be stained

A 2x8 redwood trim board has been added and the wood bleached to blend with the house trim. Matching English hollies in wood barrels complement the lights. Design: Ken Smith.

or the frame salvaged and new paneling installed.

Shade trellises can be "beefed-up" by applying what are called *plant-ons*. A 4x4 post can be enhanced by nailing 1x2s on all four sides. Beams and rafters can be treated similarly. The key to success is a little ingenuity.

PLANTS

It's much more difficult to decide which plants to save. If you're remodeling your own garden, it becomes an emotional issue to cut down an undesirable plant, especially if you're the one who put it there in the first place. Try to remember that a plant is expendable once it no longer serves its purpose. Take out the obviously dead and dying plants first. Then determine which remaining ones are still doing a good job and which ones are ill-chosen.

Transplanting is always a risk and is often attempted with the erroneous belief that all plants are valuable. Moving a small plant is one thing; anything more than 4-feet high becomes a major task. In many cases it would be better to start with a new plant.

If you decide to go ahead, here are some general rules.

● Check with a nursery to see what a container plant of a comparable size would cost. Ask your nurseryman if the plant is easy to move.

● Determine if you have an actual need for the plant in your garden and if there is a place for it.

● Choose the best time of year for the specific plant. Camellias are dormant when in bloom, deciduous plants when leafless. Palms and bamboo can be moved most successfully in warm weather, pines in the fall. Most other plants have the best chance for survival if transplanted in the spring.

● Avoid clear, hot days. Cool, overcast weather is best. Provide temporary shade protection if it turns hot.

● Take as much of the root system as practical. Move it directly into the new position. Prune back to reduce

leaf surface, apply a transplanting hormone such as Hormex® or Superthrive® and keep moist until established.

Now is a good time to correct previous mistakes and to anticipate future problems. The most common example of this is overgrowth. Rather than hacking away at a large shrub next to a walk or under a window, it might be better to remove it. However, if there is a reasonable space for a shrub to grow, don't be too hasty. Some will regrow when severely cut back and give many more years of service. Another approach: convert an overgrown shrub into a small tree by pruning the lower branches.

TREES

Where large trees are involved, it may be advisable to seek expert advice. It's truly sad to remove a beautiful old tree that can often be rehabilitated by a good pruning. Incidentally, the cost of pruning may be less than total removal. Check on the estimated value of a tree before cutting it down—you may be destroying an extremely expensive specimen.

Most existing trees are very sensitive to changes in grade. Exceptions are palm trees and native sycamores which are tolerant of fill. Soil should not be added more than a few inches deep within the area between the trunk to the outermost spread of the branches. If deeper fill is unavoidable, a wall several feet away from the trunk will at least help to keep soil away from the trunk and save the tree from almost certain death. Likewise, lowering of grade within the drip-line area should be avoided.

Orchard trees such as walnut and citrus, and native oaks are difficult garden subjects. Fruit and nut trees are normally grown with infrequent irrigation every three weeks or so. The oaks, of course, get only seasonal rain. Typical twice-weekly garden watering usually leads to crown and root diseases, especially in poorly drained soil. It's best to omit sprinklers and leave large cultivated basins at the drip-line. If underplanting is considered essential, at least use material that requires infrequent watering. Lawn, dichondra, camellias, ferns,

Inviting entry is highlighted by a well-designed trellis that seems to lead you into the garden.

azaleas and other moisture monsters are incompatible. Plants in containers or sunk into the ground in containers can also be used to keep excessive water from reaching the tree.

Don't forget to adapt site drainage, sprinklers and lighting to any changes that are made. Along with this, it would be well to evaluate what kind of maintenance situation you've inherited. Maybe you don't have the time or interest to take care of a rose garden or a lot of annuals or to do extensive hand-watering. As long as the place is torn up you might as well correct problems and make changes where desired.

One place you might want to go a little overboard is at the front entrance. Here is where you can add a personal touch and get a maximum return on your effort. This is an ideal opportunity to upgrade the paving by laying brick, tile, flagstone or wood over the typically uninspiring slab of concrete at the front door.

Where the roof overhang is lacking or minimal, a well-scaled wood trellis can turn a dull entry into an exciting, gracious one.

Don't be afraid of being dramatic. Bring in a few boulders, or cluster some telephone poles or railroad ties as accents. Add a few choice plants in containers and include some low-voltage lighting to complete the picture.

INSTALLING RAILROAD TIES

You can cut through a few ties with a hand saw if you have muscle and patience. A two-man cross-cut is better than a carpenter's saw.

Telephone pole sections set vertically in the ground are used at the corners for support and appearance.

A large circular saw is best to cut a lot of ties. A chain saw will also work if its blade has hardened tips.

Ties are combined with bricks for stairway. Photos on page 41 show the actual laying of the bricks. A tie laid along the toe of the slope keeps nuisance erosion in place.

These railroad tie steps connect adjacent walks. Try to pick ties with smooth surfaces to avoid tripping on rough spots.

RAILROAD TIES

Railroad ties aren't limited to remodeling projects by any means. However, they're so handy to add to an existing garden that it seems appropriate to include them here.

Prices have risen considerably since the days when they were available for a dollar apiece. You may still find a bargain in some areas, but $6 to $8 is what you can expect to pay now.

They're rather expensive when used as paving—the cost of the ties alone will be more than a dollar per square foot. Best uses are for steps and low walls because they're heavy enough to hold themselves in place with only 30-penny nails to pin them together. Walls higher than two ties can be reinforced with 3/4-inch steel pipe driven through 1-inch diameter holes. It takes a heavy-duty drill to go through the ties.

The most obvious use of railroad ties is in the rustic or natural style garden. Actually they fit in quite well with all but the most sophisticated designs.

FURTHER CONSIDERATIONS

Now that you've decided what structure and planting to save, you still may need additional work. If the original garden was well-conceived and suits your requirements, only minor modifications may be involved. Otherwise, a master plan is called for, incorporating existing items into the overall scheme.

Maintenance 13

The ideal garden is one which would only require care on cool, but sunny weekends—when you have nothing special planned, and when there's no important game on TV. Unfortunately, plants are like kids and pets. They always seem to need the most attention just when you have a million other things to do. However, you *can* have an enjoyable garden without being a slave. It takes careful planning and proper maintenance techniques along with a little ingenuity.

It appears that almost everyone wants a *low maintenance* garden. The problem is that no one agrees as to just what that means. What we really need to determine is how many gardening hours are actually required to maintain the average-size garden. If you have a gardener, you may be less concerned than if you do all the work yourself. But good gardeners are hard to find and they do cost money. A good compromise is to hire someone to cut and edge the lawn and you do the rest.

If you decide on eight hours per month, the design will be quite different from the 24-hour garden. No matter whether you want high, medium or low maintenance, the following items are sound ideas for most situations:

● Limit lawn to usable areas.

● Install a sprinkler system.

● Space plants with ultimate size in mind. Don't overplant.

● Work with the natural growth habit rather than fighting it.

● Select plants that are adapted to your specific climate and grow easily with little trouble from insects and diseases.

I'd classify this well-tended garden in the medium to high maintenance category. Landscape Architect: Roy Seifert.

Maintenance Chart

Category	Description	Hours per month
High Maintenance	Large lawn area, annual flowers and roses. Meticulous trimming. The *showplace* of the neighborhood.	24 and up
Medium Maintenance	Some lawn, a few annuals; neat, but not perfect. Better than most.	16 to 20
Low Maintenance	No lawn or annuals. Lots of paving and bark or stone mulches. A definite *casual* appearance. Can look run-down and shabby if not well-designed.	At least 8

This "lawn" of green gravel is very low maintenance.

Maintenance is kept to a minimum by the extensive use of brick and gravel paving, and careful plant selection. Design: Warren Jones.

Landscape architect Roy Seifert placed these large junipers just the right distance from the driveway so that they wouldn't be a problem. Likewise, he selected Japanese black pines rather than a larger species to avoid future overgrowth.

The large junipers at the left would be impossible in the small bed. Compact Gold Coast juniper is fine.

● Plant properly. Build watering basins for deep soaking. Mulch to retain moisture and limit weeds.

● Use generous areas of paving and semi-paving.

Now let's get on to the various jobs and explore ways to reduce the time they take. This doesn't mean that you have to approach it like a professional who has to take care of ten places a day. The intent is to handle the tasks you least enjoy as efficiently as possible. Then, if you *want* to spend half the day pruning your favorite tree or caring for your prize roses or merely getting out in the sun and pulling weeds by hand, you'll have time to do it.

LAWN CARE

Lawns leave the most room for improvement. First, use an efficient mower and keep it sharp and in good repair. If exercise is desirable, a sturdy hand mower is fine for most grasses. However, toughies like Bermuda grass, St. Augustine, zoysia and kikuyu require power equipment. Areas more than 2,000 square feet also justify the need for a power mower.

Reducing the size of your lawn will obviously shorten cutting time. It may not help very much. Once you

Side yards shouldn't be a maintenance chore. Three lemon bottlebrush trees are all that are needed to provide shade, privacy and beauty outside the bedroom windows. Stone mulch is clean and walkable.

putting green. You can select a less demanding type of grass, as discussed in Chapter 8. You can cut it less frequently and higher than normal. You will not only save mowing time, but most weeds will be shaded-out or at least hidden.

In a casual garden you can let the lawn grow where it may and partially avoid the job of edging. It will still need some trimming next to paving. Or you can use a spade, power edger or plastic-line weeder to try to keep a definite edge. However, the shape of the planting beds changes drastically through the years with no permanent line. Grass has a way of taking over ground covers and shrubs—especially creepers such as Bermudagrass and St. Augustine.

MOWING STRIPS

Mowing strips are essential if neat, permanent edges are desired. They relate directly to the finish grade of the lawn and are best installed in conjunction with that operation. The following are the most common types.

Redwood edging is quite satisfactory when properly installed. It's unobtrusive and relatively inexpensive. Use full, rough, heart-redwood 2x4s, not narrow stripping that breaks easily. For curved sections, laminate two 1x4s or four bender boards to a full 2-inch thickness to match the 2x4s. Material cost is approximately

It takes twice as many bricks to lay them side-by-side but this strip of used brick is wide enough for the mower.

35 cents per lineal foot. Installed, it costs $1.25 and up.

Brick and concrete mowing strips are even more practical than redwood. Lay the bricks flat and side-by-side for an 8-inch wide strip. Brick and concrete are strong design elements and should be carefully laid out lest they attract too much attention. Material cost is about 50 cents per lineal foot. Installed cost is $2 and up.

have the mower out, it's not much effort to cut a few more square feet. Eliminating narrow strips of grass and fancy edges that require lots of trimming *will* definitely save time. In some cases, you may be able to eliminate the lawn entirely. If so, be sure that what you replace it with will not be even more of a chore.

To further reduce lawn care, think of it as a meadow rather than a

Lawn is a good cover for gentle slopes. Mowing becomes difficult when the grade is much steeper than 4 horizontal to 1 vertical.

Landscape architect Dick Harrington used a redwood 2x4 as edging between lawn and volcanic rock mulch to achieve a neat effect.

MOWING STRIPS

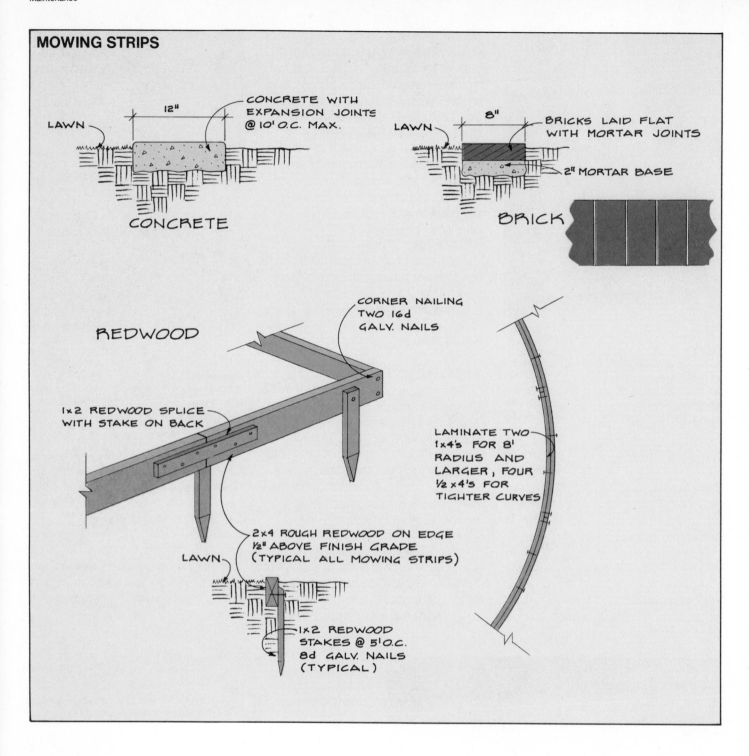

CONCRETE WITH EXPANSION JOINTES @ 10' O.C. MAX.

LAWN

12"

CONCRETE

LAWN

8"

BRICKS LAID FLAT WITH MORTAR JOINTS

2" MORTAR BASE

BRICK

REDWOOD

CORNER NAILING TWO 16d GALV. NAILS

1x2 REDWOOD SPLICE WITH STAKE ON BACK

LAMINATE TWO 1x4's FOR 8' RADIUS AND LARGER, FOUR ½x4's FOR TIGHTER CURVES

2x4 ROUGH REDWOOD ON EDGE ½" ABOVE FINISH GRADE (TYPICAL ALL MOWING STRIPS)

LAWN

1x2 REDWOOD STAKES @ 5' O.C. 8d GALV. NAILS (TYPICAL)

Steel edging is available with special splices and stakes at a cost of approximately 75 cents per lineal foot for material. The steel stakes are an advantage in soil that resists having wooden stakes driven into it.

Corrugated aluminum, bricks set jagged on end, plastic strips, large stones and similar designs are more trouble to trim around than a plain edge. Besides that, most of them are obtrusive in appearance, if not unsightly.

WATERING

Along with lawns, watering is one of the most time-consuming gardening tasks. Because of the importance of water conservation, this subject is covered in Chapters 5 and 13.

SWEEPING AND RAKING

Leaf and litter raking can be a time-consuming chore. Anyone who has had to contend with a row of blue-gum or similar large-growing eucalyptus along their property line, a giant sycamore in the front lawn, or an olive tree in a paved area, knows just how big a job it can be.

Medium-size, relatively "clean" trees are best for paved areas, lawns and places where leaf accumulation is undesirable. Carrot wood, crape

INSTALLING REDWOOD EDGING

Hand sledge is the best tool for driving redwood 1x2 stakes to hold redwood edging.

Rough redwood 1x4 edging can be made to curve by cutting notches with a saw on one side and then bending it very gently into place.

Redwood 2x4 edging separates lawn from stone mulch border designed to catch chlorine water from adjacent pool decking.

myrtle, black pine, ginkgo, Indian laurel fig, palms and evergreen pear are in this category. Use "dirty" trees only if there's room for leaves to accumulate naturally, or if they can be raked at long intervals rather than daily. Along with eucalyptus, sycamore and olive mentioned above, California and Brazilian pepper, willow, poplar, Aleppo and Monterey pines, Siberian elm and most large trees fall into this class.

Note that there are both evergreen and deciduous trees on the "clean" and "dirty" lists. Deciduous trees drop most of their leaves over a short period and seem to be dirtier. Evergreen trees drop their leaves through-out the year so you may not notice it as much. Some trees shed fruit, flowers, small twigs and bark that can be more objectionable than leaves. Large trees are more of a problem due to sheer volume alone.

FERTILIZING

Fertilization is a complex subject, confusing to most homeowners and many professionals as well. The general intent is to promote sturdy, rapid growth until the plant reaches ideal size, and then to maintain health and appearance, including flower and fruit production for some plants, without excessive growth after reaching this size. Light, frequent applications are more apt to achieve this goal rather than heavy fertilization once or twice a year, with less danger of burning involved.

For most garden plants, a complete formulation, usually termed a *commercial* fertilizer, is satisfactory when applied about 4 times a year. Other plants such as citrus, shade plants, roses and dichondra will probably respond better to special formulations, which are worth the additional cost unless very large quantities are involved. Lawn fertilizers that also contain insecticides and weed killers are okay for special situations, but there's no advantage in using them every time.

When you fertilize is especially important for some plants. Camellias and azaleas should be fertilized after they bloom. Bamboo and palms should be fertilized only during the warm months. Tender plants, such as sub-tropicals and citrus, should be fertilized in spring and summer only to discourage tender new fall growth that might be damaged by frost. Bluegrass and fescue need more feeding in spring and fall when they do most growing, while Bermudagrass, dichondra and other warm-season grasses require most of their fertilization dur-the summer. Over-fertilizing lawns results in faster growth which means more mowing and more water. Apply just enough to keep it green.

Generally, sandy soils have higher requirements than clay soils because leaching carries the nutrients

Almost all large trees drop lots of leaves. This California sycamore is in a natural setting where a pile of leaves doesn't matter.

through the root zone. Also, most Western soils have sufficient amounts of phosphorus and potassium and are mostly deficient in nitrogen. Many times, a high nitrogen formula, especially for lawns, will be more economical than a complete fertilizer. It makes no difference to the plant if the fertilizer is applied in chemical or organic form, or in dust, pellets or liquid. However, organic fertilizers should be used to enrich soil low in humus. Manures are good natural fertilizers, but are actually quite low in fertility content. They should be used with caution. Fresh manure can burn tender roots. Some sources contain weed seeds and most have considerable salt. They should be used in limited amounts or be diluted with organic material.

Iron-chlorosis is a common problem and can be treated along with fertilization. Yellowing of leaves while the veins remain green is the identifying symptom. If left unchecked, the condition will often terminate with the entire plant turning yellow and dying. A shortage of zinc will appear similar but this is uncommon. Lack of nitrogen shows more as an overall pale

green. Liquidambar, bottlebrush, camellia, azalea, gardenia, citrus, magnolia, eucalyptus and acacia are frequently afflicted. Iron chelates are more successful than iron sulphate, and should be applied when symptoms first appear. Fe 138 is best for Western soil conditions.

INSECT AND DISEASE CONTROL

Insect and disease control is another complex subject. The question nowadays is, "Are chemicals really necessary?" There *are* dangers involved in the use of most chemicals, but they are indispensible in many situations. Safety precautions should always be strictly observed and manufacturer's instructions carefully followed.

Selecting plants that are relatively free from insects and disease has already been recommended. Some degree of prevention is possible by general good care because a healthy, vigorous plant is less susceptible to attack than a weak one. A clean and trashless garden also offers fewer breeding spots for insects and disease.

Hand picking and washing-off with

the hose will keep some insect populations at an acceptable level. Application of chemical control before a problem arises is possible in some instances, as in applying a systemic to roses in early spring to control aphids. A *systemic* is absorbed into the plant and cannot be washed-off. Snail bait can be scattered before they devour any plants. Indiscriminate spraying "whether it needs it or not" usually creates more problems than it solves by interfering with the balance of nature. Most of the time, constant vigilance is the best answer. Prompt and proper treatment will usually control the problem before serious damage is done. A weekly walk through the garden with potential problems in mind is a good way to avoid a nasty surprise.

Here's where a knowledgeable nurseryman can really help. Take in a sample of your problem, a leaf or twig, and he can usually recommend the latest and most effective means of control. County farm advisors and agricultural extension staffs are also usually available for advice as are tree companies and pest control firms. If you can't figure out what the problem is, don't be afraid to ask before it's too late.

If your weeping bottlebrush or other plant has leaves that look like this, it's a good chance it's caused by lack of available iron.

The tomato horn-worm is really difficult to see. Hand picking is an effective control if you're not too squeamish. You can handle snails this way too.

WEED CONTROL

The keys to cutting-down weeding time are eliminating the weeds *before* planting. Remove new ones while they're still small—before they go to seed. Mulch around trees, shrubs and ground covers. Use weedicides judiciously when hand methods fail or are impractical. Here are some typical weeds and what you can do about them.

Broad-leaved weeds such as dandelion, oxalis and spotted spurge in a grass lawn should be sprayed with a blended mixture of 2,4-D, MCPP and dicamba, sold as *Trimec®* and *Trex-San®*.

Grassy weeds such as Bermudagrass, wild oats and annual bluegrass in dichondra or in a ground cover should be sprayed with a product containing dalapon commercially sold as *Dowpon®*. Bermudagrass roots can go down 3 feet or more. It's folly to pull it out by hand because it will come right back. Bermudagrass and other weeds in ice plant can be sprayed with 3 pounds ammonium sulphate per gallon of water when the temperature is 75 degrees or higher. It "burns" the weeds and the ice plant survives.

To control crabgrass and annual bluegrass in dichondra or grass lawns, apply bensulide, called *Betasan®*, in early spring to prevent seed germination. Spray disodium methyl arsenate after weeds have developed.

Mixed weeds in a non-planted area such as semi-pavings and bare earth between shrubs and trees should be sprayed with fortified weed oil, amino triazole, cacodylic acid or a similar *knock-down,* non-selective material. To combat future weeds in a non-planted area, apply diphenamid, sold as *Enide®* or *Dymid®*, EPTC, sold as *Eptam®*, trifluralin, sold as *Treflan®*, or a similar pre-emergent herbicide on the bare earth. A mix of diphenamid and trifluralin is very effective. This kills germinating weed seeds without harming the established plants. Diphenamid can also be applied when planting dichondra seed or on an established dichondra lawn.

For non-planted areas and semi-pavings where there aren't existing plants and you don't want to plant any, apply soil sterilants such as borate/chlorate, or simizine/amino triazole combinations.

PRUNING AND TRIMMING

There seems to be two extremes when it comes to pruning. Either the homeowner is afraid to snip off the smallest branch or he butchers the plant back to unsightly stubs. Some professionals are no better. They treat all plants either as a cube or sphere and entirely destroy the natural grace and form of the species.

Pruning and trimming are often overlooked in calculating maintenance time. Obviously, clipped hedges and shaped shrubs require constant attention. When plants are selected with their natural growth habit and size in mind, you can throw away the hedge clippers. What pruning is necessary should be done regularly to guide the plant's growth, rather than waiting until the plant becomes unshapely and oversized.

Again, there are a few general rules that are helpful. Dead wood is unsightly and a potential source of infection. It should always be removed. Traditionally it has been accepted that deciduous plants should normally be pruned during the dormant period in winter. Latest research indicates that any time is okay for most species. Spring-flowering types should be pruned during and after blooming or potential flowers will be cut off.

For most evergreen plants, light, frequent pruning is better than drastic measures at long intervals. Selective removal of stems and branches is also better than shearing. If you want dense foliage, head back the tips by clipping to induce growth. To feature a plant, clean out the inside to reveal the branch structure. This will also let air pass through a tree, lessening wind damage.

Consult a good reference book before you tackle fruit and berry vines. Choosing the wrong time and method can result in losing the crop.

PROTECTING PLANTS

Dogs, cats, deer, rabbits, gophers,

moles, children and adults can cause serious damage to a garden. Gophers and moles can be baited and trapped, with considerable patience and some luck. Sprays for dogs, cats, deer and rabbits are limited in effectiveness. They, along with humans, have to be chased away. The plants can be protected with barriers, at least until they are large enough to withstand the onslaught. Protective devices don't have to be an eyesore—a little ingenuity can sometimes turn them into an asset.

These junipers were planted too close to the walk and look ratty when sheared back. Lower types such as tamarix, *San Jose, Arcadia* and prostrate juniper could have been used.

Saving Water 14

Reduced water consumption is mandatory in many parts of the West. *Even if* rainfall is above normal, new pipe-lines and storage facilities are constructed *and* widespread use is made of effluent, the "good old days" of unlimited water are over. Drought years may come and go, but it looks like the high cost of energy for pumping and greater water consumption due to continued population growth, along with the need for increased food production, will be with us from now on.

This doesn't mean that we must abandon our existing plants or that new plantings are inadvisable. It does mean that we have to manage our water use much better than in the past. We also need to do some serious thinking about what kind of garden is really appropriate for present and future conditions.

The oasis concept still has validity, especially in the Southwest. A lush, cool, green respite from the harsh, hot desert is a desirable goal. Aside from some cool mountain areas and favored seaside conditions, the majority of the West's population truly lives in a desert or semi-desert climate. Just because we have air-conditioning and the surrounding land is covered with buildings and asphalt instead of sand and rocks, doesn't change that fact.

But there is a difference between creating inviting oases and trying to convert the entire landscape into vast spaces of water-demanding lawns, trees and other plants. In areas of water shortage we can no longer have entire neighborhoods of purely ornamental lawns anymore than we can tolerate wasted water flowing down the gutter.

If you're planning a new garden or making extensive changes to an existing one, there are several things you can do to keep water requirements low. Compare the following with the list on page 161 and you'll notice that not only will they save water, they are compatible with reduced maintenance as well.

● Limit lawn in size and to areas that will be both beautiful and usable.
● Install an efficient sprinkler system.
● Select a type of lawn that will not only get by on less water, but will survive if you have to temporarily reduce watering drastically. Chapter 8 discusses this more thoroughly.

This water-conscious neighborhood in Arizona uses stone mulch instead of lawn. Young Jerusalem thorn and common mesquite trees get by with little irrigation and are already casting considerable shade to temper the desert heat.

By concentrating lush planting around a shaded patio, you can have a cool spot for relaxing and entertaining—without having to pour enormous quantities of water on the entire yard. Landscape architect Roy Seifert tests his design with a friend.

Many drought tolerant plants have exotic shapes and striking flowers. Water-saving gardens can be beautiful.

This desert garden incorporates pebble concrete, stone mulch and a rock-covered slope rather than lawn and ground cover. Landscape architect Warren Jones enjoys shade from the well-placed palo verde tree.

● Select all plants on the same basis. Avoid plants with high moisture requirements. Birch, liquidambar, willow, coast redwood, camellia, rhododendron, azalea, fuchsia, begonia, ferns, ajuga and potentilla are all excellent landscape plants—but they need lots of water. A single specimen or small grouping wouldn't affect total water usage very much. An entire garden comprised primarily of plants demanding frequent irrigation would consume a great deal of water.

● Prepare the soil and plant properly with earth watering basins to prevent water run-off.

● Mulch to retain moisture. Even plants with normal watering requirements such as juniper, wax-leaf privet, natal plum, raphiolepis, cotoneaster, tobira, and nandina do remarkably well with reduced irrigation when they have extensive root systems and are heavily mulched. Mulching inhibits water-stealing weeds as well.

● Don't overplant. Space plants far enough apart so that they have room to grow.

● Don't feel obligated to cover every square inch of your property with plants. There's nothing wrong with bare earth between shrubs and trees.

● Plant in the fall when you have a choice. The weather is cooler and winter rains lend a helping hand while plants are getting established. Exceptions are warm-season grasses such as Bermuda and zoysia, palms, bamboo and tender sub-tropicals.

● Make extensive use of paving and semi-pavings.

WHAT MAKES A PLANT DROUGHT TOLERANT?

Some aren't exactly drought tolerant—they just have such efficient root systems that they pick-up every bit of available water within their reach. Mesquite roots have been know to go as far down as 60 feet. The reason why you can't dig out common Bermudagrass is that its root system can extend 3 feet and deeper. Ever notice the wide spacing of some desert plants? It's because a web of roots totally covers the area in between.

Water-storing stems and roots are another way that drought tolerant plants survive between rains. The barrel cactus and succulents like aloes and jade plants are obvious examples. Others merely evade the problem by dropping their leaves and going into a state of semi-dormancy when water runs low. A leafless and seemingly lifeless ocotillo bursts forth with new leaves immediately following a rain.

Fine leaves and narrow ones that turn sideways towards the sun lose less water than broad ones. This is why oleander and pampas grass withstand drought better than hibiscus. The extreme is in cacti where the leaves are reduced to spines and the stems serve in their stead.

Many leaves in the legume family, such as acacia and albizia, fold up when the going gets tough. Thick, waxy leaves like sugar bush, jojoba and carob retain water as do sticky and varnish-coated leaves of the creosote bush and rockrose. Silver and gray foliage reflects the sun. There are very few gray shade plants—it takes a lot of light for them to function.

There are many plants that will survive on little water. How they do it is important. For ornamental uses they not only need to survive, but they must also look reasonably well in the process. At the very least, they should recover rapidly without permanent injury as soon as water is applied.

SELECTING DROUGHT TOLERANT PLANTS

The following drought-tolerant plants are really tough. Under the right conditions, they truly thrive on neglect. It may be surprising, but they're not all dry looking or cactus-like. In fact, many are quite green and lush. Once established with deep roots, they'll flourish on infrequent irrigation. Most can survive and look fairly presentable with little or no water other than normal rainfall.

For various reasons, the plants on the following lists are *not* found in the lists of foolproof plants in Chapter 6. Some require extremely good drainage and are sensitive to overwatering. Some get straggly or are relatively short-lived or drop lots of leaves or have invasive roots. Many are simply not as "tried-and-true" as the old standbys.

However, used properly they can be a welcome addition to any garden where conserving water is important. These lists are arranged in order of relative hardiness to cold with the most tolerant at the top. They represent a wide climatic range, so check with your local nurseryman to select those best suited for your specific area. Almost all of them are common nursery stock or can easily be ordered. A few are uncommon or seldom grown, but are worth looking for.

Important: Even under ideal conditions, it takes one or two full seasons before most plants can be expected to shift for themselves. It may take longer where it's hot and windy, and if the soil drains rapidly. Many drought tolerant plants are sensitive to overwatering, but deep soakings at regular intervals will result in more growth and better appearance while roots are developing. Don't abandon plants too soon—wean them gradually until they're able to stand alone.

When rainfall is below normal, some supplemental irrigation may be advisable for all but the extremely tolerant types.

THE NATIVES ARE RESTLESS

Well, maybe not restless, but many of them are quite demanding in their requirements. At any rate, native plants are not a blanket answer to drought conditions. First of all, they are not all drought tolerant. Coast redwood, California and Arizona sycamore, white alder, redbud, sweetshrub, Monterey cypress, fan palm, salal, wax myrtle, Catalina currant and big leaf maple are some of those requiring normal to heavy amounts of water.

Second, many are *intolerant* of normal watering and must have excellent drainage. This is important when you have a sprinkler system that also waters other plants. Try to grow manzanita, ceanothus, fremontia, sage, smoke tree, tree coreopsis, woolly bluecurls, and most oaks, yuccas and cacti under average garden conditions. Chances are they'll perish quickly. They need special soil, climate and cultural treatment to survive.

Besides this, not all natives have desirable ornamental qualities. Many look like scraggly weeds and have to have a logical reason to be included in a habitable garden.

Before I alienate all native plant lovers, let's list some of the good ones that aren't overly fussy and are drought tolerant. Catalina cherry, incense cedar, saltbush, summer holly, coast silktassel, toyon, sugar bush, jojoba, Arizona cypress, palo verde, feather bush, coffee berry and prostrate coyote brush are excellent landscape materials. These and many others are every bit as good as a lot of the common nursery stock that comes from far-off places.

The point is that being a native doesn't necessarily mean a plant is good or bad for your garden, or that it will take less water. Neither are they all fool-proof. Or even easy to grow.

Rigidly categorizing plants as natives serves no valid purpose as far as garden design is concerned. To exclude the wealth of drought tolerant plant material from Mediterranean-type climates similar to our own would be a great mistake. It's much wiser to choose the best from all over the world.

EXISTING GARDENS

All this may be very helpful to someone starting from scratch, but what about the majority who already have gardens or "inherit" one when they buy a home with existing landscaping? First of all, some of the basic suggestions still apply, at least in part. Look the list over to see what you might benefit from.

Then thoroughly review your maintenance practices as they relate to water use. Here are some suggestions taken from my booklet *40 Ways to Save Water in your Yard and Garden,* that tell you how to cut consumption without ending up with dead or dying plants.

Most of these suggestions are sound, basic gardening procedures that you should be doing anyway. Others are more drastic and would be needed only where strict rationing is in force. Follow the ones best suited to your situation. They can easily add up to a considerable saving with little or no sacrifice of beauty.

FIRST THINGS

Make an overall assessment of your garden's watering needs. List the ways you are obviously wasting water. Develop a plan of action and stick to it. Don't be afraid to make major changes—they'll pay off in the long run. Keep close watch on your water bill or meter to see if your plan is effective. Check all hose connections, valves and piping for leaks. Leaks are more likely to occur outdoors, where they are more apt to go undetected. Even a small leak can waste hundreds of gallons of water in a single day.

Make earth basins around shrubs and small trees. Feeder roots are usually at the drip line, so if the plant is 4 feet in diameter, make the basin that size. Give plants on slopes a break. Build a wood or masonry box to hold water where it's too steep for an earth basin.

Mulch roots with a layer of bark, sawdust, leaf mold or stone several inches thick. It saves water, discourages weed growth and looks good. Plastic isn't as attractive, but it can also be used as a mulch and works very well for vegetables and strawberries. Vertical mulch trees and shrubs by drilling 1-inch diameter holes at the drip line to improve water penetration. The holes can also be used for application of fertilizer. Rent or buy extra-long bits and make sure your drill is properly grounded.

Remove weeds before they get large. They not only look bad, but they are water thieves—stealing precious moisture from nearby desirable plants. Pre-emergent herbicides kill weed seeds as they sprout and save a lot of hand labor for large areas.

Soil sampler gives a profile of underground conditions. They're available in 12 and 18-inch lengths.

No need to let the water run while you go back to shut it off when you use a spring-loaded hose spray.

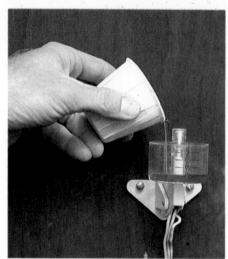

The weight of rainwater shuts off the automatic controller so that sprinklers don't come on during a storm.

WATERING

Be sure the soil is almost dry before watering. Dig down below the surface rather than just guessing, or use a soil-sampler for a deeper look. Moisture sensing devices are more fun. They tell underground conditions at a glance and come in varying lengths for shallow and deep-rooted plants. Use indoors on house plants for double duty.

Get to know how plants signal for water. Lawn and dichondra tend to lie flat after being stepped on if moisture is low. Many plants lose their gloss and start to droop a little before going into wilt. The time to water is when the plants need it—rigid schedules waste water. Try to water early in the morning to avoid excessive evaporation loss. Evening is second-best because fungus diseases then have all night to attack moist foliage. Evaporation is also higher when it's windy and more spray gets lost onto paving. Extend time between watering periods. As roots grow deeper, less-frequent watering will be required. Water lawns and ground covers, especially slopes, for a short time and shut off immediately when run-off begins. Repeat as necessary, until sufficient water is applied. If only one spot is dry, water it separately.

Place container plants over the root area of a tree or on the lawn when watering and rinsing-off foliage. Wash off vegetables outside rather than in the kitchen sink. The excess water will be put to good use.

Watch the weather reports during the rainy season. Hold off on irrigation if rain is predicted. Check how much rain actually fell. A 2-inch deluge will sustain plants longer than a 1/4-inch drizzle. A deep moisture reserve can sometimes carry them through for quite a while before irrigation is needed.

Make the most of rainfall. Dig ditches to plants under roof eaves to allow rainwater to reach them. Catch rainwater by placing plastic or wooden barrels under roof downspouts and eaves. Pure rainwater is excellent for house plants. Add a few drops of oil to the barrel of water to discourage mosquitoes. If your lot drains too rapidly, temporarily block drainage to encourage rain to soak in. Be sure to restore normal flow as soon as the soil is saturated.

Caution: Don't let clay soils and hillside lots to become overly wet.

Use a spring-loaded hose spray that lets water out only when you want it to. The fingertip pressure control and spray adjuster is more efficient than your thumb on the end of the hose.

Attach a soaker or root-feeder to your hose for deep penetration. They minimize run-off, encourage root growth and are excellent for watering large trees. Coil the soaker around the tree at the drip line and let it run for several hours. A root-feeder not only waters, but can also be used to apply fertilizer. Or you can install a bubbler or drip system. Penetration is better, evaporation less, and weed growth is minimized because water is concentrated where it's needed. Subterranean ooze-type systems eliminate surface run-off from lawns and groundcovers because they're entirely underground. Installation is discussed in Chapter 5.

SPRINKLERS

Consider installing a sprinkler system if you don't already have one. In almost all situations, watering by hand is wasteful and inefficient, besides being time consuming.

Check any existing sprinkler systems for efficiency. Adjust heads that spray onto paving. Equalize coverage so that you don't have to drown one spot in order to get enough on another. If areas with different requirements, such as lawn and shrubs, are on the same valve, install separate valves. Convert manual sprinkler control valves to semi-automatic with a mechanical timer. You turn it on for 5 to 60 minutes—the timer shuts it off. If you water with a hose, there is a model that can be attached to a hose bibb.

Better yet, convert your manual sprinkler system to automatic. This enables you to water in the early morning when evaporation and wind are lowest. Be sure to check timing periods frequently to see that the right amount of water is being applied. Install a shut-off device on automatic controllers to avoid sprinkling while it is raining. Approximately 1/4-inch of rain weighs down a simple mechanical switch which in turn inactivates the controller. If you are scientific-minded, place a tensiometer in the root-zone of your lawn or other planting area for an exact reading of underground moisture level. Connected to an automatic controller, it will allow sprinklers to come on only when actually needed.

LAWNS

Aerate lawns for better penetration. Forks with hollow tines remove cores of soil and reduce compaction. Verticut lawns to remove thatch that acts as a water barrier. Buy a hand aerator and Bermudagrass rake for small lawns, or rent a roller type aerator or machine verti-cutter for large areas. Chemical soil penetrants can also help water soak in better. They are easy to apply with a hose spray.

Raise the height of your mower to 1 inch for Bermudagrass, bentgrass and dichondra, and to 2 inches for bluegrass, rye and fescue type lawns. Most lawns are cut too short, exposing roots to drying sun and raising water loss. Be sure to tell your gardener—most of his customers demand clipped lawns.

Reduce Bermudagrass lawn watering to survival level throughout the summer. It'll perk up again with the first rain. Object to the brown color? Green it up with special lawn dye. If your front lawn is purely ornamental, consider leaving it unwatered or replacing it with a paving that absorbs water or with drought tolerant plants. This is a good time to add that parking space or circular drive you've always talked about.

PLANTS

Phase out moisture-requiring plants. Replace them with tougher types that won't keel over the first time you skip a watering. Remove water-consuming ground covers that aren't necessary for erosion control. Mulched or cultivated soil can be just as attractive. Remove sickly, unappealing and purposeless plants.

Reduce water needed for container plants. Sink pots in the ground or put one pot inside a slightly larger one and fill the space with sphagnum moss. Just moving pots out of the hot sun and wind will cut watering needs.

Change some of your flowers and other purely ornamental plants to vegetables and food-producers. Your water consumption may remain the same, but if everyone grows part of their own food, the agricultural demand for water will be lessened.

SHRUBS AND TREES

Prune back and thin out heavily foliaged shrubs and trees. Accentuating the structure can turn an overgrown blob into a handsome specimen. Fewer leaves means less transpiration loss. Don't overdo it or tender bark may sunburn and unshaded soil will dry out faster.

Experiment with an anti-transpirant spray. An invisible film on foliage reduces transpiration and is especially valuable where hot, dry winds are prevalent. Nursery shade cloth or netting thrown over a favorite plant during hot spells will also cut water loss.

FERTILIZING

Limit the use of your disposal by composting your garbage. The water savings are significant and you end up with rich humus to mulch and improve your soil. Fertilize in moderation with a complete or balanced formulation. Heavy application of high-nitrogen types encourage rapid-growing lush foliage that has a high transpiration rate. Chemical growth-retardants slow down rapid-growing, lawns, ground covers and hedges, and save both water and trimming time.

OTHER SUGGESTIONS

Put plastic trays in your sinks to

This formidable looking machine aerator is a necessity for large lawns.

A hand aerator is great for opening-up those packed down spots in a lawn where water won't penetrate.

The business end of a verti-cutter. It slices through lawn thatch to allow water filtration.

173

catch clean rinse water and use buckets to save "warm-up" shower water. Dump directly on plants or transfer to a holding barrel for later use. Be careful though, as accumulations from softened water can be injurious to plants.

In areas where every gallon is crucial, use a hose to siphon-off bath tub and shower water. Divert the rinse cycles of laundry and dishwashers to the garden. Most soaps and detergents are okay in moderation but avoid products containing boron or borax. Be sure to check with the Department of Health for information concerning use of waste water to avoid potential hazards.

Sweep paving and rake leaves rather than using the hose to blow away leaves and debris. Use a garden vacuum or air blower where the area is too large to do by hand. Wash cars infrequently, if at all. Use a bucket rather than letting the hose run. If you can drive onto the lawn, rinse

Color Key For Plant Lists

	Location & Climate	Remarks
	Interior valleys, deserts, south-facing slopes of mountain ranges.	Plants in this group perform best with heat. If you live where a sweater is necessary even in the summer, better forget it.
	California coast, low desert, favored warm slopes.	These plants are tender to temperatures only a few degrees below freezing. Don't plant them in cold deserts, interior valleys, or where frost occurs every winter.
	Northern and cool California coast and nearby areas.	These prefer it on the cool side. They are not as likely to be happy in southern interior valleys or deserts.
	All zones.	Least fussy of all. They should do well almost anywhere.

water will be absorbed rather than running off the driveway and down the street.

If you have a gardener, don't assume he is water-wise. Let him know what your conservation program is and see that he follows it. Instruct vacation-time waterers so that all your savings don't end up flowing down the gutter while you're gone.

WATER SAVING PLANTS

The charts on the following pages list plants that do especially well with very little water. There are additional plants, such as those shown here, that should also be considered and are found on the lists in Chapter 6. If you decide to use water saving plants, you can widen your selection by checking pages 90 to 113.

Sea Lavender, see page 106.

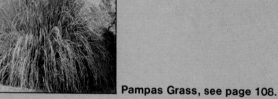
Lavender Lantana, see page 104.

Pampas Grass, see page 108.

Silverberry, see page 92.

Drought Tolerant Plants—ACCENTS

Common Name *Scientific Name*	Best Exposure/Climate & Minimum Temperature	Remarks
English Lavender *Lavandula spica*	S, W Hardy.	Small shrub. Narrow gray leaves; fragrant lavender flowers. Grows to 3' high, also several dwarfs 12" to 18" high. Well-drained soil.
Jerusalem Artichoke *Helianthus tuberosus*	S, W Hardy.	Perennial. Large, coarse leaves on stalks to 8' tall. Yellow sunflowers. Dies back in fall when edible tubers are harvested. Photo page 149.
Red Valerian *Centranthus ruber*	S, W, E Hardy.	Evergreen perennial. Blue-green leaves; magenta flowers—also white. Fast growth to 2 feet. Not fussy. Reseeds—can be a nuisance.
Red-Hot Poker *Kniphofia uvaria*	S, W All climates except desert. Hardy.	Perennial. Narrow, strap-like leaves; red-orange with yellow flowers. Various forms 2' to 4' tall. Cut back in fall. Photo below.
Mexican Evening Primrose *Oenothera speciosa childsii*	S, W Hardy.	Perennial. Profusion of rose-pink flowers. Casual filler for natural effect. Plant from seed.
Rose Moss *Portulaca grandiflora*	S, W Heat loving. Hardy.	Annual. Narrow, succulent leaves; brilliant red, pink, orange, yellow and white flowers. Looks like an ice plant. Low, creeping habit. Easy from seed.
Dusty Miller *Centaurea cineraria*	S, W 15°F, −10°C.	Evergreen perennial. Coarse, white leaves to 18" high; purple or yellow flowers. *Senecio cineraria*, also called Dusty Miller, is taller with yellow flowers. Both make good accents.
Pride-of-Madeira *Echium fastuosum*	S, W Excellent on coast. Not for deserts. 20°F, −7°C.	Shrubby perennial to 6' high. Large, gray-green leaves; striking blue-purple flower stalks. Well-drained soil. Large scale accent. Photo below.
Elephant's Food *Portulacaria afra*	S, W, E Not for cold valleys or deserts. 25°F, −4°C.	Succulent. Small leaves with wine-red stems. Sprawling branches on upright trunk to 6' and more. Use as a shrub, container plant and for hanging over a wall. Easy to grow from cuttings. Photo below.
Jade Plant *Crassula argentea*	S, W, E Not for cold valleys or deserts. 25°F, −4°C.	Succulent. Shiny, thick leaves; pink flowers in winter. Usually 3' or less, but will develop a heavy trunk to 6' and more. Prune out to reveal structure. Number one container plant. Easy to grow from cuttings. Photo below.
Crown of Thorns *Euphorbia milii*	S, W, E Needs protected location. 30°F, −1°C.	Woody perennial. Sprawling to 3' with thorny stems, bright red flower bracts. Good accent or container plant. *E. biglandulosa* is hardy with gray-green leaves; chartreuse flower bracts. Grows to 2 feet.

Red-Hot Poker

Elephant's Food

**Jade Plant and Lavender Cotton.
See page 90 for Lavender Cotton.**

Pride-of-Madeira

Drought Tolerant Plants—SHRUBS

Common Name *Scientific Name*	Best Exposure/Climate & Minimum Temperature	Remarks
Salt Cedar Tamarisk *Tamarix pentandra*	*W, S, E* Excellent for desert. Hardy.	Fine, blue-green foliage; tiny pink flowers. Survives in poor soils. Invasive roots. Rapid growth 10 to 15 feet. Deciduous *T. parviflora* and others, similar.
Spanish Broom *Spartium junceum*	*W, S* Excellent for coast. Okay inland and in desert. 10°F, −12*C.	Practically leafless, slender green stems. Bright yellow flowers. Straggly—good background or hillside. 6' to 8' high. Photo on facing page.
Toyon *Heteromeles arbutifolia*	*W, S* Best in California foothills. Okay in desert with careful watering. 10°F, −12°C.	Dark green leaves; white flowers; red berries. Withstands garden watering in well-drained soil. 10' shrub or small tree to 20 feet. Photo on facing page.
Sugar Bush *Rhus ovata*	*W, S, E* Best in California foothills. Okay in desert with careful watering. 15°F, −10°C.	Large, dark green leaves with reddish stems; pink-white flowers. Clean and lush looking. Rounded growth to 10' high. Avoid overwatering in summer.
Sweet Broom *Cytisus racemosus*	*W, S* Takes heat. 15°F, −10°C.	Small, bright green leaves; yellow flowers. Rapid growth to 5 feet. Needs well-drained soil.
Desert Broom *Baccharis sarothroides*	*W, S* Excellent in desert. 15°F, −10°C.	Bright green, long needle-like leaves; tiny, pale yellow flowers with fluffy whitish seed heads. Rounded, 3' to 6' high. Photo on facing page.
Arizona Rosewood *Vauquelinia californica*	*W, S, E* Excellent in desert. 15°F, −10°C.	Bright green, narrow leaves; small, white flowers. Dense growth 10 to 20 feet. Similar to oleander. Needs well-drained soil. Photo on facing page.
California Lilac *Ceanothus* species	*W, S* Wide range from seashore to mountains, but not deserts. Most will take 15°F, −10°C.	Many kinds of medium to large shrubs. Garden hybrids with dark green leaves and blue flowers most popular. All require well-drained soil and should not be overwatered in summer. Excellent for hillsides. Relatively short-lived.
Bird-of-Paradise Bush *Poinciana gilliesii*	*W, S* Needs heat. All but seashore and cold desert. 15°F, −10°C.	Sparse, ferny foliage; yellow flowers with red stamens. Needs well-drained soil. Fast growth 6' to 8' high. Photo on facing page.
Jojoba *Simmondsia chinensis*	*W, S, E* Excellent for desert. Young plants need protection. 15°F, −10°C.	Gray-green leaves. Slow, compact growth. Rounded form to 6' high. Photo on facing page.
Coast Silktassel *Garrya elliptica*	*S, E* Best on northerly coast. Drought tolerant, but better with water. 15°F, −10°C.	Dark green leaves with gray undersides. Decorative flower tassels, catkins and small purplish fruit. Grows to 6' shrub or small tree.
Feathery Cassia *Cassia artemisioides*	*W, S* Likes heat, but not for cold desert. 20°F, −7°C.	Needle-like silvery gray-green leaves; yellow flowers. Needs well-drained soil. Airy form, 3' to 4' high. Relatively short-lived.
Knife Acacia *Acacia cultriformis*	*W, S* Excellent on coast. Not for cold desert. 20°F, −7°C.	Silvery gray leaves, attached to stems; yellow flowers. Needs well-drained soil. Shrub or low-branched tree to 12 feet. Photo on facing page.
Catalina Cherry *Prunus lyonii*	*W, S, E* Best on coast. 20°F, −7°C.	Large, dark green leaves. Fast, upright growth 20 to 25 feet. Good screen, hedge or tree.
Feather Bush *Lysiloma thornberi*	*W, S* Best in warm desert. 25°F, −4°C.	Ferny foliage; creamy-white flowers. Looks like a small silk tree. Spreading form to 15 feet. Needs well-drained soil.

Toyon

Arizona Rosewood

Bird-of-Paradise Bush

Jojoba

Spanish Broom

Desert Broom

Knife Acacia

Drought Tolerant Plants—TREES

Common Name *Scientific Name*	Climate/Culture & Minimum Temperature	Remarks
Tree-of-Heaven *Ailanthus altissima*	Withstands all conditions. Hardy.	Tropical-appearing foliage, interesting structure. Brown seed clusters look like flowers. Rapid growth to 25 feet and more. Spreads by suckers. Deciduous.
Goldenrain Tree *Koelreuteria paniculata*	Withstands all conditions. Okay in lawn. Hardy.	Open structure. Yellow flowers followed by brownish pods. Slow growth to 20' high. Deciduous.
Texas Umbrella Tree *Melia azedarach* *'Umbraculifera'*	Okay all but seashore. Hardy.	Dark green, lacy foliage. Lavender flowers; yellow berries are poisonous. Rapid growth to 25' and more. Brittle and dirty. Deciduous.
Chinese Pistache *Pistachia chinensis*	Okay all but seashore. Okay in lawn. Hardy.	Lacy foliage with brilliant fall color. Needs pruning to develop good form. Grows to 30' and more. Deciduous.
Athel Tree *Tamarix aphylla*	Excellent in desert. 10°F, −12°C.	Grayish, needle-like foliage. Smoke-like texture at a distance, straggly up close. Good windbreak. Invasive roots. Photo on facing page.
Australian Willow *Geijera parviflora*	Okay in lawn. 15°F, −10°C.	Willow-like leaves and form, but not as dense. Well behaved. Grows 25' high.
Chilean Mesquite *Prosopis chilensis*	Good for all deserts. Not for coast. 15°F, −10°C.	Bright green, fine-textured leaves; few thorns. Fast growth to 25 feet. Almost evergreen. Common Mesquite, *P. juliflora,* has deciduous gray-green leaves, thorns. Photo on page 169.
Silver Dollar Gum *Eucalyptus polyanthemos*	Okay on coast or inland. 15°F, −10°C.	Round, gray-green leaves—old leaves are narrower. Picturesque silhouette. Fast, upright growth to 30' and more.
Blue Palo Verde *Cercidium floridum*	Good for all deserts. Not for coast. 20°F, −7°C.	Sparse foliage; blue-green bark; yellow flowers. Prune for low-branching form to 25 feet. Little-leaf Palo Verde, *C. microphyllum,* is similar with yellow-green bark.
Carob *Ceratonia siliqua*	Best with heat. Not for cold deserts. 20°F, −7°C.	Dark green, dense foliage. Brown pods are source of carob powder. Grows to 30' and more. Well-drained soil best. Can be grown as a large screen or multi-trunk. Photo on facing page.
Bottle Tree *Brachychiton populneum*	Loves heat, but not for cold deserts. 20°F, −7°C.	Shiny, light green leaves. Upright growth to 30' and more. Drops leaves and pods. Good screen or windbreak. Photo on facing page.
Bailey Acacia *Acacia baileyana*	Good on coast. Not for cold deserts. 20°F, −7°C.	Fine, blue-gray leaflets; yellow flowers. Well-drained soil best. Rapid growth to 20' and more. *A. b. 'Purpurea'* has purplish new growth. Relatively short-lived. Photo on facing page.
Silk Oak *Grevillea robusta*	Not for cold deserts. 25°F, −4°C.	Dark green, fern-like foliage; orange flowers. Fast growth to 50' tall; narrow pyramidal form. Drops leaves, brittle branches. Photo on facing page.

Bottle Tree

Carob

Silk Oak

Bailey Acacia

Drought Tolerant Plants—GROUND AND SLOPE COVERS

Common Name *Scientific Name*	Best Exposure/ Climate & Minimum Temperature	Height	Remarks
Prostrate Germander *Teucrium chamaedrys 'Prostratum'*	S, W Loves heat. Hardy.	6" to 12"	Dark green leaves; rosy lavender flowers. Do not overwater. Cut back to renew. Space 12" to 18" apart.
Snow-in-Summer *Cerastium tomentosum*	S, W Coast, inland and desert. Hardy.	6"	Small, silvery gray leaves; white flowers. Needs well-drained soil. Cut back to renew. Space 12" to 18" apart.
Stonecrop *Sedum anglicum*	S, W, E Hardy.	Flat	Tiny green leaves; pinkish-white flowers. Good small scale ground cover. Space 9" to 12" apart.
Croceum Ice Plant *Malephora crocea*	S, W, E Hardiest ice plant 10°F, −12°C.	6" to 12"	Cylindrical, gray-green leaves; reddish-yellow flowers. Many other species not as tolerant of cold. Best on slopes. Do not overwater. Photo below.
Australian Saltbush *Atriplex semibaccata*	S, W Not for cold desert. Fire resistant. 15°F, −10°C.	6" to 12"	Small, gray-green leaves. Not refined, somewhat straggly. Fast growing and deep rooted. Usually sown from seed by hand or by hydroseeding. Photo below.
Prostrate Manzanita *Arctostaphylos* species	S, W Wide range, seashore to mountains, but not deserts. Best northerly. Most will take 15°F, −10°C.	Flat to 3 feet.	Most have small leaves, reddish bark, white-pink flowers. *Vine Hill* and *Little Sur* selections are excellent. All require well-drained soil and should not be overwatered in summer. Space 3' to 4' apart.
Prostrate California Lilac *Ceanothus* species	S, W Wide range, seashore to mountains, but not deserts. Best northerly. Most will take 15°F, −10°C.	Flat to 3 feet.	*Point Reyes* has small, leathery dark green leaves; lavender-blue flowers. *Carmel Creeper* has large, shiny dark green leaves; bright blue flowers; grows rapidly. All require well-drained soil and should not be overwatered in summer. Space 3' to 4' apart. Relatively short-lived. Photo below.

Prostrate California Lilac

Australian Saltbush

Croceum Ice Plant

Common Name *Scientific Name*	Best Exposure/ Climate & Minimum Temperature	Height	Remarks
Bush Morning Glory *Convolvulus cneorum*	S, W Not cold desert. 15°F, −10°C.	2 to 3 feet.	Silvery gray leaves, white morning-glory flowers. Needs well-drained soil. Good hanging over a wall. Relatively short-lived. Space 2' to 3' apart.
Rockrose *Cistus* species	S, W Best on coast. Okay inland. Not for cold desert. 15°F, −10°C.	2 to 4 feet.	Crinkly leaves; white, pink and spotted flowers. Do not overwater. Fire retardant. Space 3' to 4' apart.
Noel Grevillea *Grevillia noellii*	S, W, E Best on coast. Not for cold desert. 15°F, −10°C.	3 to 4 feet.	Bright green needle-like leaves; small, rose-red and white flowers. Graceful, arching habit. Needs well-drained soil. Space 4' to 5' apart.
Dwarf Coreopsis *Coreopsis auriculata* *'nana'*	S, W Not for desert. 20°F, −7°C.	6"	Long leaves, orange-yellow flowers. Remove faded flowers. Use as an accent and as groups in small areas. Space 18" to 24" apart.
Prostrate Acacia *Acacia redolens* *prostrata*	S, W Best on coast, withstands salt-spray. Also will take heat. 20°F, −7°C.	18" to 3 feet.	Gray-green leaves; yellow flowers. *'Ongerup'* is similar or synonymous. Space 5' to 6' apart. Good on large slopes. Photo below.
Rosea Ice Plant *Drosanthemum hispidum*	S, W, E Not for cold desert. 20°F, −7°C.	4" to 6"	Tiny, crystalline leaves. Sheets of bright lavender-pink flowers in spring. Forms a trailing dense mat that roots as it spreads. Plant 12" apart. Photo below.
Trailing Ice Plant *Lampranthus spectabilis*	S, W, E Not for cold desert. 20°F, −7°C.	6" to 12"	Small, fleshy, gray-green leaves. Covered with spectacular red, pink, rose-pink or purple flowers in spring. Nondescript out of bloom. Plant 12" to 18" apart. Photo below.
Coralpea *Kennedia rubicunda*	S, W, E Good on coast. Not for cold desert. 20°F, −7°C.	Climbing to 20 feet.	Large leaves; red flowers. Rampant vine-like growth. Prefers water. Usually planted by hydroseeding.
Cape Honeysuckle *Tecomaria capensis*	S, W, E Good on coast, likes heat. Not for cold desert. 25°F, −4°C.	10 to 15 feet.	Dark green, shiny leaves; bright orange-red flowers. Large, sprawling shrub. Needs well-drained soil. Space 6' to 8' apart. Photo page 62.

Rosea Ice Plant

Trailing Ice Plant

Prostrate Acacia

Sources Of Information

Although I've tried to include as much information as possible, additional questions will undoubtedly still arise as you work on your landscape. A surprising number of them will answer themselves with a little thought and common sense. Where to get the answers to the more technical ones?

As mentioned several times before, a good way to learn how to do something is to watch a craftsman do it. Second best is to look at the finished results. I built an entire house this way, from the ground up.

The people that sell a product quite often know a great deal about it. An *experienced* person at a building supply company, lumber yard or nursery is a potential gold mine of information. Contractors are of course the ones who really know how to do their specialty, but they're not in the business of dispensing free, or even paid advice. You have to hire then to do the work in order to benefit from their knowledge.

Now we come to the "experts." Landscape architects and designers have been discussed in Chapter 2, along with landscape contractors, gardeners and nurserymen. You can get some help from your building department—but mostly on the application and interpretation of the rules and regulations. Individuals are often courteous and helpful. Generally the approach is from the negative side, with prohibition the keyword. But, that's another book.

State agricultural extension offices usually have county farm advisors available to answer questions concerning plants, soil, insecticides and similar subjects. Also, state universities will often offer advice. My experience has been that farm advisors and university personnel are very well qualified and their publications are excellent. Check under County Government in the phone book and look for farm Advisor or Cooperative Extension Service, or call your nearest state university.

Various industry associations will answer written questions—but that's not much help when you want to finish up a project on the next weekend. Their publications are often very good and can be acquired before you start work. Describe what you need and they'll either send it to you free or let you know what is available at what is usually a nominal cost.

Brick Institute of America
1750 Old Meadow Road
McLean VA 22101

California Redwood Association
617 Montgomery Street
San Francisco, CA 94111

Portland Cement Association
Old Orchard Road
Skokie, IL 60076

Southern California Solar Energy Association
City Administration Building
202 C Street, 11B
San Diego, CA 92101

Western Wood Products Association
150 Yeon Building
Portland, OR 97204

Commercially prepared material such as nursery catalogs; spa, hot tub and pool booklets; sprinkler and lighting pamphlets; and fertilizer, weed killer, insecticide and similar product description sheets are some other free or low-cost publications available.

Botanic gardens and arboretums frequently have lectures and printed material in addition to demonstrating plantings. Evening adult classes in horticulture, home landscaping and gardening are available in most localities. It's a good idea to check on the instructor's background to see if you're dealing with a qualified expert.

Don't overlook the federal government. Write to the Superintendent of Documents, Government Printing Office, Washington, D.C. and ask for *List of Available Publications of the U.S.D.A.*—Bulletin No. 11—45 cents.

The library and book store are not intended to be last resorts—you might find what you're looking for faster and more easily there than through the other sources. It is confusing however, because there are so many publications available. Most of them are technically okay, but fall short when it comes to design esthetics. Also, when plants are involved, some books ignore or only superficially recognize the tremendous differences in growing conditions in different climates. Look through the racks carefully to see whether or not a book is zoned for your specific region and if it offers real information that applies to your needs.